Accounting Fables

Accounting Fables: Tales of Race and Racism in the Borderlands of Business

BY

ANTON LEWIS

Governors State University, USA

emerald PUBLISHING

United Kingdom – North America – Japan – India – Malaysia – China

Emerald Publishing Limited
Emerald Publishing, Floor 5, Northspring, 21-23 Wellington Street, Leeds LS1 4DL.

First edition 2025

British Library Cataloguing in Publication Data
A catalogue record for this book is available from the British Library

ISBN: 978-1-80117-070-3 (Print)
ISBN: 978-1-80117-069-7 (Online)
ISBN: 978-1-80117-071-0 (Epub)

Printed and bound by CPI Group (UK) Ltd, Croydon, CR0 4YY

INVESTOR IN PEOPLE

Contents

Foreword

My wife and I make a point to introduce the importance of politics to our children where we can, particularly where it pertains to race and racism (no surprise there, then). It is the year of the 2024 US presidential election, and we made sure to catch as much of the Democratic National Convention hosted in Chicago as we could. As unabashed Democrats, we were lucky enough to see the ever-wonderful Michelle Obama's speech at the convention, among many others. Her use of the term "Affirmative Action of Generational Wealth" (AAGW) caught my eye. Now, there is a term that distills much of the ethos behind my research and passion for Critical Race Theory and its application to the Accounting profession. It is the net result of unaccountable whiteness, uncritiqued and untroubled.

To be white in US society, and I would argue that this applies to the bulk of dominant majority white societies, is to be born with affirmative action, which confers privilege and protection of property rights as a precursor to wealth acquisition among a multitude of other advantages. This is the unnamed white right to all, in perpetuity, vehemently denied by whites but plain to see for those who are not that favored hue. It is to go wrong and end up being right by design. So deep is this belief in the white psyche that it is an almost incomprehensible concept to accept, let alone dislodge consciously. Its genius lies in its structural nature and "taken for granted-ness," invisible to most. And to be clear, AAGW affects all. An example is medical care, where African American women are much more likely to die from medical complications in childbirth than any other female demographic. Underpinning this is the racist hidden belief in the medical profession that Black women feel less pain, and so are often denied close medical attention when complications arise. Within the Law, it is a well-known fact that Black and Brown bodies make up the majority of the incarcerated in US prisons while representing a fraction of the populace. Studies reveal that endemic racism in the legal industrial complex makes this so. Where one can describe it as the complicated reciprocal relational web between the Legal profession, government agencies (Federal and State), and related industries, its adherence to profit and vulnerability to lobbying sees the creation and effective maintenance of the school-to-prison pipeline for poor Black and Brown children. Once branded a criminal, wealth acquisition becomes nearly impossible. And … I could go on ….

For me, the buck stops with accounting and its role in perpetuating AAGW. In the zero-sum game that we have constructed, that is, racialized society, for whites to possess an affirmative action of wealth attainment means that those discriminated by race have their wealth chances severely curtailed over generations.

It means Black and Brown communities with poorer housing with an inability to earn and invest in wealth-generating assets because they have been steered away from such practices. It means worse educational outcomes because of school funding based on property taxes. It means Black businesses that do grow cannot flourish, as too few Black accountants, bankers, and financiers exist to help and guide those who most need success and profitability. It means Black communities become trapped in a smaller, ever-shrinking bubble of wealth-generating opportunities. It's such a simple concept, hidden from public debate for far too long, that must be unpacked now.

For this reason, I have written Accounting Fables, among others. I charge that the profession in the USA and worldwide can do more for the Black Accounting Other and the communities from which many come. But the profession must separate itself from its ideological malaise and entertain, if not embrace, the unlikely and the impossible as potential routes to navigate choppy racial waters. It is how we fight white affirmative action, even though resistance is strong and the stakes are high. Then, as Michelle Obama pleads with us, we must take the higher road while stopping those who "fail forward," those raced (white) and classed upward (the 1%) who see this injustice as their birthright from continuing to do so. Ultimately, it is to dream that we can envision better, so I get to tell my Black children, and by extension, all kids, that fighting for what is right is the only way. As adults, we must then put our words into action.

Anton Lewis

Critical Race Theory Counterstories

> [...] Using fantasy and dialogue to uncover enduring truths. (Bell, 1987, And We Are Not Saved, p. 6)

The question I pose in this book is how do we create connection? It begins with empathy, where understanding can grow from this fertile ground. Specifically, racial understanding is a much-needed balm for our troubled times. However, how to do this has always been elusive. It was not until I discovered, "many moons ago," the writings of Derrick Bell in *And We Are Not Saved* and similar work that I perceived the potential of tales to do what needs to be done where, connection, sympathy, and understanding of racism are concerned. The power of parables, myths, and counterstories to reimagine the known and the staid has inspired a generation of critical race theorists across numerous disciplines to heed Bell's call. It is an unequivocal demand that we take up literary arms to discover new ways to draw compassion and responsiveness from those ensconced in whiteness. Telling tales to foster deep feelings from the willfully ignorant allows for the creation of long-sought-after meaningful connections between races while championing mutual respect across differences. More formally, it is to champion the cause of practiced storyteller Aja J. Martinez, to see tales as a multifaceted approach:

"[Where] CRT counterstory recognizes that the experiential and embodied knowledge of people of color is legitimate and critical to understanding racism that is often well disguised in the rhetoric of normalized structural values and practices" (Martinez, 2014). It is here that counternarrative differs from traditional fiction. The Critical Race Theory (CRT) method can upend what is taken for granted, what I call "white stream thinking," that flow of thought that moves ideas, solutions, and ways of being in one direction, ebbing on the tides of whiteness. Nevertheless, the right countertale can begin the process of swimming upstream against this tide by problematizing received wisdom, contradicting the powerful societal undercurrent that is the status quo, which valorizes the conceit that the white way is the right way. Moreover, that is the only way that counts. This is the power of a particular type of story to "counter scrutinize" the certainty of taken-for-granted theoretical notions and sympathize with empirical data that is often the backdrop of a tale retold on behalf of the liminal and forgotten.

Furthermore, in doing so, create characters from sources and situations drawn from past events, personal histories, or existing literature to aid the process of racial critique. It allows tales to shield the vulnerable, protecting those who cannot do so themselves (Martinez, 2022). I see this within the Accounting context as a way to spotlight the abject failure of the profession to engage with race and racism in its own house adequately and the need consequently to protect the Other from the institutionalized fallout of this debacle (Lewis, 2020). In many ways, this has already begun. Although not common within Accounting literature, examples of counterstories exist, written by forward-thinking critical Accounting scholars who have already applied storytelling methods to significant effect across various subjects. From Sopt et al., comes a paper, cutting edge in scope, challenging ideas of what outer space can mean to a firm's notion of accountability, grounded in traditional Accounting and decision-making processes when reinterpreted through narrative inquiry conducted by children (Sopt & Cohen, 2024). Twyford, Tanima, and George recount tales of the cruel treatment of refugees at the hands of the Australian government, showing the revelatory power of counterstories as an accountability mechanism, making those who are invisible visible, documenting harm perpetrated through government offshore immigration policy (Twyford et al., 2022). A reimagining of a future sustainable world is told by Atkins et al. (2015) as a scientific counternarrative rebuttal against corporate environmental activities, often reported in the form of environmental, social, and governmental assurance reports, ones which often omit the voices of those most affected by the corporation's harmful actions. Such counterstories exemplify "talking back" to positivistic notions of what constitutes authentic Accounting knowledge, opposing the de facto epistemic dominance of "fact, not fiction" narratives in the Accounting academy and beyond. Within this crucible of struggle, the "known" can be unmade, and other ways of knowing are brought into view. The field must get its own racial house in order. The importance of doing so is where we turn our attention to next.

Why Tell a Different Tale?

The stories we tell one another matter, as do those that are not told. The most ubiquitous are majoritarian stories detailing the unspoken, enforced reality of the dominant/majority group. This is the tale not overtly told but whispered every day by the voice that never speaks, and it is the most powerful, drowning out all others. This voice comprises prevailing principles and opinions that validate white actions as correct (Love, 2004). In a dominant majority white environment like Accounting, such stock stories are typical, attributing differences of the racial Other to harmful societal tropes. Here, the Black woman Accountant is an overcontrolling, emasculating overachiever. The Latina Accountant is fetishized, exotic, and sexy. The Asian male accountant, as a model minority, is seen as numerically gifted but also negatively feminized, seen as not masculine enough for leadership roles, compounded by stereotypes of his poor social skills (Jun et al., 2023; Lewis & Allen, 2016). Each is lesser in some way than what the industry values most: the pale male Accounting professional who exudes authenticity (Lewis, 2012). This stock story is a tale of white male privilege juxtaposed against the deficit social position of his race and gendered contemporaries. These grouped suppositions are the yardstick against which the worth of the Other is determined, effectively flattening and muting any voice of resistance against it. Typical is the idea that Blacks are not good at mathematics and so cannot succeed in the numerical field of Accounting, "proved" by the low number of Black accountants in the industry, echoed with similar tropes explaining low numbers of Hispanic CPAs as well. (Dey & Lim, 2023; Gabre et al., 2017).

Russo's Ruse – A Majoritarian Tale

Stock stories can cause terrible harm when deployed correctly to the correct audience. What follows is my account of what I call Russo's Ruse, a recently formed majoritarian tale that speaks to the "evil" of CRT. Much like a crooked pendulum on a racial clock, I suggest that progress swings toward positive change and back to the negative. It explains how we move from President Obama to President Trump only a few years later. What I describe as racial physics comes into play here, underpinning how the pendulum works. The narrator of this particular pernicious tale is Christopher Russo, a sometime conservative filmmaker and blogger. Around 2020, he penned a blog, "when diversity training is all about feeding racism," on the Manhattan Institute website, and as his viewpoint gained traction, his conflated take on diversity training turned into a definition of CRT. It is this tale of the nefarious nature of DEI as CRT (which it is not) that seeped into the Republican imaginary, sitting well with the notion that DEI has gone too far and that reverse racism against whites is now the status quo – redefining CRT as racial cynicism.

And why does this matter? Again, tales have power, and after an invite from Tucker Carlson, former host of Fox News, Russo again railed against CRT as a fundamental threat to the meaning and existence of the USA as he knew it. It was usurping common sense to become the "default ideology" of the federal bureaucracy that is the USA and now used as a weapon against its white citizens. As this majoritarian tale grew in popularity and reach, like the nine-headed Hydra, it touched many areas, becoming as difficult to slay as the Hydra itself. Ruffo called on Fox viewers to end "CRT brainwashing" by executive order, and sure enough, his story soon reached the Trump White House, where Fox News found friendly ears. Some while later, Ruffo was granted an audience with President Trump (an avid Fox viewer), subsequently becoming the chief architect of a memorandum that forbade the issuance of federal monies related to training on CRT, White Privilege, or Implicit bias. The key was prohibiting any activity deemed to portray the USA as innately racist and evil. This is elaborated upon further by Executive Order 13950, created to "Combat Racial and Sex Stereotyping," adding procedural teeth to the essence of what has just been mentioned (Goldberg, 2023; Lopez & Sleeter, 2023). Its effect? To declare open season on CRT, with draconian punishments in tow, for example, if a firm engaged in DEI training, it would not receive federal funding or contracts. Although revoked by the incoming Biden administration, the path forward for Russo's Ruse was clear; this method was efficiently employed at the state level to push baseless allegations against CRT teaching in schools (but remember that CRT was never taught in schools in the fashion that Russo and his acolytes portray). This tale fused with others, weaving a narrative about the unfairness of Harvard's use of race as a criterion in college admissions. After substantial pressure, it was subsequently overruled by the conservative-leaning Supreme Court, ensuring the retraction of affirmative action across the US Higher Education landscape (Lewis, 2023) – another win for Russo's Ruse.

But why does he keep winning with this now tired but effective play? The way I see it is that Russo and, by extension, the Republicans of our modern times tell better tales. Having said this, please note that I admire a well-played game and take my hat off to the Russo Ruse. It is masterful in its low cunning and exceptional ability to inculcate fear and loathing of the Other in the Republican base and many moderates. It is a playbook that President Trump knows all too well and employs with masterful craft. I put my hands up, giving a slow round of applause. Instead, I reserve my ire for moderates and Democrats left standing in their wake. This is a case of simply not being able to tell the proper tale, a tale with power, one which can reach the hearts and minds of people who progressives have foolishly written off as deplorable. Russo's Ruse as a narrative has shown its power to herald change and upend and flip over the DEI and CRT status quo. The question is, can those who count themselves as CRT theorists, me included, Anti-Racists and the like, rise to the storytelling challenge already set? Can Russo's Ruse be matched with a counternarrative of equal potency?

While that remains to be seen, this book takes up a similar herculean task, facing off against Accounting's master narrative that this book wishes to challenge using counterstories to highlight the inherent color-evasive nature of the profession. To mention race or racism within its walls remains taboo. Although this is a core theme of colorblindness contained within the stock story of Accounting, this majority voice must be challenged if the voice of the raced accountant is to be heard. Fortunately, the academic Barbara Love shows us how she believes counternarratives should challenge the US education of Black children to redress deficiencies. I reinterpret the questions she poses, asking them instead of Accounting:

(1) How, in Accounting's master narrative, has the liminality of the racial Other been shown? Can a countertale be told of the raced accountant that remedies this? Can a differing, more equitable reality be described?
(2) In Accounting's master narrative, is the voice of the Black subordinated worker heard? Is their view taken seriously? Or is their voice ridiculed, dismissed as inconsequential? What if counterstories could reverse the course of whitestream Accounting, turning its milky hue darker, enabling the white world of Accounting to empathize with and "get" the Black experience within its walls?
(3) Where Accounting's master narrative is concerned, what is the overarching aim of this stock story? How can its purpose then be subverted using counterstories, challenging its core meaning and function to "change the waters we swim in" as racialized Others in this space?

(Lewis, 2024; Love, 2004).

As a specific CRT technique, counterstories aim to answer questions using core CRT tenets, which are foundational ways of viewing and interpreting race and racism in society. This line of questioning and the answers gained, grounded in theoretical principle, is where Russo's Ruse and other stock tales are found wanting and perhaps bested. It is to these fundamentals of theory that we now briefly turn.

Canons of a Critical Race Theory of Accounting (CRTA)

At its heart, CRT is a malleable theoretical lens. It can be a round peg that snugly fits into a square hole, giving it the ability to quickly adjust racial interpretation over time, keeping in lockstep with racism's ever fluid nature. It is this stickability, its capacity to cling on to racist practice, as it twists into a myriad of contrary forms, and then contests it, which marks it out as a singular tool in my mind. Omi and Winant have long identified racism's plasticity as a racial formation; for them, race logic is fluid and unfixed. It is a kind of "racial superposition," where racism exists in multiple states of social meaning, repetitively altered by political struggle (Hosang et al., 2012; Omi & Winant, 1986). Fitting well with Stuart Halls's revelatory insight that what racial difference implies at any given point is on no occasion still, it is always "on the move," never rooted, constantly fluctuating, as a floating racial signifier (Hall, 1997). I conceptualize this as the idea that we all recognize traditional racism found in society. However, it exists in distinctly varied forms in disparate settings such as law or Accounting. Variation is due to raced sociohistorical political struggles peculiar to any given profession. Racism then occurs as a pliable process of domination, spreading to where it is needed, filling in the nooks and crannies of professional life, winding and warping, enabling it to effectively do its work of subjugation. Cleverly, allowing it to go often unrecognized and be actively misunderstood for what it really is. Its hegemony over long periods remains untouched. That is why I argue that specificity be used wherever possible when investigating race and racism relating to a given field using the CRT way. As this relates to racism in Accounting, it necessitates an expansion of the traditional CRT paradigm, "accounting", for the profession's past and present political strife, probing how this becomes expressed as future racial practice. This is where I believe a variant of CRT that I have coined, "Critical Race Theory of Accounting (CRTA)," has benefits when exploring race and racism. More flippantly, we must always be on the move to see what the "Man" does next.

This Is the Way

As an ardent fan of the Disney series *The Mandalorian*, I could not help but crib the titular refrain "This is the way," which is the creed of these intergalactic bounty hunters. So then, what is the creed of the critical Accounting scholar employing a CRT framework to explore race and racism in Accounting? CRTA, as I have defined it in my previous text on the topic *Counting Black and White*

Beans, Critical Race Theory in Accounting (Lewis, 2020) has many of CRT's central canons but also highlights others as relevant tools of inquiry particular to the field. A brief list of CRTA organizing principles of racial exploration of Accounting as I conceive them follows. For a more in-depth explanation of these concepts, please read *Counting Black and White Beans*, as mentioned in the text and referenced in this chapter.

Racial Realism – Racism as the Mundane

In Accounting, the unspoken denial of the ubiquity of institutional racism is replete. To examine the profession using CRTA accepts that racism does exist in a myriad of forms and is central in decision-making. However, it also recognizes its taken-for-granted nature and "gets real about" resolving pervasive racial practice.

Ahistoricism – Accounting for a Racist Past

Accounting has a racial past, keenly forgotten if not willfully ignored. It has hitherto existed as racial technology through the need to account for the trade of African bodies taken during the middle passage from Africa to the New World as enslaved people and then valued as assets put to work in plantation settings. Production of economic slave information was central to the success of colonialism across the 17th and 18th centuries, a fact which modern Accounting finds unsavory and tacitly denies. Moreover, Accounting as a profession also has a long history of obfuscating the entry of Black and Brown candidates into its ranks in the form of direct rejection by white-led bodies such as the AICPA and ICAEW, not allowing full membership because articles could not be completed. Another tactic employed by the ACCA was the subtle appropriation of fledgling Indigenous Black and Brown Accounting projects such as those of Trinidad and Tobago, Jamaica, and Kenya, to mention a few (Annisette, 2000; Bakre, 2006; Sian, 2006), seeking their self-determination. Only to be quashed by their more significant influence and supposed authenticity of the ACCA's whiter, more trusted, larger Accounting body.

White Fragility – Racism as Taboo

An unspoken rule exists within the profession in dominant majority white spaces that mentioning race and racism is off-limits and should only be engaged in as it pertains to the possibility of gaining assurance work from other firms that need DEI help from Big 4 firms or mid-tier rivals. Engaging in race chatter runs the risk of provoking white fragility on the topic, which is a painful brittleness that happens around the subject of race for whites. It is an intense dislike of race talk because they find it painful. Such unwillingness to engage with racial reality (our first principle) makes it extremely difficult to discover and then implement racial remedies that might repudiate the hindered progress of the racial Other. This cannot be achieved if people of all hues will not engage in meaningful dialogue, this includes within the DEI training space where white fragility is often at its highest. It should also be noted that similar rules defining the salience of racial reality in Accounting also subtly posit that Black colleagues, in particular, must restrain their voice about race and racism, burying any emotions they have around the topic lest they provoke sanction (Wingfield, 2010). It, in turn, leaves raced accountants isolated and alone as a result, doubling down on their feelings of marginalization.

Challenging Meritocracy – A Rigged Game

CRTA pushes back against industry mores that tout the meritocratic nature of Accounting. Suggesting instead that a "shadow structure" exists, one that seeks to promote the preferred archetype of the field. This is the pale and male accountant, the most trusted, to be placed on influential client projects and receive favorable evaluations from managers, an event seldom experienced by their Black, Brown, and women colleagues (Lewis, 2012; Upton & Arrington, 2012). Once Accounting has accepted the existence of bias, a chance exists to construct policy to promote a fairer environment where all can succeed through effort, as originally professed.

Intersectionality – Interweaving Inequities

CRTA recognizes that inequity in Accounting is multifaceted and intertwined across multiple identity categories. Subordination rarely has a favorite, and it seeks to oppress all. Therefore, redress must address inequality in its innumerable forms, be it race, gender, class, or all the differing marginalized identities in between, which must also be fought for if social equality in the profession and beyond is to be achieved.

CRTA as Multi-disciplinary

As alluded to at the beginning of this chapter, CRTA possesses fluidity, which is crucial to its sharpness as a critical construct. Making explicit its requirement to combine divergent and even contradictory ways of knowing where necessary. This is a cohering of epistemics, utilizing varied critical lenses, revealing wide-ranging experiences in diverse settings for the purpose of creating social justice.

Accounting for Tales – The Giving Voice to the Voiceless in Accounting

Finally, CRTA valorizes the voice of those customarily silenced in Accounting as an act of resistance. Telling oppositional tales is to "clap back," to the standard story which depicts a deficit existence for the Othered accountant. It is authentic truth-telling from a position of liminality that can, as already mentioned, topple the status quo, readying the profession for another way of being, one not entangled inside concealed disparities or reduced life chances for the stigmatized. Doing so encourages Accounting students, practitioners, and the academy to dream of other different cultures and discussions, which can topple the prevailing consensus that racism does not exist – allowing for the visualization of opposing Accounting worlds (Boyce & Greer, 2013). It is worth noting again that these principles are not final, set, or exhaustive but instead represent a guide to applying CRTA in research within Accounting.

Existence in the Negative?

But how is this done? Noted CRT storyteller Richard Delgado sees the creation of counternarratives as a form of "Counter reality" constructed by outgroup members subjected to racism at the intersection of other inequities (Martinez, 2014). Now, another truth emerges, like the production of traditional photographic film. Firstly, a counter-truth as an idea is captured. Secondly, it must be developed so that the accurate picture of the way things really are can be made clear; racialized existence emerges from the photographic negative that is the counterstory told. Thirdly, this explanation of racial realism is "imprinted" onto the white racial imaginary, subverting them from their normalized view of the world given to them from their consumption of stock stories. They are given a view of the subaltern world for the first time. As a fan of the Netflix show *Stranger Things*, I liken the upcoming Accounting Fables in this book to the "Upside Down" in the show, which is an adjacent universe to ours. Those in this upside down become strangers in a strange land, where everything appears unnervingly familiar but inverted. Consequently, countertales have the potential to alter the perception of whites to perceive Accounting's own Upside Down, as Love implores:

> By listening to the counter-stories of people of Color, white people can gain access to a view of the world denied to them by white privilege and white domination. (Love, 2004, 233pp.)

A compelling counterstory is a Trojan Horse of cultural insight (Yosso, 2006), allowing subjugation to be relatable to all, and this often means it is personal. It is to expose the unfairness of the vulnerability of those who cannot do so themselves, an act of protection enabling counternarratives to hold dominant majority whites responsible for the formation of this circumstance. At the same time, it is deeply personal, an effort to invoke sympathy for the unnoticed, demonstrating itself to be a tool of accessibility that is a principal characteristic of any counterstory. But whether Black Accounting lives matter is a tale yet to be told meaningfully. It is worth repeating that the use of the Accounting Fables that I will shortly tell is a clarion call to implement Accounting's literary imagination to crack some of its most tricky and sticky problems; race and racism are perhaps the most historically intractable.

Counterstory as Methodology

CRTA Counterstories, as a method, track CRT and act to dislodge the complacency of what counts as valid knowledge in Accounting. In this way, the whimsical fables in this book are counter-hegemonic, using the non-academic voice to reject familiar stock stories claiming white Western epistemology as the lone arbiter of authentic valued knowledge. It is to bring the outsider's voice to the fore, exploring what it means to endure being Black in Accounting. But positivists have long condemned this as invalid, citing it as unscientific, not rigorous or relevant, of belonging in sociology, not the hard technocracy of Accounting.

CRT traditionally meets such criticisms by explaining that counterstories are often constructed through Composite Characters (CC) usage. Martinez opines that this is a specific CRT construct which adds to the richness of qualitative inquiry by incorporating data in several ways. CCs permit information about the politically vulnerable to be recounted in a manner that is least risky to their well-being while incorporating quantitative study, empirical analysis, surveys, and semi-structured interviews within its structure. Current and past sociological, legal, or other relevant historical knowledge is included. Finally, personal and professional lived experience rounds off the construction of particular types of CCs, who fit archetypes and ideas found in extant research. Authors then reconfigure these constructs to become mouthpieces of research conclusions grounded in specific historical and political situations to resonate with the reader the importance of challenging racism and other forms of discrimination where it stands. Allowing for thoughtful consideration of the matter at hand, accepting its difficulty while retaining the essence of meaning.

This is the methodological approach I have used to construct the CC found in the stories ahead, recognizing that lived experience and cultural knowledge of People of Color have value, are genuine, and are indispensable to the unpacking of racism, often camouflaged in everyday ordinariness (Martinez, 2014). This means that the upcoming fables, as literary methods, do not seek to provide answers but instead, at best, attempt to reframe the dialogue of race and racism in Accounting and, at worst, provoke difficult conversations.

The Risk of Counterstories

However, having outlined the many pedagogical benefits of using the counterstory method in Accounting, risks still remain. Fundamentally, the danger exists that what I produce here will not be appreciated or understood, and most readers will not appreciate what has been attempted. As Derrick Bell noted in his work, risk exists in the novel (Bell, 1987), particularly in the CRT/Sci-Fi approach that is unique within Accounting academe. But is it welcome? Furthermore, and perhaps this is what any author fears the most, peril exists in the production of tripe! That is to say, one fears when writing counterstories that you will be the purveyor of a poor story that cannot produce any of the benefits to the reader I have outlined. Martinez captures this beautifully, revealing her feelings around her once harshly critiqued work:

> […] this method is the most challenging for me as a counterstory writer as well, and my own first attempt at it … I was told "reads as bad fiction." (Martinez, 2020, p. 61)

It is my fear as well. The dread of being the purveyor of lousy fiction cuts the deepest, not for vainglorious reasons and not for pride. No, it is that fact that I will have failed to reach those who must be reached with a message of racial awareness, which is most important. It is the fear of failure. Yet this handwringing's upshot is bravery, which is always called for in such work. Fear of the accusation of lousy fiction also exists as an attack on the voice of the racial Other by bad faith actors, those intent on muting the message, again attacking what is different because it is diverse. It is easier to destroy than to nurture and create. But if truth be told, to resist self-doubt is to give what is required. Having pride in one's voice is the work that must be done. It is the work of racial realism that is foundational to the CRTA way, one which I encourage the reader to begin to think about. Truly, what tale can you tell? How can you be brave and push the boundaries that need to be pushed? I hope that the Fables that follow do all this and more.

References

AICPA. (2019). *Trends in the supply of accounting graduates and the demand for public accounting recruits*. https://us.aicpa.org/content/dam/aicpa/interestareas/accountingeducation/newsandpublications/downloadabledocuments/2019-trends-report.pdf

Annisette, M. (2000). Imperialism and the professions: The education and certification of accountants in Trinidad and Tobago. *Accounting Organisations and Society*, *25*, 631–659.

Atkins, J., Atkins, B., Thompson, I., & Maroun, W. (2015). "Good" news from nowhere: Imagining utopian sustainable accounting. *Accounting Auditing & Accountability Journal*, *28*(5), 1–21.

Bakre, O. M. (2006). Second attempt at localising imperial accountancy: The case of the Institute of Chartered Accountants of Jamaica (ICAJ) (1970s–1980s). *Critical Perspectives on Accounting*, *17*, 1–28.

Bell, D. (1987). *And we are not saved: The elusive quest for racial justice*. Basic Books.

Boyce, G., & Greer, S. (2013). More than imagination: Making social and critical accounting real. *Critical Perspectives on Accounting*, *24*, 105–112.

Dey, M., & Lim, L. (2023). Do social networks improve the chance of obtaining challenging assignments? Evidence from Black accounting professionals. *Advances in Accounting*, *63*(100677).

Gabre, H., Flesher, D., & Ross, F. (2017). CPA credential perceptions: A case study of Hispanic accountants. *Accounting Education*, *26*(1), 54–77.

Goldberg, D. (2023). *The war on critical race theory*. Polity.

Hall, S. (1997). *Re: Race*, The Floating Signifier [Message posted]. https://www.mediaed.org/transcripts/Stuart-Hall-Race-the-Floating-Signifier-Transcript.pdf

Hosang, D. M., LaBennet, O., & Pulido, L. (2012). *Racial formation in the twenty-first-century*. University of California Press.

Investigator, Q. (2020, 12/22/20). It Ain't What You Don't Know That Gets You Into Trouble. It's What You Know for Sure That Just Ain't So. https://quoteinvestigator.com/2018/11/18/know-trouble/

Jun, S., Phillips, T., & Foster-Gimbel, O. (2023). The missing middle: Asian employees' experience of workplace discrimination and pro-Black allyship. *Journal of Applied Psychology*, *108*(108), 225–248.

Lewis, A. (2012). *A critical analysis of the Black accounting experience in the U.K. Tales of success and failure in the British professional workplace*. Lambert Academic Publishing.

Lewis, A. (2020). *Counting black and white beans. Critical race theory in accounting*. Emerald Publishing Limited.

Lewis, A. (2023). Keeping our promise. *The CPA Journal* (November/December), 1–80. https://www.cpajournal.com/2024/02/07/keeping-our-promise/

Lewis, A. (2024). Black women in accounting and the backlash to DEI. *The CPA Journal, XCIV*(3/4), 1–80.

Lewis, A., & Allen, T. (2016). Looking through a glass darkly: Reflections on power, leadership and the Black female professional. *The Journal of Values Based Leadership, 9*(2), 1–16.

Lopez, F., & Sleeter, C. (2023). *Critical race theory and its critics*. Teachers College.

Love, B. (2004). Brown plus 50 counter counter-storytelling: A critical race theory analysis of the "Majoritarian Achievement Gap" story. *Equity & Excellence in Education, 37*, 227–246.

Martinez, A. (2020). *Counterstory. The rhetoric and writing of critical race theory*. CCC/NCTE.

Martinez, A. Y. (2014). A plea for critical race theory counterstory: Stock story versus counterstory dialogues concerning Alejandra's "Fit" in the academy. *Composition Studies, 42*(2), 33–55.

Martinez, A. Y. (2022). The catharsis for poison: A counterstory retrospective on composition studies' 50th anniversary. *Composition Studies, 50*(1), 90–94.

Omi, M., & Winant, H. (1986). *Racial formation in the United States from the 1960s to the 1980s*. Routledge.

Sian, S. (2006). Inclusion, exclusion and control: The case of the Kenyan accounting professionalisation project. *Accounting, Organizations and Society, 31*, 295–322.

Sopt, J., & Cohen, N. (2024). Children, imagination, and outer space exploration: Implications for space accountability systems. *Accounting, Auditing and Accountability Journal, 37*(5), 1312–1344. https://doi.org/10.1108/AAAJ-12-2022-6177

Twyford, E. J., Tanima, F. A., & George, S. (2022). Critical race theory, counter-accounting, and the emancipatory potential of counterstories. *Accounting, Auditing & Accountability Journal*, ahead-of-print(ahead-of-print). https://doi.org/10.1108/AAAJ-12-2020-5035

Upton, D. R., & Arrington, E. (2012). Implicit racial prejudice against African Americans in balanced scorecard performance evaluations. *Critical Perspectives on Accounting, 23*, 281–297.

Wingfield, A. (2010). Are some emotions marked "Whites Only"? Racialized feeling rules in professional workplaces. *Social Problems, 57*(2), 251–268.

Yosso, T. J. (2006). *Critical race counterstories along the chicana/chicano educational pipeline*. Routledge.

Prologue

Dear reader, perhaps our greatest folly is that "we think we know when we do not." Put more succinctly by Mark Twain, "The trouble with the world is not that people know too little; it's that they know so many things that just aren't so."[1] And it is with this thought in mind that we begin a journey, to a place out of sight, out of reason, beyond hope and adjacent to despair. It is in the moment amid moments, the boundless empty between one reality and another that Elder Gods of old reside.

They are many. Their actions beyond comprehension, plaguing the affairs of man since we crawled out of the sea and then a little later, subsequently popping down from trees, deciding that walking upright wasn't a bad idea at all. By the way, more than a few Elder gods considered getting rid of us right there and then because we looked like a potential irritant. In many ways, it is for good reason that we of the modern age choose to ridicule the idea of gods and monsters such as them. After all what would we do if it were true? What would our existence mean if we saw ourselves as the "ants" we are compared to them? The ontological ramification is quite terrifying if this belief holds. Creatures such as these are the stuff of Eldritch horror, a personification of fear, dread, and loathing. In days past Shamans, druids, and clergy, have known of their existence and omnipotence, naming them "Daemons" over eons. Sometimes worshiped and revered. Always feared and never trusted. But balance exists here as well, for some of these perfidious many-angled ones, have been known to fight for the cause of humanity, to champion "good" and defend what is right, even as their brethren do the opposite. Regrettably, these "good ones" are too few in number, getting less each millennium. Haven't you ever wondered why things seem to be getting worse with the world? This is why.

Elder Gods take many forms and their pantheon is quite extensive. Rather than outline all of this, it makes more sense to highlight one or two of the more egregious players that are the hammer which smashes against the anvil of torment that besets human life. For instance, "Karkadium the sorrowful" has delighted for millennia in pitting man against woman since apple eating became fashionable in the Garden of Eden, the result of which has been an age-old recurrent

[1]Please note that although this quote is commonly ascribed to Mark Twain contestation exists as to whether he originated the phrase. It has been suggested that others used it first (Investigator, 2020).

tsunami of harm leveled against women for eons. He really is the most outrageous misogynist and is sorry for nothing. Not one iota. Unfortunately, it is this trait, the inherent inability to say sorry for anything nor ask for directions when lost upon pain of death, that men inherit from Karkadium to their eternal shame, thus making women's life absolute hell. He puts the toxic into masculinity. Yet his sister – Karkadia is no less insidious or ambitious. It is she who supports the machinations of an all-pervasive patriarchy that poison's men's hearts (as well as many women) and it is she who has seen to it that the power of a woman's voice is unfairly muted, professionally gagged in the workplace, having to exist in a male centric world Karkadium manifested. And all would be lost if it were not for a number of great women. Titians of their age, strong enough and selfless enough to challenge her invasive and inescapable influence as well as that of her brother. Such is the ilk of women like Audry Lourde, Emily Pankhurst, and the late US Supreme Court Justice Ruth Bader Ginsburg (eternal heroines), whose actions challenge the Gods of old themselves. The torch bearers of equality and fairness in a world where it has been sorely needed. But unseen, endlessly skulking in the shadows, their valiant efforts are perpetually confounded by the unseen mischief of the Elder twins successfully thwarting women's emancipation. It they that let women know that a monster lives in everyman. It is they that let men know that a witch exists in every woman. And we wonder why we "can't get along," never mind as the great one once said, "Let's get it on."[2] I mean who doesn't need healing right now ....

Another of note is the God of the Low, "Eseru Ezeru", as some on earth have named him, better known as "EewU" to the other Elder folk. It is he who keeps those of poor means in their place. The socio-economically challenged are his, and his alone to be toyed with and kept without property, without a feeling of worth, to know in their hearts that they are valueless. They are the perpetual poor unable to attain wealth or get more than just enough to eat. They can never achieve what is needed for a decent life. In many countries, it seems as if his influence is waning but in truth, he is just gathering his full strength, his secret is that he knows on a planet like Earth with scarce, limited resources it is only a matter of time before those who have means utilize their power to horde more than they need of everything, subjugating the countless poor who do not have the influence or money to resist. They will eventually be forced into his never-loving arms and told to love Capitalism as a religion. After all this timeless one has time on his hands.

Lastly, we turn to Enki Abyd, an Elder God of stature, somewhat different from his brethren, and our protagonist of sorts. This trickster God has had many names over the centuries you may recognize, from Loki of Norse mythology to Anansi the spider deity from African and West Indian folklore. His role in our lives has traditionally been one of puncturing arrogance and teaching through folly, and pranking. Think about some of the most humiliating situations you've undergone. Had a bad day at work and your boss is basically being a dick? Is he a bully who delights in making underlings feel worthless? Is he

[2]I refer here to the song sung by Marvin Gaye "Let's get it on."

good at it? At breaking point you succumb to a fit of rage, just once, emailing your best friend about the latest incident using colorful expletives to describe him. And it's only after relaxing that evening with a cooling beer do you realize with horror that the reply all email went to your boss and the entire office! Or how about when you go to your new job for the first time knowing that as a woman in the workplace you have to hit the tone just right. Make sure your personal brand is on point. You have bought just the right dress that says professional, classy, and corporate. You saunter into the office and begin work. It's been two hours before you get up and head toward the rest room before the office manager stops you, smirking in that knowing way. He lets you know that nightmare upon nightmares, you accidentally tucked your skirt into the back of your underwear! Nobody said a thing. This is all Enki Abyd.

He is the devil incarnate I hear you cry! Nope, he is not. We will come to him later though since he and Enki sometimes go for a pint at the expanded Hell's Kitchen bar and Grill in downtown Sau Paulo for shits and giggles. No, these pranks have a purpose, humility forces us to be real with ourselves and our situation. Such things remind us not to take ourselves too seriously and laugh when we can, and cry when we need. This is the stuff of humanity. But to be fair it is a bloody pain at the time. In this way Enki is a good figure (kind of) for humanity. But don't be fooled, he is no hero, and just like all the other Elder Gods mercurial in behavior and attitude. To say he sees humans often as pets might be a bit too generous. But as a Trickster god he does not like to lose, and he must understand the line between right and wrong, good, and bad if he is to pull off the best tricks for his own amusement, while teaching the way of wisdom. Often bending and twisting us to the point of breaking, as and when he pleases, because… well…he is a God just like the rest.

So, the tale I now put forth pulls back the curtain of what truly ails the earth, or should I say whom ails the earth. Revealing grotesque beings pulling the strings of humanity's fate. Just one of endless planets under their thrall in the universe. Unfortunately for us, however, earth is always a popular choice with the Elder ones, such is our bad luck. We concern ourselves at this moment with our particularly unpredictable central character Enki Abd,[3] sat in an enormous, dank, and forbidding cavern, deep in the nether regions of the long-forgotten pit of Angst. It is here that we find the great Trickster God residing in the moment amid moments, sat pondering on the Rock of Pondering in the middle of the misty sulfur lake of Shame and Desolation. He's been at it for some time by all accounts. What consumes him so? He is wondering about the Grandmaster of Race. How and why, he came into being? How he has been charged with defeating him and how he has utterly and completely failed to do so since his "birth," and with it the creation of race and racism as we comprehend it today. But first a little context is required, which we come to next.

---

[3]For more exploits of Enki Abyd in the area of accounting and race please read the counter story "Deamon Days," in *Counting Black and White Beans: Critical Race Theory in Accounting* by Anton Lewis.

Reference

Investigator, Q. (2020, 12/22/20). *It Ain't What You Don't Know That Gets You Into Trouble. It's What You Know for Sure That Just Ain't So*. Retrieved from https://quoteinvestigator.com/2018/11/18/know-trouble/

Introduction

Is Accounting Racist?

The above statement is quite a bold one to make to say the least, if not offensive and deeply provocative to many. So why claim this in the first place? Previously, as a Black Accounting professional, I personally experienced institutional racism in Accounting. Later, as a doctoral student studying the experience of other Black accountants, I found racism to be commonplace for them. Now, as a scholar, I find racism pretty much unremarked within the Accounting academy apart from a few critical voices. The irony here is that this really isn't a surprise. It's an open secret that dare not speak its name. I compare it to speaking aloud the name of Lord Voldemort in J. K. Rowlings' Harry Potter book series. To mention Accounting and racism in the same breath is taboo (Lewis, 2015). So what I do within this book is invoke racism as the dark Lord's name loudly, what it is and where it resides. I play around with racial ideas and context in the form of narrative fables.

But no matter the perspective race still remains muted and on the whole invisible in the profession, particularly in relation to itself. Arguably, for those staunchly against the idea, minds swivel to a Black/white binary, where whites see race baiting and reverse racism as the clarion call of what is to come. But why shouldn't race talk simply be a statement of fact? Why does it incite such a reaction and why is it so problematic for industry, and Accounting academe, to openly admit this is the case? Oddly, I ask ChatGPT fairly regularly "Is Accounting racist?" And the bot response below of "no," to me typifies the nonsensical nature of discourse around the subject:

> The field of accounting itself is not inherently racist. However, there have been discussions and studies highlighting issues of racial disparity and discrimination within the profession.

ChatGPT Response

The blanket statement that the field is not fundamentally racist is presented as an article of fact by ChatGPT. But how do we conclusively know that it isn't? Then an admission of the presence of racism as disparity and discrimination is admitted to. For me, it doesn't make sense. But on reflection, this is the veiled line

Accounting Fables: Tales of Race and Racism in the Borderlands of Business, 1–9

Published under exclusive licence by Emerald Publishing Limited
doi:10.1108/978-1-80117-069-720251002

adopted by the profession itself with little critical evidence to back up its claims either. Yet, type the very same question into the competing Copilot Chatbot and the opposite response is conclusively given:

> Yes, racism exists within the accounting profession. Black and Brown individuals face obstacles, including underrepresentation and microaggressions. Addressing this issue is crucial for progress and equity.

Copilot Response

Which one is it? Why do I use chatbots in the first place to answer such questions? It's not really appropriate academic rigor. I agree with this assertion apart from the fact that AI-generated responses are rapidly becoming the norm of where the public and professionals acquire information about the world. This is why it matters. Given this point, the contradictory responses of two popular chatbots are confusing to all.

As you might have guessed, I fall down on the side of racism being endemic within Accounting. But lay public and the profession, like these chatbots seem to oscillate. Sometimes recognizing race and racism in the financial services and then sometimes not. I would proffer to say that the public if ever polled would be in favor of the view that Accounting is not on balance inherently racist. You see Accounting itself works hard to deny the possibility of such a thing. It's almost as if an Accounting Fragility, analogous to White Fragility,[1] exists, preventing deeper analysis. So Chatbot Copilot assertions of racial practice in the industry cannot be taken seriously, perhaps it's a hallucination? Is this because we see the profession as a mere technocracy devoid of bias because it's just about the numbers? Or is it that, as I have argued elsewhere, the profession cannot afford the reputational risk of not being considered the trusted unbiased arbiter of facts and figures that such a discovery might engender? Either way, I have been at this awhile now and I thought it was time to poke the proverbial bear one more time but in a markedly different way. Telling tales about this controversial area is the way forward for me as indicated earlier. Using the right tale, I might sneak in racial critique through the side door of consciousness, encouraging analysis through wry humor. Let's hope so.

Again, industry and the Accounting academy's first reaction to the idea of exploring race and racism through stories in and about Accounting is to dismiss it out of hand. For them, stories have no place in the profession, just like racial analysis. I beg to differ. Accounting is all about telling stories. What is a net income statement or balance sheet but a story of the economic activity of a firm? And as an industry, we work extremely hard to safeguard the veracity of these types of

[1]"White fragility" refers to the mood of disquiet that descends upon whites when challenged in dialogue about racism (DiAngelo, 2018).

tales, told in a particular way, so that Accounting professionals are trusted and believed, because important business decisions are based on their narratives. So why cannot racial tales be adopted in a similar manner, told in a particular way to promote trust, because here too important racial decisions are made in relation to policy and behavior. Pronouncements (on Diversity, Equity and Inclusion (DEI) for example) occur from this that can adversely affect the life chances of People of Color both inside the industry and the wider business world beyond. Again, I reiterate that it is for this reason I have written Accounting Fables, to tell contrary tales as important as any traditional Accounting equivalent about the existence of race and racism inside the profession and outside it. I simply ask what does this mean and what might we discover?

The Accounting Imaginary

For me, the best stories are the most imaginative, the ones that grab you as a reader and will not let you go. This is the art of literary connection if you like. It's the same thing that happens when I explain an Accounting concept in the classroom and I see the eyes of my students light up with understanding, eager to explore more. An anti-banking method takes place, where knowledge imparted by the author is not dictated or autocratic but instead is eagerly and empathically absorbed. This is what is needed in Accounting across the board, but particularly where discussions of race and racism are concerned. This is the value of an expertly told counternarrative, which solicits change in a most welcome way, as Richard Delgado (2007) states succinctly:

> Stories, parables, chronicles and narratives are powerful means for destroying mindset – the bundle of presuppositions, received wisdoms, and shared understanding against a background of which legal and political discourse takes place.

Altering opinions, seeing matters in a differing light has become the challenge of our time, let alone changing hearts and minds. To do so directly has proved difficult for many reasons, including the weaponization of what was once taken for granted knowledge, now often replaced with "alternative facts," that is in reality thinly veiled disinformation. An example of which was famously championed by White House advisor Kellyanne Conway who wished to sway public sentiment toward her with such "facts." It is within this maelstrom that I see advantage in creative tales that extinguish such outlooks, in a way that (hopefully) does not disenfranchise the reader who can still enjoy the tale the idea is wrapped in. Imagination does this work and has done so before within Accounting and other areas. As previously mentioned, Atkin et al.'s futuristic sustainability narrative, outlining what a sustainable future world might look like with the aid of Accounting practice is exemplar. In this world the reader is placed in a setting where received wisdom is challenged, and deeply held beliefs questioned but in the safe arena of the fantastic, protected by the certainty that this isn't real. In this environment, the mind can roam the realm of "What If" (Atkins et al., 2015) possibilities. This is how the truth of racism is revealed through the mechanics of telling the right resistance tale, grounded in allegory and fantasy. It exposes the veracity of racism for all to see in an undeniable fashion, for a mind that has been prized open from the torpor of its color-evasive state, most typical of professionals in institutional settings such as Accounting (Lewis, 2016; Martinez, 2020). Making the wantonly unobserved seen is the function of fables in this book.

"Eating Humble Pie" (Accounting's Racial Hubris)

I began this chapter accusing Accounting of racial denial and my belief it needs to be shaken out of its indolence, stunned into action by harmful exposés of the Black experience and those of the stigmatized in general. However, its inability to do so smacks of racial hubris. The Big 4 are happy to help other organizations with their DEI issues (for lucrative billable hours), but never admit their own "mea culpa" that the profession is itself institutionally racist and they do next to nothing about it. As many Critical Accounting academics have attested and the AICPA's own 2019 Trend Report acknowledges minimal Black CPA representation of 2% exists in the USA, while a UK contemporary body in the same year reported a sobering 84% of its membership as white, with a mere 11% being from an ethnic minority group (Lewis, 2020). On both sides of the Atlantic, the profession has successfully erased its own complicity in the creation of this situation and its salience to the Black and Brown racialized experience with its own walls. So, the question becomes how best to shake it out of this complacency, this dangerous over-confidence that everything is more or less fine in terms of race and racism, so long as it's never mentioned in relation to itself? Stories have the power to prick the balloon of Accounting's confidence in its self-professed meritocracy which is anything but that. By showing racial reality in sometimes altered, occasionally humorous ways, this high and mighty stance can be laid low through the use of satire, very much in the Black literary tradition of greats such as Richard Ellison's *Invisible Man* or Richard Wright's *Black Boy* to name a few. It is this ability to hold up a fun-house mirror to the profession and beckon it through into a twisted racial wonderland that holds the power to shake the foundations of Accounting Fragility and bring racial hubris down low. Parables paint an effective picture of the silliness of racism denial, a farce to be sure, which propagates belief in the fiction that Accounting is getting near racial equity, while secretly accepting it doesn't exist. And to my mind it is once again Derrick Bell (1992) who shows the way of resistance, urging us not to forget that the creation of that racial "Eureka," moment involves inviting originality into existence. This is the importance of the use of counternarratives that are the fables of this text. I posit "that which destroys must be countered by that which creates." If racism exists it must be stamped out, replaced instead with an inspirational path forward. This is the test.

"Brilliant but crazy Derrick Bell … he set a tone" (Bell & Southerland, 2021)

Charles Ogletree captures the quandary that is Derrick Bell, and his work to shock the legal profession into recognizing Racial Realism, in the opening of his 1995 Derrick Bell lecture. He recounts numerous instances of Bell's actions which seemed mad at the time, for us to find later that indeed he was the racial soothsayer of our time. From resigning from Harvard because of a lack of Black women representation, to later resigning again from the Deanship of The University of Oregon Law School, because his faculty voted to prevent him from offering a place to an Asian woman, Bell was the definition of inflexibility when fighting racism at the intersection of gender. This at a time when the school minority was predominantly Asian, and no Asian faculty existed (Bell & Southerland, 2021).

His "folly" was soon at work again, this time surfacing during his tenure teaching Constitutional Law at Stanford Law School back in the 1980s using the lens of slavery. An action that prompted predominantly white law school students to claim their teaching was substandard, leading them to eventually audit other faculty member's courses in protest. Surreptitiously, in response to these claims, Stanford Law Faculty of the time had the idea of creating a public series of Constitutional Law lectures allowing disgruntled students to supplement what they deemed lacking in Professor Bell's class. Ultimately, the series was stopped by a protest of Black Law students in support of Derrick Bell. It was they who highlighted its ultimate racist intent, laying bare efforts to undermine one of the few Black Law professors at the time in Stanford, by white faculty in collusion with discontented white students. So successful was the shinning of this light into the dark recesses of institutional racism at Stanford Law School that its own Dean, Paul Brest, subsequently penned a statement of contrition in the *SALT Equalizer*, a publication of the Society of American Law Teachers, opening the door to racial change at the school (Callerous, 1987) at his behest.

Was Derrick Bell simply a crazy man for crazy times? I think not. But unconventional couched as "crazy" is the only tonic that shakes up the status quo of racial practice. Frankly, to do this, you have to be a bit nuts, which for Derrick Bell meant being ethical to the core, being ethical until it hurts. He simply called upon us to do likewise (Bell, 2002). This is why, I believe, decades after his passing, Critical Race Theory (CRT) today has come to the fore in taking up his mantle of disruption, one which Derrick Bell championed so well. After all he is one of the progenitors of CRT, a paradigm standing tall today, even as it becomes a pariah idea for the Republican right to rally against. Yet, even against this difficult backdrop an unexpected gain has accrued, CRT for good or bad cannot be ignored nor relegated to the dusty annals of academia. CRT today follows on as an ode to Bell as an active threat, it will not and cannot be ignored, its victory lies in its relevance good or bad. He showed those, like me, committed to anti-racism, that only "dangerous" work can do the heavy lifting required. A costly fact that the Black Panthers and Stokely Carmichael among many have found out to their triumph and cost. Personally, for me Bell's true brilliance lies in the "conceptual claymores," embedded in the tales he told. Repeatedly, as the reader walks through the entertaining visage of his fictions, their assertions are abruptly "blown away," time and again by the force of racial realism presented. Awakening some to a world they have not seen before. Now they can perceive a path forward, seeing the road toward racial empathy lie ahead, one to tread carefully if they so choose.

It is with this reverence for what Derrick Bell has achieved that I in some small way wish to emulate in Accounting. Sadly, I am no Derrick Bell, and my only wish is to try and match his peerless spirit and creativity. Instead, I present my own interpretation of Bell's way offering what I have termed Accounting Fables, as my own take on Bell's parables. They are versatile and wide-ranging in scope, touching on race and racism in Accounting, business, and society. I have already begun the process by giving a comprehensive description of CRT counterstories, citing examples of cutting-edge critical scholars who continue his narrative tradition both past and present. I query why we lack stories in Accounting and why we believe it is antithetical to standard financial storytelling. In doing so I challenge myself to explain why it is this way, and why telling CRT stories must exist as a counterpoint in Accounting space. Explaining specifically why I have tried to emulate Bell in taking a fantasy and science fiction approach to counterstory telling as methodology.

In keeping with the continuity of my last book, *Counting Black and White Beans*, the story of the Trickster God, and millennium-old anti-racist, Enki Abyd, is continued and expanded upon. The reader is afforded a richer, more textured vision of Enki's, home, the *Space between Spaces*, where he and Other Elder Gods reside. Moving forward our 1st Fable, "The Grandmaster," recounts how the "Grandmaster of Race and Racism" came into existence and his effect on the world. Throughout the book, the Grandmaster represents a central idea of CRT. He is emblematic of the intractability and fundamentality of race and racism in society, particularly Accounting and business. He is an articulation of the overarching futility of believing that race and racism can be defeated in society and instead underlines its permeance. Meanwhile Enki Abyd epitomizes the reality that we must fight against it anyway no matter the odds, equivalent to that of a novice chess player trying to outplay a Chess Grandmaster in the racial game of life. The beginner at best may take a piece here or there but ultimately the Grandmaster will win the game. Such is the fluidity and intransigence of race and racism that is a hallmark of its enduring nature (Bell, 1987). Here, we who fight against race and racism are the novice, explaining why so little progress has been made against racial practice in society's institutions and beyond.

The 2nd Fable, "Infection" wonders what might happen if a Black woman scientist and her male colleague discover a cure for a hidden malady in whites that has been an infestation of ingrained racial apathy. Its effect over hundreds of years has been to all but destroy race-based empathy in whites and effectively diminish any that might somehow be produced over time. The parable is that endemic racism robs whites of compassion and therefore humanity and always has done. Anti-racism in this context is not just the pursuit of saving the racial

Other but is in fact an act of redemption for whites to save themselves. However, a question in the tale is asked, should a Black woman scientist and Black male business professor actually reveal this discovery to the world? Should they profit from it as intellectual property? Could they even keep it? Continuing in this vein the 3rd Fable, "Unbearable," is set against the backdrop of bird watching while Black.[2] In the story I ask what does it mean to be Black in every setting? A great-granddaughter of one of the first cohorts of US African American business professors reads old letters recounting his encounter with creatures from another world. His telling of repeated meetings with them explores the nonsensical nature of race and racism if it were explained to beings from another star system, with no understanding of anti-Black discrimination, and how it relates to the idea of White Supremacy. The 4th Fable, "Hot Chicken. Hot Haircut" starts as an exploration of the mundane, as a Black father and son engage in the simple activity of getting a haircut and buying some spicy chicken, which quickly devolves into an odyssey all too familiar when interacting with Black business. How and why Black entrepreneurship has been intergenerationally injured, and neglected is problematized in this tale.

Within each counterstory runs the underlying reality that race and racism exert a costly influence in nearly every aspect of Black life, muting agency, increasing psychological battle fatigue,[3] both inside and outside the professional workplace. But what if significant redress was made in this area? Such, a moment seemed to germinate as the world absorbed the horrific killing of George Floyd at the hands of racist Minnesota police officers in May 2020, resulting in global Black Lives Matter protests and societal repentance. In that moment many white CEOs of Blue-chip companies pledged multi-millions to help mitigate the effects of race and racism, seemingly acknowledging its widespread harm in all aspects of society, specifically in their own sectors and beyond. Yet, unsurprisingly, a few years later, these grand promises proved all too hollow and the majority were reneged upon (Lewis, 2023). The 5th Fable takes this idea and wonders what might have arisen if promises made by powerful white business leaders were kept. Perhaps held together by a talismanic white male Accounting leader and ally. But the truth of the matter is that no matter how earnest the wish, institutional racism in organizations makes dismantling embedded racial practice nigh on impossible, even with full-throated support of the C-Suite, championing a clear anti-racist agenda. To do so is to push against the overwhelming whiteness of most firms, one that mechanically resists such attempts, ultimately doomed to fail.

---

[2]This phrase relates to an incident in New York's central park where a Black male bird watcher Christian Cooper asked a white woman, Amy Cooper (no relation), dog walker to leash her dog as per park rules. In response she called the police citing harassment by a threatening black man.

[3]Racial Battle Fatigue is the extreme tiredness and tension caused by having to manage unending racial microaggressions, leading Blacks and other racially stigmatized groups to suffer varied types of psychological, emotional, and physiological harm as an outcome (Acuff, 2018).

To genuinely attempt such a feat in our world is ultimately foolish, and to this end, we discover the white male hero in this narrative is in reality an entity from another universe. In his alternate reality, racial parity has been achieved in Accounting and society as a whole, meaning that it must be technically possible in our world. At least in theory. Our 6th Fable, "White Racism Sunglasses," asks the simple question, what happens when technology reaches a point that a device is created which makes colorblindness an actual reality? What does this mean for professions and businesses structured by racial hierarchy the populace no longer perceives?

As we move to the next parable, I draw inspiration from Aja Martinez' book *Counterstory* that gives a first-rate unpacking of CRT storytelling method to identify a differing approach to use; counterstory as autobiographic reflection. Here, authors present their own experiences and lives as stories to explore race and racism in the CRT way. This has the advantage of creating a pragmatic spin on the application of theory, giving it real-world significance, and revealing intricacy of meaning, in multi-faceted ways (Martinez, 2020). In a nod to this method, the 7th Fable "Talk Radio" locates me in the tale for the same reason. I take part in a fictional late-night radio show, there to discuss my conceptualization of CRT in Accounting and deliberate upon what this might mean as it traverses the neurodiverse Black Accounting experience. However, the Grandmaster of race and racism calls into the show and matters take a decidedly different turn. Our 8th and final Fable, "Jinn and Tonic," takes us to a contemplation of racial life and death within Accounting. We see both a Black woman CPA intending to commit suicide and a mythical Jinn spirit who has something to say about all this at the bottom of the East River, in New York. This tale analyzes the typical experience of Black women professionals within the Accounting profession. What they often suffer, and what a concrete ceiling consisting of an impenetrable mix of racism and sexism can do to Black women's psyche and career progression, probing Accounting's possible future in this light.

It is my hope that each fable reaches some part of you, the reader, that you enjoy and perhaps raise a wry smile at some of the more humorous situations. But in truth I really want you to join me in a much more serious examination of deep-seated racial practice in the profession that I call home and the racial reality of business as a whole for the stigmatized Other.

References

Acuff, J. (2018). Confronting racial battle fatigue and comforting my blackness as an educator. *Multicultural Perspectives*, *20*(3), 174–181.

Atkins, J., Atkins, B., Thompson, I., & Maroun, W. (2015). "Good" news from nowhere: Imagining utopian sustainable accounting. *Accounting Auditing & Accountability Journal*, *28*(5), 1–21.

Bell, D. (1987). *And we are not saved: The elusive quest for racial justice*. Basic Books.

Bell, D. (1992). *Faces at the bottom of the well: The permanence of racism*. Basic Books.

Bell, D. (2002). *Ethical ambition. Living a life of meaning and worth*. Bloomsbury Publishing.

Bell, J., & Southerland, V. (2021). *Race, rights, and redemption: The Derrick Bell lectures on the law and critical race theory*. The New Press.

Callerous, C. (1987). Derrick Bell's experience sparks change at Stanford. *SALT Equalizer, 1998*(2), 1–8.

Delgado, R. (2007). Legal storytelling: Storytelling for oppositionists and others: A plea for narrative. In A. K. Wing & J. Stefancic (Eds.), *The law unbound! A Richard Delgado reader* (pp. 3–20). Paradigm Publishers.

DiAngelo, R. (2018). *White fragility. Why it's so hard for white people to talk about racism*. Beacon Press.

Lewis, A. (2015). Counting black and white beans. Why we need a critical race theory of accounting. *European Journal of Contemporary Economics and Management*, *2*(2), 1–13.

Lewis, A. (2016). A critical race theory discussion of neutrality and colorblindness in accounting. *Advances in Public Interest Accounting*, *19*, 113–134.

Lewis, A. (2020). *Counting black and white beans. Critical race theory in accounting*. Emerald Publishing Limited.

Lewis, A. (2023). Keeping our promise. *The CPA Journal* (November/December), 1–80. https://www.cpajournal.com/2024/02/07/keeping-our-promise/

Martinez, A. (2020). *Counterstory. The rhetoric and writing of critical race theory*. CCC/NCTE.

Chapter 1

1st Fable: The Grandmaster

A wager was all it took to create one of the greatest harms to befall the world and birth one of the more recent Elder Gods. Enki Abd is used to such bets and rarely fails to win because one's money should always ride with a trickster God which Enki is. And success would have been the outcome had he not foolishly bet against the one entity who defined the notion of deceit, cunning, and loss – Old Nick, Enki's close friend and mortal enemy. If the Elder Gods can be described as having a leader it would be him. The exact nature of how the wager came to be is detailed elsewhere[1] but know that Enki challenged Old Nick, Beelzebub, or Mr Morningstar as he is known to others, to create a pestilence to plague man like no other. This was the genesis of racism. But what neither realized was the true extent of its success. It was so complete, its ability to render intergenerational harm so effective that it birthed itself as a new fully formed Elder God, "The Grandmaster" of race and racism. In truth, although he tried to hide it, Old Nick was as proud as any new father could be. Of course, he had to conceal his favoritism because … well … Elder Gods don't do offensive human emotions. I mean the very thought is repugnant but nevertheless, Mr Morningstar was delighted. And what was the visage of the Grandmaster? Who could tell for sure? Most perceive him to be an older white male, extruding an aura of wealth and menace. Particularly if you are Black. In the 1970s, African Americans simply referred to him as "The Man," an apt descriptor for the Grandmaster. This is no beast in the classic sense. In fact, he is rather refined in a deceitful kind of way, with a flinty look in his eye. He misses nothing. But why call himself the Grandmaster?

Because to him the existence of race and racism in the affairs of man is a game, one that he ultimately always wins pretty much every time, but even so, he still cares deeply about it. Similar to a Chess Grandmaster he is ahead of any move used to redress race and racism and always finds a way to win eventually. He effectively represents the stickability of racism, its ability to confuse and confound even when you know what it is. But when finally recognized and challenged, craftily morphs into what it is not, forcing those who consider themselves anti-racist

[1]The full tale of exactly how this wager came into fruition can be found in the book *Counting Black and White Beans. Critical Race Theory in Accounting* (Lewis, 2020).

Accounting Fables: Tales of Race and Racism in the Borderlands of Business, 11–20

Published under exclusive licence by Emerald Publishing Limited
doi:10.1108/978-1-80117-069-720251005

to wonder in our more modern times where have all the racial foxes gone? And when did hens have such big sharp teeth?[2] This is his most elusive trick, enabling racism to incessantly transform over time, aiding its ability to deceive in the service of subjugation and power. Put simply it changes to fit circumstance.[3]

However, the Grand part of his name alludes directly to a heartfelt pet project of his own making, the Klu Klux Klan. For it was he who sowed the idea into the addled minds of six youthful Confederate veterans in 1865, Pulaski, Tennessee. Turning what was nothing more than a hay seed social club into an engine of misery and despair. Somewhere deep in what Klansmen call a "mind," unconscious homage was paid to the Grandmaster as their spiritual guru. This is how their first leader became Grand Cyclops, his assistant Grand Magi, with a Grand Turk created to meet and greet new recruits. All this was a subliminal kissing of the ring of the Grandmaster so to speak, an act he greatly appreciated. After all, racial terrorism plays a significant part in unerring white domination over the African Other. In return, the Grandmaster instilled his nefarious resolve in a new horror, influencing new recruits to be called "Ghouls," an apt descriptor of crimes to come. The Klan therefore became a laboratory of sorts, allowing the Grandmaster to implant one nightmare into the Klan imaginary after another, testing out what worked and what did not in the service of racial strife and struggle. Thus, cleverly allowing Klan behavior and thinking to become racism's muse in an odd sort of way. Emanating from this experimentation arose the dread tactic of the night ride. Ghouls cloaked in white hoods and gowns would visit Black homes in the dead of night, often gifting them "Strange Fruit" sung so sorrowfully by Nina Simone. Such was the triumph of this tactic it evoked memories of the terror of prewar slave patrols (Klanwatch, 2011). And for his part, the Grandmaster was greatly pleased with the doom he had seeded into the mind of many a white person for generations to come.

The Grandmaster also bids us not forget his other great invention of doom and discord, reminding you the reader that such racial terror has its antecedents in colonialism. A foregrounding of what was to come in the New World, imported from the Old. Empire building through the colonial project was his doing. Whispering to King Leopold of Belgian of the glory of the Congo that could be his if he wished. Cajoling the monarch of Britain, Queen Victoria, to plunder the wealth and land of India, recasting it as the "Jewel of Empire." Disguised as one of her most trusted servants, the Grandmaster ushered in the "art of the take," causing an epidemic of land theft and slavery to wash over Old Europe, stealing Black and Brown wealth in the self-professed cause of "defending civilization." The tale told to validate pilfering was that the native was too simple, childlike and

---

[2]I borrow here from the anthropologist John L. Jackson Jr's conceptualization of racism disappearing as racial foxes that have left leaving "hungry sheep" smacking their lips, showing how racism transforms to deceive (Jackson, 2008).

[3]See counterstories chapter for a review of the fluidity of race and racism in the context of Omi and Winnat's Racial Formation and Stuart Hall's Floating Racial Signifier.

savage to manage their resources themselves, all in the service of racial capitalism. It was the white man's burden to do so (as it still is today), usefully providing European nations the moral justification to jockey for position for lands and peoples which were not theirs at the barrel of a gun. A grab for power creating templates of suffering for years to come.[4] Key was making sure Black and Brown bodies were robbed of self-determination under pain of death, infantilized for good measure, and internalized gratitude to the oppressor for their generosity. The Grandmaster's ploy ensured the complete white conquering of native lands, bodies, and minds. Naturally believing their own inherent racial inferiority and supplicating their needs in preference for white. A requirement of colonization lives within society today as racialized self-hatred and obedience leaving the Black and Brown Other in ceaseless pain, neck deep in sorrow, and mistreatment. And he, the Grandmaster, did not think it too much for the next scheme beckoned.

In fact, only one mortal – Professor Derrick Bell (2005) – correctly identified the true nature of the Grandmaster in his assertion of Racial Realism; that racism is an irreducible and enduring ill ever present in the affairs of humanity. Indeed, the endlessness of racial practice is a precise characterization of the Grandmaster himself for in reality they are one and the same – the permanence of racism and the existence of the Grandmaster of race.

It was this very assertion however that helped fashion an ideology to challenge his reign, an effective weapon to be used against racism and therefore the Grandmaster himself called Critical Race Theory (CRT). Through its analytical lens any notion of a historicism is dismissed, meaning that to reveal the machinations of the Grandmaster, one must look to the racial practice of the past to account for a racist present and a racist future. Humanity cannot magically move beyond itself into racelessness as some pundits have claimed society is right now, because examination of times past shows race and racism to have operated as a nervous system in dominant majority white society. Effectively parceling out privileges to "deserving" white inhabitants, while branding darker citizens of color worthless. In this polarity, Blacks are positioned at the very bottom of the racial hierarchy and whites at the top. The CRT way illustrates that the racial past is but a pale reflection of the present. It is to see the world "but through a glass darkly." It is to see the world as it really is.

This is how (in the context of the USA) when slavery was finally abolished, it was replaced by Sharecropping – debt peonage that is economic slavery by proxy. Fine work once again by the ever-inventive Grandmaster. Subsequent Black codes at the turn of the century made sure the prison industrial complex swelled with Black bodies, accused of violating thinly veiled racist vagrancy laws, a neat trick expanded exponentially upon by the Grandmaster as a war on drugs later in the 1980s. A policy couched in tough policing politics, that served up Black bodies to an unquenchable prison industrial complex in existence to this day. After all,

[4]Racial capitalism illustrates how racial exploitation and capital accumulation combine to extract social and economic value from marginalized peoples who are most often Black and Brown (Andrews, 2021).

the benefit of slave labor was that it was "free," after initial purchase costs Black bodies could be worked incessantly (often to death), until significant returns on capital were garnered. Black and Brown bodies now predominantly make up the US penal system and have long been put to work in a similar fashion to produce goods at near free rates, and where this is not the case dark bodies at rest still serve as a central economic driver in the most rural, least educated, and predominantly white areas. This pragmatically enables a non-college-educated white male to be a prison officer, giving benefits such as a salary, and pension security advantages (Alexander, 2010; Davis, 2003).

How very crafty of the Grandmaster to ensure that the US penal system, masquerading as reform is in fact a capitalist profit project, guaranteeing economic and social benefits to the forgotten of rustbelt America. Economically, the prison is often the largest business in the town in which they reside.[5] The Grandmaster, ever thinking and plotting, pulled strings years ago needed to guarantee urban schools of poor Black and Brown children are forever seen by white society as culturally inclined to criminality. Institutionalization of a prison mentality is complete as armed police officers are stationed in the majority of schools, seen as "safety officers" in predominantly white schools, protecting white children from the dangerous Black Other, and de facto "Prison officers" in urban schools, defending greater white society from Black and Brown students getting out. This is how Black children are shown the way to the "Big House" of the State Pen (Prison) early, securing the racialized school to prison pipeline with frightening alacrity until these profit-producing institutions are fit to burst.

Such is the art of the Grandmaster that he has seen to it that racism continues to seep into the US judicial and political system, fueled by white fear of the Black Other. So much so that it is now "normal" for Black and Brown bodies to be imprisoned for minor infractions, mediated by a white institutionally racist legal industrial complex, which in the past championed notions of immediate large prison terms for crack cocaine as opposed to powder for no conceivable reason apart from the fact that Blacks predominantly used crack and whites used powder (Alexander, 2010). It is the control of Black bodies for economic gain not so different to that of slavery that is the natural way of things, or the New Jim Crow as noted academic Michelle Alexander adroitly puts it. It's genius really. It's the Grandmaster at his best.

These are but a few examples of his strategic playbook. We will of course examine more, but right now, Enki is still in mid ponder ….

> "Why can't I beat him? I beat everybody, at everything, all the time but I've not bested the Grandmaster once, not in a way that matters. Damn it! It makes me embarrassed to be a Trickster God, let alone a lesser of God of Gambling."

---

[5]Towns like Lockport, IL, are supported by Statesville Correctional Center (one of the largest prisons in the USA). In Warden, OH, the Ohio State Petitionary, a maximum security prison has long revitalized the local economy.

For sure, it is a curious sight to see a God ranting, and a little later, mumbling, in an incoherent manner to himself.

"More."

The voice half belched and half gurgled out the statement out of a newly formed bubble of sulfuric acid from the Lake, culminating in a popping sound.

"More of what?" murmured an exasperated Enki.

"Everything" was burped out next.

So, what did the lake mean by this? Enki went into pondering overdrive on the rock of pondering. This could take eons, he mused. If he took the Grandmasters chess analogy seriously then he had to admit that Enki Abyd was nothing more than a talented novice doomed to lose every time he played against him. To win he needed to learn more, see things differently, act and think in unpredictable ways, still reconciling himself to the reality at best he might win the odd piece, but the game is always lost. It all seemed so hopeless.

But wait … the raucous, stinking, fizzing lake had actually given him a new train of thought to go by. A path of which to follow if you will. This was no accident. You see it's a little-known fact that lakes like peace and quiet. They just want to be. Plus, they are bloody good at just being. In fact, nothing irritates a lake in the earthly realm or in the dominion of Elder Gods than people trying to find peace with their pesky "troubles." This is why the lake beside Enki was so animated. It just wanted him to shut up and go away! Over eons, lakes discovered that initiating inspiration actually got mortals and gods to get up and leave. It really is the reason lakes in any universe are tranquil places where one gets the best ideas. Just remember that when that Eureka instant arrives you should immediately leave out of politeness. Anyway, at the moment the lake in its inspiration frenzy had run up against the Achilles heel of Elder Gods. Boredom. I mean really what do you do if you are eternal and omnipotent? You run out of things to say and on top of everything you've literally heard it all before. You've engaged in unthinkable, unconscionable acts of depravity and saintly acts of kindness because … well why not? The short of it is that you become unimaginative. Unable to think in differing ways, or to question what you see or why you see it and for Enki this was acutely true as he viewed the question of race and racism. What could he do about this vexing problem? And the panicked lake thought "This will not do!"

"People."

This time the belching bubble burst forth in a pungent stinky blood red liquor toward the slimy wall of the stalactite filled cavern. Weirdly, it almost sounded like a hiccup. It meant humans. They irritated Enki for sure, but their capacity for imagination, confusion, chaos and irrationality far exceeded the abilities of the Elder Gods. In truth, as a species, they are nuts. It's a core reason that the Elder ones love to mess with them in the first place, after all its just so damn funny to do. I mean look at the damage they do to their planet without anywhere else to go … incredible. But how to coax this out of them? The sad truth is having said all this they can also be the most irritating dullards and quite gloomy creatures. But with the right persuasion you can coax their inherent natural gifts of imagination, pandemonium and creativity. If you can do this then you have something to work with. This mattered to Enki's ambitions where the Grandmaster was concerned. The lake was on a roll now ....

"Stone."

Tranquility settled from one end of the shore to the other and it seemed that this would be the last wisdom burp that the lake had to offer this day. The bubbles were subsiding leaving the lake still and lifeless, if such a thing can be said of a body of liquid sulfur that was pissed off and exhausted. Enki knew what it meant though. It was the "Fable Stone." One of many objects of mystical worth housed in the "Palace of Taking," in the region that the Gods inhabit, containing a multitude of objects found, and robbed, from Earth and other planets deemed far too powerful for mortals. Think of it as the Elder Gods "Hanger 51."[6] It contained within it the legendary *Tribulum Arcanca,* an ancient tool that was a wooden framework, with parts of metal attached beneath the belly, usually dragged over grain by an animal, such as oxen. But this magical *Tribulum Arcanca* had an unreasonably heavy slab of rock, the Fable Stone, attached beneath. Its gift is the ability to bequeath its user with an unlimited bounty of whatever seed was sown, no matter the time of year or weather conditions. In addition, as one plowed, dreams of the impossible and the wonderful occurred meaning that hours passed away in joyful minutes. And these dreams came true ....

When detached from the Tribulum itself, the stone also allowed which ever human who touched it to breach space, time, and reality and access their inherent ability to act differently and behave chaotically, to seamlessly access their own natural creativity, and supercharge their imagination. This got Enki thinking. He could use his own Eldroth[7] powers alongside it to fabricate newly imagined worlds, using them to explore and test racial remedies or create portals to differing universes guided by the wishes of the stone. All hidden from the prying eyes of the Grandmaster. He just needed a few humans. Oh, and there was just one small fly in the ointment. Those who touched the stone tended to die. Hmmm .... Enki murmured. He would have to clear that bit with his old drinking pal Death. Still, it is a start.

The wailing wind seemed particularly brisk that day as Enki Abd made his way toward the inner sanctum where the *Tribulum Arcanca* lay. This new approach really had him excited. He had always needed a radically different strategy to engage the Grandmaster of race and racism on his own terms. Business might well be the key. On a previous occasion, the Accounting profession on Earth had been a test case for his experiments in racial redress. Sadly, it proved less than fruitful, but this would be different. He needed to view race and racism in a newer way. Or perhaps older. Given the deep harm and unfairness that is racism, it is easy, Enki deliberated, to forget that much of its power to harm was/is predicated upon economics. After all, Africans were transported to the "New World" to build it and not for just for a jape and a wheeze. The money involved was vast and

[6]This refers the movie *Raiders of the lost ark*, where the powerful Ark of the Covenant was kept for safe keeping.

[7]The innate powers of a Daemon, beyond human reckoning.

fortunes amassed quickly when a Black man or woman was reduced to chattel and worked on the land as such. Once again, we find the Grandmaster behind the scenes encouraging (and still does quite a bit) racism to be expressed as racial economic logic to keep people as "working cattle," and their offspring in such a state in perpetuity if possible. As highlighted earlier at the start of our tale, this was how great wealth accrued to slave holders in the British Empire through remote ownership of Sugar Plantations in the British West Indies in the 18th century (Davie, 2005) and the white Southern Plantation plutocracy (Baptist, 2014) with much the same effect in America. If truth be told it was the very back bone of the economic miracle that was the USA at its inception and contributed mightily to the industrial/economic behemoth that was the British Empire, be it through the action of slavery or its history of colonial domination of Black and Brown people across the globe over the same period. It is to see the backbone of racism for all intents and purposes as fundamentally economic with Accounting technologies of the time acting as tools of subjugation. It is about the ultimate marshaling of wealth and resources to white ingroups to the detriment of Blacks and Brown outgroups for the most part.

In reality the Grandmaster is the "Plantation master's master" if you like. The plantation was integral to his plan of racial subjugation from the beginning. And to be fair, the business of the plantation was simply an expression of what modern business is now except veiled by an imperceptible colorblindness according to his design. Not obvious or quite as crude but effective in its current exploitation of Blackness at this moment. The Black worker is trapped by the ideology of "Neo Plantocracy," a system of racial conquest as commerce still stuck fast as a fly is in amber. In this way, the Grandmaster continuously sees into existence a rejuvenation of the racial hierarchy of whites at the top and Blacks at the bottom for each generation. It is Plantocracy in microcosm, rearticulated for a new more enlightened era that is anything but, permitting hidden oppression to continue to reside across business. Worse, a new cadre of non-white masters in the C-Suite (Asian, South Asian, Latino/a, and Black CEOs) adhere to the Grandmaster's way of whiteness as rightness, making sure white centric influence spreads across diversity efforts, hobbling it through non-performativity (Ahmed, 2012). It is why DEI policy often fails as it was never knowingly meant to succeed, there to be seen to do diversity but never attain it. This is "slavocracy"[8] in all but name, concealed, but nevertheless an expression of Blackness in bondage still, where Blackness is really social death (Wilderson, 2020). And we wonder why Blacks do not progress in such environments in great numbers. This arrangement speaks to his design that is White Western hegemony underpinning continued exploitation of the Global South by the Global North (Winant, 2001).

However, if Enki is to inflict a grievous blow to the Grandmaster, then exploring economic racial realism is required. Perhaps Blacks cannot withstand

---

[8]Slavocracy is a group predominantly governed by slaveholders, who wield political and social power similar to the dominant group of slaveholders in the USA in the 18th century and later.

this social/professional death that the Grandmaster has constructed, and therefore must initially accept it. That is not to welcome it, nor be crushed by it, but simply accept it until a time of their choosing, and then strike back. What the Grandmaster has missed is that this social death is itself a social construct and therefore can be blown up, but from the inside, by those who "know their place." This is the ultimate trick that the trickster god must play to checkmate the Grandmaster. But it is almost impossible for the Black actor to accomplish. It would need luck and hope. Luck Enki can engineer but HOPE disappeared some time ago. She is nowhere to be found. Enki suspected it was the Grandmasters doing. It should be noted that one of the few rules the Elder Gods possess is that no God can harm another in thought, deed, or action. HOPE was a daemon, one of the oldest who regrettably disappeared ages ago. She is the reason people on Earth are so hopeless because well … they don't have HOPE. Alas, Enki has no proof to accuse him let alone find the Goddess himself. But he has a plan ….

The *Tribulum Arcanca* in the inner sanctum lay on its side surrounded by an assortment of other untold artifacts with the potential to relieve humanity of global suffering or conversely inflict worldwide harm. Quick as a flash Enki hoisted up the device and wrenched the stone from its millennium long home embedded within the mahogany that was the Tribulum. Nothing more than smashed matchsticks remained. Enki could be quite impatient when a good idea takes hold. Think of a Lego-obsessed six-year-old ripping apart a new set eager to get building and losing the necessary pieces in the process to get the job done. Oh … and add a dash of godly domination and pique for kicks. You get the picture. It was time for Enki to make his way once more toward the mortal realm and he had much to do. Humans are such frail things, and would once again be integral to his plans, but they are fickle, where would he find one to begin this journey with? Indeed, where geographically would he start? For such a small planet these talking apes seemed to infest every nook and cranny. Picking the right one from the right place is just plain difficult.

His indecision was rife, another worrying trait that seemed to infect the Elder God's more and more these days most likely from prolonged exposure to humanity, an unsavory attribute that has not gone unnoticed by Old Nick. Enki decided that he would stick with what he knew best. America. It is widely considered the Grandmaster's home turf, so where better to start his project than in "racism's heartland" for want of a better word? Of course, it would be easier for him to also persuade Death down for a jar or two as well. It's a little-known fact that Death really does like an American Pale Ale from time to time. It is a habit he picked up on his frequent sojourns to the States for work. Between the gun lobby, 1st amendment rights and inner-city poverty he has been kept quite busy. Death of course likes to be kept busy.

Enki decided that Indianapolis, Indiana, would be the best place to start. A spot rich in opportunities to find his first victim or "helper" as Enki had decided to name or more accurately "frame" his hapless accomplices. If dismantling the business of race and racism was to be Enki's task, then it seemed fitting that he begin at a business school, and the Met Indy school of business of Indianapolis

Metropolitan University would suffice. It had suffered an unfavorable relationship in its past with the Ku Klux Klan, not unlike other institutions such as Valparaiso University[9] to the Northwest of the state. Met Indy's claim to fame was that a Grand Wizard graduated from the business school in 1978 and was subsequently implicated in a spate of race-related gun killings of African American worshipers at Black Churches, by clan members of the area, an unfortunate trend that continues to our time.[10] Enki whipped up a quick "Scry cloud," used mostly for predicting the future but also as a teleportation system to instantly get from one location to another. In this case, Met Indy was the target. As he ventured into the swirling mists of effervescent purple, and blue, he thought perhaps he could grab a quick Big Yummy Tummy burger, quite a popular chain in Indy on the way down, but then recanted as he was pushed for time after all. And in an instant, he was gone.

References

Ahmed, S. (2012). *On being included. Racism and diversity in institutional life*. Duke University Press.

Alexander, M. (2010). *The new Jim Crow. Mass incarceration in the age of colorblindness*. The New Press.

Andrews, K. (2021). *The new age of empire*. Bold Type Books.

Baptist, E. E. (2014). *The half has never been told. Slavery and the making of American capitalism*. Basic Books.

Bell, D. (2005). Racial realism. In R. Delgado & J. Stefancic (Eds.), *The Derrick Bell reader* (pp. 74–77). New York University Press.

Davie, S. S. K. (2005). Accounting's uses in exploitative human engineering: Theorizing citizenship, indirect rule and Britain's imperial expansion. *Accounting Historians Journal, 32*(2), 1–3.

Davis, A. Y. (2003). *Are prisons obsolete*. Turnaround Publisher Services Ltd.

Hersher, R. (2016). *Jury finds Dylan Roof guilty in S.C. Church shooting*. https://www.npr.org/sections/thetwo-way/2016/12/15/505723552/jury-finds-dylann-roof-guilty-in-s-c-church-shooting

Jackson, J. L. (2008). *Racial Paranoia. The unintended consequences of political correctness*. Basic Civitas Books.

Klanwatch. (2011). *Ku Klux Klan. A history of racism and violence*. https://www.splcenter.org/sites/default/files/Ku-Klux-Klan-A-History-of-Racism.pdf

Lewis, A. (2020). *Counting black and white beans. Critical race theory in accounting*. Emerald Publishing Limited.

---

[9]In 1923, the Klu Klux Klan very nearly acquired Valparaiso University, eponymously referred to as "Ku Klux Kollege," by some, after falling into financial hardship during the period (Taylor, 2021).

[10]In 2015, 21-year old Dylan Roof was found guilty of murdering nine African Americans in the basement of the Emanuel African Methodist Episcopal Church, a historically Black Church, in Charlston, North Carolina (Hersher, 2016)

Taylor, S. (2021). *Ku Klux U: How the Klan almost bought a university*. https://blog.history.in.gov/ku-klux-u-how-the-klan-almost-bought-a-university/
Wilderson, F. (2020). *Afropessimism*. Liveright Publishing Corporation.
Winant, H. (2001). *The world is a Ghetto. Race and democracy since World War 2*. Basic Books.

Chapter 2

2nd Fable: Infection!

The figure of a slightly built man, African American, danced menacingly in half-crescent moonlight against the Indianapolis sidewalk. Bryon Jones, an Associate Professor of Management in the College of Business of Indiana Metropolitan University was in a hurry. So little time and so much to do he murmured, as if like the white rabbit of Alice's imagination,[1] he had a mysterious Wonderland to visit. Indeed, the man did have whiskers, and he did twitch them when nervous … but in truth "mystery" dodged the Building of Biochemistry, his stated destination, which he rushed toward as if his life depended upon it. Honestly, never had such a dull and mirthless bunch of academics been lumped together in one space. Moreover, the building was state of the art, new, and "cheap" at a mere $13 million dollars. And yet it oozed a lifeless, dull tedium, that had to be seen to be believed and yet because of this, in quite a perverse manner, it was something to behold. But Bryon Jones had a more interesting destination in mind within the building itself; the Center for Infectious Disease and Tropical Medicine (CIDT Med), where Professor Annie Ball sat hunched over an electron microscope, engrossed over her disturbing findings, entertaining an expression of what can only be described as disbelief mixed with joy and just a dash of dread.

The Breakthrough

As Bryon Jones rushed up the six flight of stairs toward the top floor where the Center resided (the elevator still didn't work), his old, battered briefcase clattered against his thigh, giving him an ungainly gait. Flushed and out of breath he burst into the laboratory blurting out:

"I'm here, Annie, I made it!"

"Bryon … you have to see this."

She managed to make this statement without moving an inch, motionless, huddled over a sensitive piece of equipment. Bryon's spritely jaunt up the multitude of stairs had left him in a state of extreme perspiration to put it kindly. Composing

[1] I refer here to the white rabbit which leads Alice into Wonderland in *Alice in Wonderland* by Lewis Carroll.

Accounting Fables: Tales of Race and Racism in the Borderlands of Business, 21–33

Published under exclusive licence by Emerald Publishing Limited
doi:10.1108/978-1-80117-069-720251007

himself after a minute or two (he really was not the healthiest of men), he then joined the only Black woman tenured full Professor at the University. And to be fair the institution was lucky to have somebody of her caliber working there in the first place. She really was a prodigy in her field, and typically like so many brilliant Black women academics in the Ivory Tower, it had no idea what to do with her. She, like Bryon, was marginalized within her college, discounted by the university as a whole, and had to fight tooth and nail to get her research agenda of Race and Disease taken seriously (Krusemark, 2012). They basically put her in CIDT Med as a "photo opportunity" to show off their brand-new science building and their lovely new token diversity professor for maximum optics. Cynical I know but it happens all the time.

Isolation and kinship first brought Bryon and Annie together as kindred spirits, enduring life in a Predominantly White Institution, one chockful of racism and sexism that of course would never be admitted. As it happened his investigations into race and business had interesting synergies with her work, a valuable benefit against the gloom of their academic life. Which brings us back to the scene before us, begging the question, why at nearly midnight were two Black academics taking turns, viewing something both appalling and astounding on a dark, dank Saturday night in an empty building in downtown Indianapolis? What finding could bring a business professor and a scientist together in such a fashion?

Enki Abd knew of course. As usual, he was lurking in the shadows at the other end of the lab. Waiting, watching, peering at events as they unfolded. He loves to lurk a lot and this is a valued pastime for many Elder Gods. To sulk and skulk. It's just such fun. Have you ever felt when you are alone that somebody is watching you? Staring? But you cannot see them, perhaps existing at the edge of your peripheral vision. Or you wake up with a start, from a deep sleep, looking for the briefest moment at the daemonic figure at the end of your bed? Yep, it is one of the "Masters of Misrule." Why? Why not? It is a classic jape and wheeze. Some of them go as far as to sit on the chest of sleeping humans just watch their horrified expression as they wake up to see an actual real-life Daemon seated on their chest. Such is the shock of being in physical contact with beings of such immense power that people being sat upon become instantly paralyzed, trapped within their own skin. The best of it is that 'rational' humanity has come to describe this practical joke as "sleep paralysis," explaining away the very real experience of having an omnipotent God sat on your chest. Regularly. This of course makes it even more fun to the masters of space, time, and cruelty. I mean for them terrifying and unnerving humans is just so entertaining, after all one must do something to while away the eons .... However, Enki was not in this precise corner scrutinizing unfolding events for "shits and giggles," no he had a reason and these two were part of his plan.

"Good. I see you have finally found it" announced Enki as he stepped toward the two professors.

How people react to mind-bending terror is a sight to behold. One can really tell a lot about a person. For example, the mild-mannered Bryon instantly dropped to his knees and began mumbling, praying, and gurgling all at the same time. It was an odd sort of ad hoc worship. On the other hand, Annie just stared, as if she were looking at a cross between a fish and a Muppet. You know, like she was looking at something that made absolutely no sense.

"Get up human and stop degrading yourself," gestured the God.

Babbling, wailing, and weeping was all Bryon could muster as he gazed upon the immensely imposing, tall, impossibly Black ethereal figure looming ever larger over them both. Dear reader, pray you never see a Daemon for real. It is not pleasant and usually requires a change of pants for most.

"Tell. Me. What. You. See" barked the impatient deity.

"It's an infection. A virus. Incredibly virulent, and ruthless in its ability to infect as both an airborne pathogen and easily transmitted by touch, and ingestion" proffered Annie.

"But … it does not kill people." pressed the being of power.

Both academics shook their heads while shaking themselves.

"Then what does it do? You woman doctor speak!"

"It's … a … Soul Eater, I think?"

An impish smile crept across the face of the seldom-smiling Enki.

"Go on …."

"What I mean is that this virus specifically attacks the area of the brain where empathy and understanding reside. It destroys it and that seems to be its only effect. The disease kind of causes a psychological syndrome of racial apathy and denial in the mind, while the rest of the body is left intact. But here is the really confounding piece, the bit that Bryon and I just can't get. It only affects white people for the most part." Annie, relaxed a bit more as her never-ending curiosity edged out her fear as she spoke. She was ready to explain more.

"The effect?" They finally have it mused the God to himself.

"Well … it means specifically that the majority of those considered white for the last few hundred years have been infected with a contagion that robs them of their ability to be empathetic toward other races of people. It is particularly acute where Black African and indigenous people are involved. The upshot is that it has produced a race of 'moral monsters' as Baldwin once said."[2]

Annie had moved beyond fear or doubt and was now in full flow, compelled even to reason out the full ramifications of this matter to the other worldly being.

"This 'Sickness,' if you will, is trauma within the souls of whites, to their intrinsic humanity. Its similar in some ways to the CTE[3] degenerative brain condition. Just like multiple hits to the head, the 'soul,' as I define it, that part of understanding and empathy that exists for other races is continually damaged. But it is an impairment that they themselves on their own cannot see. Exposure has already taken place within the familial setting, and symptoms activate with

---

[2]Baldwin's "moral monsters," quoted from the motion picture, *I Am Not Your Negro*, is an evaluation of racism and the moral weaknesses of persons (usually white), who continue the system (Peck, 2016).

[3]Chronic traumatic encephalopathy is a disease of the brain brought about by multiple head injuries over time that can include concussions. It has been prevalent in professional athletes who played heavy contact sports like football and ice hockey.

early racialized experience for whites, intensified by society which has long standardized racial practice, normalizing and compounding this unseen injury in equal measure. But the effects on Black and Brown people are not so hidden and are immediate and devastating. Because over time it prevents the vast majority of whites being able to do what is racially right or to conceive of racial justice. They are doomed, unable to understand the true harm of intergenerational destruction caused by racist practice. Essentially preventing them from knowing how to do the right thing regarding race, as a group or independently. Robbing them of sympathy and placing them outside the norms of regular humanity. By default, deep at their core, beyond rationality and reason, the 'Sickness say's' that the Other, particularly the Black and Brown,/indigenous Other is not worthy or not valuable. Their malady makes them believe they are one step above their brothers and sisters of color deep in their heart. This is now a bit out of my area Mr …."

"It's Enki Abd, I'm a Daemon. But more of that later perhaps. Continue."

And Annie could not help herself, she began to launch into another diatribe, barely noticing the quivering figure of Bryon next to her. Her wits were about her in full working order, as she resumed relating the findings of her analysis.

"Mr Abd."

"Enki, will do."

"Enki, sir, I believe Bryon could better explain some of the economic welfare ramifications a little better than I if only he wasn't a gibbering mess. Can you do something about that?"

"Humans …."

With the raising of a single eyebrow, below what could be called eyes at a push, Enki removed most of the fright and uncontrolled worship Bryon was experiencing. Feeling more himself he stood up and addressed the deity in front of him.

"Lord Enki, my sire[4] … Annie is quite right of course. It's where my research on race and business dovetails with hers. Essentially the effects of the disease are that whites on the whole feel absolved of racial responsibility, for any past action they or their predecessors have levied on racial Others. Often, the older they are the more difficult it becomes to engage in any sort of 'Racial Realism'[5], as coined by the scholar Derrick Bell, that shows the history of extreme harm to racial Others or its continued existence right now. To paraphrase Bell somewhat, racial equality under these conditions is impossible. Worse for Black and Brown people, among the gamut of many considered Other, persistence in trying to achieve racial equity is a fruitless exercise. That goal is unachievable because of racial apathy found in whites, thus causing over time increased exasperation and hopelessness in the racialized, damaging their hearts and soul (Bell, 2005). Perversely a knock-on effect also occurs for Blacks existing in predominantly

[4]As has been explained in Enki Abd's previous exploits, men cannot but worship and revere beings such as him. They bow and scrape in the presence of real power. Women of course have learned reserve in this respect.

[5]Bell suggests that racial realism pushes us to cast off the notion that legal or moral arguments drive racial progress in society or will bring about racial equality.

white working environments. When in settings such as Accounting or technology among many others, with traditionally low diversity, equity and inclusion (DEI), they find themselves suffering racial exhaustion. White racial apathy defines the contours of 'WhiteWorld's'[6] space, everyday racism abounds, that is subtle and unchallenged. It is endured relentlessly by the racialized and as a result they experience negative physical and psychological effects i.e., the more guilt free whites feel about racism the more dangerously fatigued and harmed they become. To paraphrase the academic Hadnot, in a paper by Joni Acuff – we are all holograms now; shadows of who we really are, disappearing within ourselves, in the (racialized and sexualized) workplace, sick and psychologically scared thanks to life lived under the present tenets of business-as-usual Corporate America (Acuff, 2018)."

"Very interesting" purred Enki.

"But my Liege, there is more. Interestingly, a few whites exhibit an unexplained immunity to this sickness and naturally identify with and act decently toward racial Others, treating them as they would any other white person. They tend to be anti-racist. But we don't know why yet."

"Yes. These types do seem to resist his little games quite well, don't they?"

"Excuse me but 'who' are you talking about exactly?"

Enki gave Annie a derisive glance for her insolence and then uttered.

"The Grandmaster of Race and Racism. He created this little bug of yours. It is he who guides it on its unalterable trajectory, fomenting chaos in its wake. But do not concern yourself with worry. It is not for mortals to comprehend. Be still and focus on the task in hand. You have a decision to make, don't you?"

Both Annie and Bryon nodded, frozen in perplexed agreement, minds intent on what was to be done next.

"You two Black academics must decide if you should reveal this discovery to the world or not. It has been at the back of your mind since you discovered its true nature, and you are torn about the possible effects. For you both see all too well what might occur, and it doesn't look good. Bryon, you perceive that great wealth is just around the corner for whoever licenses and produces this as a cure. Just as pandemics in past periods led to tremendous profits for Biotech companies which developed vaccines, you see the same happening here; an antidote to racial apathy in whites that might bring relief to lifelong battle fatigue suffered by Blacks and other groups. At a price of course. But you cannot help feeling that ultimately it will somehow work against People of Color in the end, but you just cannot put your finger on it. Indeed, you might well be correct for the Grandmaster is a maestro of strategy. Annie, you recognize that for you on a personal level it might mean a possible Noble prize and the expansion of a new scientific area of study – racial disease. But you too cannot shake the feeling that an inoculation against racial apathy, that is to all intents and purposes a vaccine against

[6]WhiteWorld is the place that exists when only white perspectives matter. Whiteness is the de facto standard against which other raced perspectives are marked deviant in this interpretation of racial reality (Gillborn, 2008).

a "strain," of racism, is too good to be true. You cannot shake the feeling that perhaps you have missed something. As a Black woman deep down you feel it will fail but why?"

Annie looked at Enki with a mixture of admiration and dread, this powerful creature with dim smoldering red-set eyes, always morphing, always changing, seemed to have read both their minds. Nothing can be kept from him, no secret, no plan.

"But I have a solution."

Within his spindly, gnarled hand claw, he revealed the ageless Fable Stone, which he then thrust toward them.

"I now give you the chance to see the possible future effect your finding will have upon the world, both good and bad. This will aid you in your final decision."

An almost imperceptible, sly smile scuttled across the face of the Prince of Pandemonium.

"Of course, there is a price …."

"Oh, great one what is it?" chirped Bryon, ever so eager to please.

"No, you get to know once you agree to 'see' what the stone has to show" he hissed and rhymed.

"That's a terrible deal!" Annie piped up.

"Yesss …" was the abysmal reply.

But Bryon and Annie knew immediately. The choice was not a choice, even though they knew the price would be unimaginably high. They were compelled to do so. A solemn nod from both signaled Enki to approach nearer with stone in hand. As soon as it was in reach, as if beholden, Bryon placed his hand upon its precious marble-like surface, quickly followed by Annie following his lead, putting her hand over his. Instantaneously, a strong smell of sulfur engulfed them, a gush of wind appeared from nowhere which swirled around them, forming a diminutive cyclone if you will. And finally, the lights dimmed. The stone began to produce an unsettling radiance, pulsating a spectrum of color, drawing all into its vortex, sucking in all so that even light could not escape. Enki looked on motionless as both were scooped into its heart, that of a miniature Black hole, conveying them to another time and place. Into the Dreamscape.

The Vision

For the liberal left it was a clarion call. Finally, meaningful, empirical proof had arisen that racism, or at least a fundamental aspect of it could be identified and bested by the US exceptionalism. By US science! It made fundamental sense to scores of Democrats that racism was not central to the core of US society or a principal ill of societies the world over as many Critical Race Theorists (Degado & Stefancic, 2001), and anti-racism (Kendi, 2019) protagonists would have us believe. No, it was a disease, and every disease has a cure. Liberal news agencies like MSNBC and CNN had a field day. Not since the heady days of the first Trump administrations open policy of race baiting and dog whistling had race and racism hit the newsfeed so fast and so hard (Drum, 2019). Of course, in this partisan political world in which the US resides, every action has an equal and opposite reaction. And it came to pass that a hastily made stock story was molded and championed by an acolyte of the Grandmaster, Mr Jack Duso. One dutifully expanded by conservative news outlets and other right wing media pundits. Its key thrust was that the cure was "Fake news," and that America doesn't need a cure for an illness it never had! But in this moment, for once, the narrative making machine, which had hitherto, effectively, muted anti-racist practice, culling Black authors from school libraries, and destroyed DEI offices at universities, failed to sway public opinion. For once, overwhelmingly, the US public weighed on the side of the cure. This outcome produced riches beyond reason for Spicer LLC, the large Biotech conglomerate that had reacted first to the explosive paper of Professors Jones and Ball, and they by all accounts had been placed on a short list for a Nobel peace prize because of it. Indeed, the review process had been extraordinarily quick given the nature of the subject matter. For this, they had Enki Abd to thank. It was he who subdued the usual stymying of race-based research submitted to top journals. An occurrence the noted Accounting academic Marcia Annisette has long taken issue with, in relation to the dearth of race-based research around Accounting, for instance, questioning why Accounting academia, and by extension editors of top tier journals and lower, have been pretty much silent on the issue of race (Annisette & Prasad, 2017)? In a similar vein, the *Harvard Business Review* noted comparable lethargy in the sphere of science (Ileka et al., 2020). Instead, the opposite occurred when their manuscript was submitted to the esteemed science journal *Nature* to instant critical acclaim. Because of this, Bryon and Annie stood to gain handsomely in terms of recognition, wealth, and good fortune. Things looked on the up in this Brave New World of racial awareness.

They hovered within the cyclone peering deeper into the aperture showing them the possibility of what could be. They saw before them a national mood of jubilation, buoyed by the prospect of finally vanquishing the ill of racism due to their discovery. Ironically, little distinction was made of the fact that the "cure" could only reduce one facet of racism, and that others remained. Instead, the public saw this as a new dawn. The mood translated into political gold for the Democratic Party, who pushed wholeheartedly to get the "Cure" vaccine ready a.s.a.p. A national rollout was planned, accompanied by the certainty that this time it would work! This would not be another botched attempt as per the disastrous COVID-19 rollouts of yesteryear. But as with all things in the land of Uncle Sam, partisanship took hold and opposition to the national rollout spewed forth from the usual suspects.

State representatives of Mississippi, Texas, and Indiana instantly roiled against the idea of a forced imposition of the cure for "racism" that did not exist in the view of these conservative-leaning states. Worse, it was an infringement of personal freedom once more. But their super majority in the Senate would make sure such plans never came to fruition. More positively, Corporate America took the opposite stand and advocated for voluntary taking of "The Cure" as it was coined. Business seemed to have learned from the racial ructions of the terrible times of the George Floyd episode, for once they seemed to genuinely accept and enact calls for meaningful anti-racist policy called for by Black Lives Matter campaigners. Interestingly, out of the Big 3 global Accounting firms, only All World Financial (AWF) took the most progressive position. They advocated for afterwork "Cure" parties, a demonstration of their anti-racist credentials, also acting as a networking event for Black minorities within the firm, something that Accounting had become more accustomed to in recent years (Gelles, 2021). To be fair AWF's reputation had been tarnished years earlier after a nasty affair regarding a Black manager's claim of disparate racial treatment from a senior partner. Curiously the whole issue was only resolved when both manager and partner one day inexplicably disappeared within hours of each other. The case was never solved.[7]

All in all, the great and the good of Corporate America (white male CEOs and partners) quickly cited this as a victory of capitalism over racism, noting the "magic of the market" as the engine of free market efficiency that overcame a historically intransient problem. And the irony of yet another Black innovation being hijacked by the white world of business, while disregarding the Black and Brown or Native pioneer was lost on them. In this regard, it was business as usual. Black intelligentsia resisted this new stock story as it had resisted so many others, rightly pointing out that the celebrated history of the US capital markets was actually one of parasitic exploitation of Blacks. Tracing the thread back to when Black bodies themselves were the "Cure" for the desperate need for labor of an ever-expanding "New World," one which thirsted for African American involuntary productivity, valued then as enslaved commodities to be bought and sold, becoming the economic bedrock of Pre-emancipation America (Baptist, 2014). Today was no different. A valuable Black asset was again coopted for white advantage. However, this time, corporate public relations ensured a positive spin on this tale, couching the "Cure" as good for business, fitting in snuggly with the decade's old unproductive and harmful narrative of the business case for diversity.[8] In this sense to promote the cure, to be seen as racially progressive, was a practical move bolstering the image of AWF, and the other large Blue-chip companies which followed suit. It seemed to be working, America through their cure push was coming to terms with the centrality of race and racism in its past and looked toward a brighter future.

Bryon and Annie gazed agog at the future events they were privy to, hovering, weightlessly sustained by the vortex. All this was beyond their wildest hopes

---

[7]To find out how and why both protagonists vanished read the counternarrative "Daemon Days" in *Counting Black and White Beans. Critical Race Theory in Accounting*.

[8]Note that the Business Case claims diversity improves company performance due to special abilities and viewpoints perspectives, and collaborative techniques minorities possess from their different life experiences. However, research by Georgeac and Rattan shows this rhetoric to be instrumental in nature, negatively messaging to stigmatized groups that their worth to the firm lies solely with their specific identity and are therefore evaluated according to the firm's bottom line in. This produces social identity threat in the marginalized, reducing their sense of belonging for those within the firm and dissuading others from joining it (Georgeac & Rattan, 2022)

and dreams. The ever-changing rainbow light emanating from the Fable stone, to which they seemed magnetically attached, was as intoxicating as was the prospect this vision would be reality. Indeed, the very idea of a cure for Battle Fatigue caused by microaggressive behavior in workplace and beyond added to their euphoria. Only Enki remained expressionless. His all-knowing stare did not alter. He did not move. Not one inch, instead announcing:

"Watch on mortals, more is to be told from this tale of what will and could be ...."

Counterattack

It was termed the "Blacklash" by whites opposed to the cure. A not so clever pun on the word backlash, a thinly veiled epithet, devised by hard-right conservatives, to conjure images of lashings "owed" to uppity negroes, in the eyes of these whites. How dare they demand equality from their betters and try to pressure them to take a cure they did not want nor need? The outraged opposition grew quickly, mainly from the Republican Party, and connected think tanks stating that a national rollout of the "Cure" was in fact a violation of the 1st amendment right of free speech, and their unassailable right of assembly to challenge the supposed merits of the "cure." The usual tactic was employed through coded dog whistles and fearing mongering ideologies propagated by Republican think thanks, reminiscent of the attacks on Critical Race Theory and DEI a decade earlier, that successfully removed diversity teaching in schools, universities, and workplaces in half of all states. Successful anxiety peddling by Fox news and other conservative media outlets soon saw legislation created temporarily stopping cure rollout in several states. Additionally, the rollout had been botched yet again at the Federal level, not too dissimilar to the Obamacare rollout years earlier, by the Democratic administration. This led to tax increases for the public and a political repercussion on the horizon at the ballot box for the Democratic incumbent. Of course, it did not matter that free speech had not been curtailed by the left or by anybody really, nor had anyone been forced to take the drug. If anything, the cure would only be a fraction of the nation's health budget, but at the State level, Republican Governors implemented drastic taxes on the Cure and fought this move all the way to the Republican-leaning Supreme Court where victory was assured. The rollout soon wheeled into reverse at the cost of People of Color across the land. Any physiological and psychological benefit gained quickly evaporated as hopes of significant reduction in everyday racism through the cure effect vanished and renewed racist practice returned like a boomerang (Williams et al., 2019).

But frankly, all that was needed, as so often is the case, was the right story to hit the right cord, one of white burgeoning anger and frustration that somehow their racial dominance in society was on the brink. They were now threatened with having their own knapsack of white racial advantage removed, and that could not hold (McIntosh, 1997). Such is the power of the right story told at the right time. The stock story was effective, allowing whites to revel in the belief that they had a right to their racism, to enjoy it even, to coddle and nurture their indifference to the plight of other races. After all, this new story showed that in reality the cure induced "injury" to white empathy (an effective fiction that peddled the cure as the real problem). Adding to this stock story was the age-old idea that civilization has actually benefited from the "White Man's burden" of raising society upon his back, to a new technological age, while simultaneously civilizing savage ill-educated Black, Brown, and indigenous peoples both past and present. And so it was that racism's Cure gave rise to an even greater harm, virulent and malignant in nature, the tale of white peoples "right" to racism and the goodness of manifest destiny. Its lurking power, the cementing of this truism in the white imaginary, successfully spreading from the minds of avowed racists to colonize the thinking of white liberals and some minorities as well.

Predictably enthusiasm drained in the business world for the Cure and DEI itself started to come under attack once more. It was not in the interest of AWF to promote the vaccine anymore as it became clear a "business case for the absence of diversity" had taken hold of public sentiment fueled by the new stock story that was anti-cure rhetoric. Again, it no longer made sense to promote an anti-racism cure for white racial apathy.[9] Funds that once flowed to Democratic lobbyists pushing the "Cure Bill" disappeared, leaving it to "die on the vine" so to speak. Not long after, company-driven "Vaccine parties" vanished, leaving a "litigious down pour" in its wake for Spicer LLC, the company which had initially benefited so well from Annie's and Myron's discovery, virtually bankrupting the once-prominent pharmaceutical company. Yet, another demonstrably fake tale surfaced created once more by the much loved Republican phony, Jack Duso. He had a gift and his plans worked wonderfully. His newest tale, "hot off the fake press" so to speak highlighted the original "dubious" Cure results, exposed unsurprisingly by the Duso Foundation. Other assorted Republican think tanks took aim at Annie's previously peer-reviewed work throughout her career, attempting by stealth to discredit its findings. Pushing the fiction that this was a disgruntled Black woman's quest, aided by her feckless Black male academic accomplice to create vaccine slavery for whites. The "Cure" was nothing but Black revenge against America's original sin and so any finding no matter how beneficial or scientifically proven could be not trusted. They were America's number one enemy now. Conservative media outlets flooded the airways with this narrative and Duso's refrain that "White America, never, ever will be slaves," became a popular slogan. As absurd as its sounds this quickly became a mantra, taking hold quickly, increasing racist incidents exponentially across the nation. Subsequently, a review of Annie's and Byron's jointly submitted manuscript was demanded including the mechanics of the peer review process itself. The fix was in. Their work was this time questioned in unseemly detail, picked over for minor irregularities until "faults" were found. As a result, both were academically hauled over the coals so to speak by the very institution that pronounced their genius not long ago. Anne's scripts became

---

[9](Lewis, 2020). See *Counting Black White Beans* book for an exploration of how the fictional multinational Accounting firm AWF previously back tracked on the business case for diversity in the CRT counter story "Daemon Days."

plagiarism target practice by well-funded Republican plagiarism centers, created to undermine Black scholarship, particularly that of Black women (Lewis, 2024). Spicer LLC was in the crosshairs of white public outrage as well and its share price plummeted like a rock.

As for Bryon and Annie their fate was sealed. No national rollout, their assets from the Cure frozen as a Federal Civil Rights investigation opened up against them, and they were compelled to endure a hastily convened Senate hearing to investigate their "plan" to enslave white America through "Cure Coercion." For Annie, the prospect of the Nobel Prize up and vanished like a "fart in the wind." With their professional reputation and financial situation in tatters, seen as hucksters, they both retreated to their university. But only to find that here, even though they were both tenured professors, discussions were underway at the Trustee level to see if they could be removed for bringing the name of the university into disrepute. A By-law was hastily proposed to the Faculty Affairs Committee to ratify the notion that any form of defamation, intentional or unintentional, should be a sackable offense. Although clearly preposterous should it go ahead the idea was to fight it in court should the two Black academics resist until they broke financially or psychologically. It was an ignoble end to an honorable idea, the death knell of a discovery that could have changed the quality of life of people the world over for the better. But in the end once again didn't.

Postscript

As quickly as the swirling tumult of the Vortex arrived it dissipated, leaving the Fable Stone, looking drab. The dimmed lights now flickered back to normality fully illuminating the CIDT Med laboratory. Stunned and silent, breathing heavily stood Bryon and Annie, and of course the Triskter. It was Bryon who broke the silence.

"It's not a done deal yet. We must bury this."

"It would seem so Bryon. Five years of my life, and a momentous discovery gone, but yes, it's done with" groaned Annie.

Both academics seemed childlike in their expectance for Enki Abd to do something. To sooth or redeem this situation for the better.

"Mortals, I can do nothing for you. This is a possible truth that may or may not come to pass. But I think both of you know the odds. You feel deep within yourself the stakes at play and the phantom player with whom you have had a dalliance with."

"Yes, as I peered into the stone, as I inhaled its vapor, there was something or someone else at work, guiding, moving situations against us, against the potential for good that the vaccine might create."

"Well done, Annie, for a human you are reasonably perceptive" murmured Enki's skin.

"The being you felt was the Grandmaster of Race and Racism. It is he all those who wish to redress the system of racism must challenge unknowingly. It is he who holds of the keys to racial emancipation and always has done. Therefore, the cure could never work. It attempted to work against his design and it is a powerful thing to attempt to undo. As ever it is his genius to poison the effectiveness of any solution to racism so that it will never work. He has made sure that whites will never truly feel for the racial Other because their apathy is linked fundamentally to their self-interest in keeping the status quo in check. Any 'Cure' will have to cure whites of their inherent self-interest, accrued by being racist, and disavow the multitude of intergenerational benefits it bestows both knowingly and unknowingly. It will require institutions steeped in racism to reform and be reimagined. No cure can achieve this, because before a critical mass of empathy can be generated, racial practice enacted by Whiteness springs into action, sensing the shift of racial privilege and destroys it like a racist T-cell, using your medical parlance. In this regard, racism in many ways has its own immune system to resist and ultimately expel foreign bodies of Anti Racist practice. This is the gift of the Grandmaster."

"Oh, holy one, noble Enki, what about this price?" queried Byron unwisely.

"Ah yes, thank you for reminding me Byron (as if he, a God forgot anything), it's time to introduce you to my old drinking buddy Death."

The color instantly drained from the faces of Bryon and Annie.

"Like most things in life and ironically in death, this is all a bit unfair" announced the God.

"A bit!" shrieked Bryon.

"It's a cosmic balance, time like, paradox thingy you mortals just cannot fathom. In my quest to upend the Grandmaster and his racism construct there must be sacrifice. And unfortunately, you two are it. It's for the greater good."

"This isn't right I need more time! What about my family? My work? I was so close ..." Annie was near frantic now as all would be in such a situation.

And matters would have continued in this manner, the pleading, the begging, the wailing some while more if another ethereal figure had not appeared at the opposite side of the room. Taller, ganglier, more frightening than Enki himself could ever be. Oozing menace, judgment, and finality. Also, he looked oddly bored, leaning against his enormous scythe.

"Ready?"

Death said the words that came from no particular direction, with a kind of savage amusement.

"Ready" retorted Enki.

"Friday still on at the Dark Nemesis Café? Usual spot at the usual time? 35th Wabash and Pilsen?" queried Death.

"Aye and its your round" Enki blithely retorted.

Turning to the two terrified academics Enki absentmindedly remarked

"He never forgets, not once in eons. Our drinks are the only thing keeping him (Death) from jacking it all in I tell you" and with a side whisper leans into them both noting:

"things could be better at home really. I'm looking into a therapist ...."

With that an enormous thunderclap exploded above, rain beat heavily against the windows, as Death elongated his limbs to the end of the laboratory, jointly scooping up the shaking academics into his never-loving grasp. Slowly the trio receded into a mirthless gloom that was once the corner of the laboratory to which they had devoted much of their life, where they disappeared entirely never to be seen again.

Now Enki had something to work with. He had witnessed how the Grandmaster was adept at producing racial feedback loops that propagated racial dominance automatically and without assistance. He had seen that his model of racial dominance can be subverted, at least for a little while. The strategy of the Fable Stone was working; the imagination of the humans was giving Enki much needed insight. He just needed more victims come helpers. And he would get them.

References

Acuff, J. (2018). Confronting racial battle fatigue and comforting my blackness as an educator. *Multicultural Perspectives, 20*(3), 174–181.

Annisette, M., & Prasad, A. (2017). Critical accounting research in hyper-racial times. *Critical Perspectives on Accounting, 43*, 5–19.

Baptist, E. E. (2014). *The half has never been told. Slavery and the making of American capitalism*. Basic Books.

Bell, D. (2005). *The Derrick Bell reader*. New York University Press.

Degado, R., & Stefancic, J. (2001). *Critical race theory: An introduction*. New York University Press.

Drum, K. (2019). *Donald Trump's race-baiting presidency: A Listicle*. https://www.motherjones.com/kevin-drum/2019/06/donald-trumps-race-baiting-presidency-a-listicle/

Gelles, D. (2021). *'There is a bigger role': A C.E.O. pushes diversity*. https://www.nytimes.com/2021/03/05/business/tim-ryan-pwc-corner-office.html

Georgeac, O., & Rattan, A. (2022). The business case for diversity backfires: Detrimental effects of organizations' instrumental diversity rhetoric for underrepresented group members' sense of belonging. *Journal of Personality and Social Psychology: Interpersonal Relations and Group Processes, 124*(1), 69–108.

Gillborn, D. (2008). *Racism and education. Coincidence or conspiracy*. Routledge.

Ileka, K., McCluney, C., & Robinson, R. (2020). *White coats, black scientists*. https://hbr.org/2020/09/white-coats-black-scientists

Kendi, I. X. (2019). *How to be an antiracist*. One World.

Krusemark, S. (2012). The campus as stage: A qualitative study of the hypervisibility and invisibility of African American female identity in the built campus environment. *Journal of Research on Women and Gender, 4*, 25–51.

Lewis, A. (2020). *Counting black and white beans. Critical race theory in accounting*. Emerald Publishing Limited.

Lewis, A. (2024). Black women in accounting and the backlash to DEI. *The CPA Journal, XCIV*(3/4), 1–80.

McIntosh, P. (1997). White privilege and male privilege: A personal account of coming to see correspondences through work in women's studies. In R. Delgado & J. Stefancic (Eds.), *Critical white studies: Looking behind the mirror* (pp. 291–299). Temple University Press.

Peck, R. (Writer). (2016). *I am not your Negro*. Magnolia Pictures.

Williams, D., Lawrence, J., & Davis, B. (2019). Racism and health: Evidence and needed research. *Annual Review of Public Health, 40*, 105–125.

Chapter 3

3rd Fable: Unbearable

The 1st Letter

It was a cold windswept New Jersey day as Dorothea Revere sorted through the eighth box of assorted memorabilia in the attic of her deceased parents' family home. She had always wondered about the experience of Grandpa Joe, a Redtail pilot who flew sorties over Germany in World War Two. He was one of many Black servicemen celebrated openly as American heroes but privately within their own towns and homes besieged by white racists thugs, angry that any value be placed on "uppity negroes." It must have been a bitter pill to digest. In fact, Grandma hinted he was never really the same after experiencing whites drive them from their starter home in a white neighborhood, bought just after Joe returned from the war. Dorothea assumed this was the reason they moved to the safer, more secure enclave of Cherry Blossom Hills, New Jersey, a suburban retreat within the Black city of East Orange. Her grandparents, father, and mother had grown up in that large ramshackle house, which still stood long after her parents' passing. Now she found herself back gain, elbow deep in the arduous task of foreclosing their family home, part of the probate process left for her to deal with. Her folks while somewhat successful had typically been unable to retain their wealth like so many Black families in the USA before them, instead passing on next to nothing of worth to their heirs except a house with multiple liens against it full of negative equity and bad memories. The very thought of such matters reminded her of a study which compared Black versus white prosperity in 1992, uncovering the worrying fact that while median Black income was roughly 60% of white income, the median net worth of Blacks amounted to a measly 8% comparative to whites. Worse still, only 25% of white families experienced 0 or negative assets, but greater than 60% of equivalent Black families had no wealth at all (Keister, 2004)! Sadly, it seems that little has changed today, as a 2024 report investigating Black Chicagoan wealth exposed that median income there was more or less zero (Bhaskaran et al., 2024). It was all very demoralizing, and that her family should be part of such a statistic was even more galling. The racism is just so unbearable! Yet as the administrator of the estate it was her responsibility to figure out what

Accounting Fables: Tales of Race and Racism in the Borderlands of Business, 35–53

Published under exclusive licence by Emerald Publishing Limited
doi:10.1108/978-1-80117-069-720251010

had personal significance and what did not, and what was to be left to creditors after foreclosure was done with.

In truth, it was long grueling work, taking time away from her that she could ill afford, but at least only one unopened box remained, after which she resolved to call it a day. It was there that she discovered three letters, the first shorter than the others, all dusty brown, frail but somehow alluring. It was difficult to explain, but she felt compelled to read the first letter. After all, it was written by a former lodger in the house that her father had spoken of on previous occasions. Oddly, nobody could remember his actual name but instead simply referred to him as the "Lecturer." Pride was the general feeling conveyed about having a Black academic in the home who was the first African American business professor at New Jersey Polytechnique University's (NJPU) Cahill School of Management. But on a personal level he was a remote and aloof figure, a lonely man who kept to himself. He had an edgy manner, one which quickly unnerved those who spoke with him. Dorothea peered intently at the 1st letter as it began:

> 6/1/1985
>
> To whom it may concern,
>
> I must relate these terrible events less I go mad! But to whom can I speak of such things? I write to calm my mind, my feelings, and my heart. What I will speak of shortly pertains to the color line as W.E.B. Dubois framed it[1] and that of the stars above and those who inhabit them. My tale is one of a life ruined long before being "taken" was a thing. My story begins in 1981, where I was appointed as an accounting faculty member at Cahill College of Business for several years. As the only Black faculty member I had been fighting a losing battle to be placed on the tenure track path within the College, while at the same time seeing less qualified white males from less prodigious alma mater's breeze through and within a few years gain tenure. I was sure it was my research agenda of investigating race and business, and commitment to helping Black professionals, particularly in accounting that saw me perpetually marginalized, unable to publish in noted academic journals in my field. An effective method I discovered of keeping me ineligible for applying for promotion or tenure track positions elsewhere. I simply did not have the required published manuscripts to do so. And let us not forget that institutional racism was also rife in Cahill College, a reality which mirrored the university as a whole. I was stuck in "mud" at this first hurdle, frozen in place. One which I could not move from. It was soul destroying, but my relationship with my students of color, my research into discrepancies of experience between Black accountants and whites in New Jersey kept me motivated. But like so many Black academics, over so many years, no matter what I attempted, no matter how brilliant I tried

[1]Dubois (2005) outlines the fundamental problematic of race to modernity US society.

to be, I was incessantly sidelined because of the color of my skin and the nature of my "odd" research agenda (Hammond et al., 2022). And that this should happen in "raceless liberal" academe incensed me further! After a lifetime of racial prejudice I had sought refuge in the Ivory Tower but to no avail. Even here I felt the ever present heel of racist practice crush me as if it were pressing against my throat, stifling my breath, making it so that I could not breathe. How many suffer as I do? How many of my Black brethren continue to do so? Will this be forever? When will we all be able to breathe freely (Thomas & Hollenshead, 2001)?

It was November 1984 when it happened. I had seen unusual lights in the night sky while driving through isolated country roads on my way back to Cherry Blossom Hills before, but I had always put this down to an unseen plane or weather balloon or some such thing. My drive home usually necessitated travel across fields where other traffic seldom passed. Normally, Sam Cooke was the artist of choice during my laborious drive home. His dulcet tones soothed the ever present resentment which regularly tightened my chest and quickened my pulse whenever I thought about NJPU and my work situation. But this evening was different. As I passed the same old farm, nearing the same old bend on the route I always took, things slowed down. Sam's voice became a slow drawl, the very wind itself became frozen. And light! I was bathed in an ethereal light! Flooding the space where my old Lincoln car should have been. Then with a blink of an eye I was elsewhere. Floating as you might expect with such alien abduction accounts. Then nothing for several minutes. Silence. Darkness.

Oddly, I was not scared. I felt serene and calm. I had not experienced this sort of feeling of contentment since I was a child. After what seemed to be an age, I awoke with a start, at the wheel of my Lincoln which was parked on the other side of the road. It seems on this drive home I pulled over because I was falling asleep. A quick power nap as a precaution must have been my reasoning as to why I did this. But two things concerned me. Firstly, no self-respecting Black man I knew would ever pull to the side of the road late at night and sleep in his car in a white rural setting. It is a recipe for disaster. One call to the police by concerned white residents or farmers and things can quickly spiral out of control in a way that often leaves Black men dead at the hands of white police (Italiano, 2020). Secondly, I had slept for several hours, and it was now 4 a.m. in the morning but my car clock had stopped at 10 p.m. Why? This had never happened before, and I was not tired after work. It was unusual. Nevertheless, it was important that I get home to bed as quickly as possible and grab what little sleep I could. I resumed my journey home this time staying awake. Sadly, this would not be the only curiosity I would have to deal with in the coming weeks, months, and years. Of that you will find out more in my next letter.

L.

Dorothea drew in a sharp intake of breath. She had been triggered by this tale from the past. The persistence of racism in the life of the Lecturer decades ago now reached out to her as she recalled her own participation in the youth protest against "Permit Karen" a few years previously. The media outlet TMZ reported that the entire event stemmed from a dispute between a Black couple and a female white neighbor over the right to install a stone patio on their property. The altercation was captured on video showing "Permit Karen" alleging physical assault by the Black husband against her and her subsequent call to the police (TMZ, 2020). What was most infuriating was the entitlement. The belief that racial redress was the sole purview of white femininity. In fact, it was literally textbook stuff that Dorothea herself had begun to explore in her classes on race and history as a history major at NJPU. What came to mind here was Critical Race Theorist Cheryl Harris's idea of a "property right in whiteness," gleaned from assigned class reading. She outlines the reality that whiteness is treasured property in racialized society, conferring privileges, assumptions, and benefits, which constitute it as an asset (Harris, 1995), perhaps as valuable as gold if not more so. It is an advantage whites vigorously protect with force and commonly deploy police against Black and Brown people as a proxy to do so. Permit Karen in Dorothea's view did just that. Her property right in whiteness allowed her to both demand her Black neighbors know their place in the US racial system and allowed her to trespass upon a Black family's property multiple times to make demands and then subsequently utilize the police as a weapon of terror to reinforce her white racial right. This is what angered Dorothea the most and why later that day she chose to protest with a mix of young white allies and People of Color to resist such racist action. But the reality that this age-old struggle, forged during the creation of this nation, is still being fought with no end in sight struck her hard. She still struggles as the Lecturer did. Unfortunately, he did not have whiteness as an asset as it was something he could never attain, and as a result suffered professionally for it. Meanwhile her lack of whiteness as property means she battles just as hard years later against the Permit Karen's of this world, and the racialized US legal system designed to make them as unaccountable as possible. Frankly, it was all too much. Karen's arrogance, her lack of reflection, it was gruesome to behold. Conversely though, it was that very fact that forced Dorothea to fight back harder, calling out white racial property rights where she could. Without noticing, absent mindedly, she had been pawing the yellowing paper of this first letter all along, knowing more lay within. Why did the Lecturer fall asleep in that manner at the side of the road? Why did he lose time? What were those lights in the sky? Looking at her right hand, she wasn't even aware that she had now picked up the second letter, so lost in thought had she been. It had been a long day and she should go home, but not just yet. She could not resist the urge to know more about the plight of the Lecturer, whatever that might be.

The 2nd Letter

The wind rattled the longstanding sash window frames of her grandparent's house. It was now late evening as Dorothea gazed into the second faded letter, holding it gingerly between her finger and thumb. She noticed that the Lecturer's handwriting had become slightly erratic and in places, somewhat illegible, perhaps marking his increasingly agitated state of mind. The letter began thus:

8/06/1986

Dear reader,

I woke up with a start on what seemed to be a long sliver table. It was cold and I tasted a bitter metallic flavor in my mouth. I was clothed in the pajamas I had worn to bed, but my slippers were nowhere to be seen. At first, I squinted due to the brightness of my surroundings, although not strapped to the table I was nevertheless unable to move. Frozen ridged against the freezing cold surface. Slowly, two figures emerged from the darkness. As my focus steadily returned, I could not quite believe what or rather who met my gaze. It must be a dream. Because before me standing tall was the noted singer, concert artist and activist Paul Robeson and next to him, no less in stature stood Ida B. Wells, an early Civil Rights behemoth, and advocate for women's rights. This had to be a dream.

"No Lecturer, this is no dream. What is happening and what will continue to happen is very real" uttered Robeson.

"But this cannot be real. Both of you are dead!" Blurted the Lecturer.

"Very observant. Yes, these are but facsimiles of people you consider vital to what you term the struggle for Civil Rights in this land you call America. We wear such 'skin' to put you at ease, images we have taken from your mind that make you feel comfortable."

"Then why? Why take these forms and why take me? What are you really?"

Ida B. Wells stepped closer to the Lecturer as if to make her point crystal clear.

"We are not human but are instead what you erroneously refer to as 'Alien.' We have been observing your species for some time, witnessing your progress both technological and social. You are here because we have questions."

"But why me? I am nobody. Not successful, not interesting and certainly not brilliant."

"You are correct on all counts but that is precisely why your 'common' view is so important. You are representative of the 'every man/woman' experience of being Black in America. This thing you call race, this attack upon personhood you call racism, makes no sense to our kind. We find it perplexing, and you are here to explain it to us."

I spluttered out a laugh. It was ridiculous that I, a mere jobbing academic had to explain race and racism to civil rights titans. In truth all they needed to do was to step outside in the cold light of day in any American city in their current form and their questions would be immediately answered, perhaps fatality.

"Why?" both captors stated aloud in perfect harmony.

"Are you reading my mind? I only thought that!"

"Yes" Robeson said, emotionless and in a monotone manner.

Without skipping a beat Ida B. Wells continued his sentence as if they were one voice.

> "It is an ability our people have possessed for many generations. It makes lying harder and allows us to connect in an empathic feeling way humankind currently can never understand but apparently sorely need."

I pondered for a moment, clearing my mind, and began to explain as best I could.

> "The Black skin you wear now is what US society judges to be inferior. With this skin you are less likely to be employed, more likely to live in poverty, more likely to have terrible housing, and much more likely to be imprisoned. From birth it is probable that you will experience terrible health outcomes through societal neglect, and as a result die earlier than the national average of many other races. Often through no fault of your own" (Alexander, 2010; Dymski, 2009; Williams et al., 2019).

> "This makes no sense. We wear this skin to comfort you since humans find difference alarming, but we are many things, many skin tones and textures, many thoughts, and ideas. Also, we know a truth that you do not. We know that we are one people 'under the groove,' irrespective of what we look like or what we are perceived to be."

Again, both civil rights leaders spoke in perfect unison and continued to do so. It was disconcerting. The Lecturer paused for a moment considering what had been said and then replied.

> "Yes, it can be tricky to get a grasp of this matter unless you are part of this world and reside within it. You are right of course … and wrong. It makes no sense because this thing we call 'race' is truly a fiction that has been created. But it was created for a reason in the US and beyond."

"What is this reason?"

> "I'm assuming that in your viewing of humanity you have come across slavery?"
>
> "Yes, we know of this concept of human bondage. It has blighted human history from before the age of the Greeks to that of modern human slavery today. But to us this concept is not raced in a manner we understand. Slavery has happened to both whites and Blacks, men and women and many derivations in between since antiquity."

"Ah … lets be careful now in how we discuss slavery here. Yes, I agree that slavery has been a constant facet of human existence since time immemorial, but it was not until the 16th through to the late 18th century and beyond that Transatlantic Slavery was institutionalized as well as globalized. It is here we find the 'atomization' of Black African peoples, the complete destruction of culture, language, sense of self and inherent humanity. All to turn enslaved people into a Backhoe or Bobcat!"

"Atomization?"

"Yes, it's my way of conceptualizing the sense of loss in the Black psyche which is chasm like. I refer here to the idea that Black Africans who endured the middle passage, who were transported in filthy depraved conditions in the hulls of slave ships to the New World, who then lived through the horrors of plantation life where death and degradation were constant companions, had the very essence of their sense of being destroyed figuratively, and literally at an 'atomic' level. Their social being ripped apart 'atom by atom,' to be forged anew into something different but not always better. I argue therefore that African Americans, Black British and many other Afro heritage groups within the global Black diaspora, who exist as a darker minority, of which slavery is their legacy, and who still live within white majority environments, do not start at the same baseline of culture, or collective action. Their ability to act or react as a social actor in society is substantially different, thwarted if you like before birth, unlike that of all other races. How can it not be? And this experience is singular to this subset of the Black diaspora, no other nation ethnicity or race has ever experienced slavery in this manner. Additionally, Black 'atomized' social actors must still to this day exist in racist societies which continue this same assault all be it in subtle and not so subtle ways, continuing the destruction of a sense of self and place in society."

Breaking the choir, Ida B. Wells murmured.

> "But what does this achieve?"
>
> "I have on other occasions suggested that "atomization" of captured Africans was required to turn a fully formed human being into a Bobcat."

"What is a Bobcat?" the perfect union of speech resumed.

"Well, they are industrial machines that help build things in our human modern world. Except in the period of Transatlantic Slavery that I spoke of just now, no such technology existed. The cutting-edge technology that did exist at that time however was that of slavery, where dehumanized Africans were made into functioning automatons, or mindless cattle, through 'atomization' to build a nation. It is here in America where the Southern Plantocrisy used Africans purposely, stripping people of everything that makes life worth living to pick cotton and cut sugar cane to export around the world to make their white masters rich. It was the art of raising a nation off the backs of Slaves. Thus, racism derived in part from Transatlantic Slavery makes perfect sense because whites needed to build a nation and make vast profits in the process i.e., seeking profit and economic gain at the expense of Blacks and those considered non – white. Racism was and still is a foundational factor of business and commerce in the United States because it is encoded in the DNA of the nation, perpetually fulfilling its function of conferring a horde of benefits to whites at the expense of Blacks (McIntosh, 1997). It is the essence of Racial Capitalism core to American life that is irremovable (Melamed, 2015). At best it can managed, at worst reveled within. Subsequently, to be white is to have value, while to be Black is to be valued less (Glaude, 2016). All to make sure that a racialized hierarchy exists to position those considered white with the best possible opportunities to gain success, wealth, and a long life, at the expense of those considered Black or racially Othered. This is why race and racism is the essence of the American experience, one deeply tied to a Black and white binary which sees economic success for whites and economic failure for Blacks, mirroring society's racial hierarchy in perpetuity. The economy and society, its institutions and legal systems are designed to make this assertion an intergenerational reality.

I was in full flow now.

"It's all just so Horrifically White!" The words spat out of my mouth like venom.

With curious intent both Wells and Robeson approached the silver table and the Lecturer found that he could sit upright to face his pseudo-Civil rights captors. This time Ida B. Wells spoke on her own.

"What is this Horrific Whiteness that you speak of?"

I took a moment to compose myself, wanting to make sure I could be clear in my description of the term. A minute or two later I cleared my throat and began again.

"Well, it's a term that seems to have developed locally in Cherry Blossom Hills, a predominantly Black neighborhood in New Jersey where I live. It is tricky to define exactly but I will give it a go. Specifically, to me being 'Horrifically White' is the way that whites, often in power, (but not always) are socially conditioned over generations to be critically unaware of race or racism. It is the power for any white person to racially shock through word, deed, or act, where Black people and People of Color are concerned. It is the power to cause fear and repugnance in the racially stigmatized. On a personal level, as a Black man, it's when white people do things that are just so unacceptably 'white,' that it causes fear, pain and suffering to me, simultaneously, all done in a manner that exudes entitlement to do so. It is the reflexive assurance that this world is theirs, and Black and Brown interlopers will be punished for trying to conceive anything else. It is to be so tightly wrapped in whiteness that you cannot look at whiteness critically. It's a racial prerogative of the worst kind, informing white racist reality, consciously and unconsciously guiding act and deed. This is where whites go to normalize white racist action and feel naturally permitted to do so. It is an instinctive reaction in many. I really need to give you a practical example, but I am struggling a bit."

"It matters not. We believe that we know of such an instance." Both uttered at the same time back in chorus mode.

> "Really? I'd like to hear it."
>
> "Very well. As you might have well surmised you reside within a vessel able to traverse vast distances from our Homeworld to here. To do so we have mastery over of what your gifted scientist Albert Einstein conceived of as spacetime, enabling us to pick where and when we visit your planet. In about two and a half decades from this point in time, in New York City, a racial altercation will be recorded between a white woman, her dog, and a Black male bird watcher. It will quickly become world newsworthy. She will be known as Central Park Karen."
>
> "Really? I want to know more about this Karen lady. What else does she do?"
>
> "As a point of clarification, your human media classified her as a 'Karen,' a derogatory term describing a type of uncritical, entitled white woman who uses the threat of extra judicial violence from your constabulary to enact their wishes against People of Color, in particular Black people. Previously they have been referred to as 'Becky' as well. Her actual name is Amy Cooper[2]. For 'Central Park Karen,' the issue arose while she was walking her dog. The Black male bird watcher asked for her to leash her cocker spaniel canine in Central Park, pointing to signs calling for dogs to be

[2]Note that for reasons of preserving the timeline he will quickly forget Amy Coopers (Central Park Karen) name and any recollection of the abduction. This is why he frantically writes these letters.

> leashed in the area. She refused, instead provoking an argument, which led her to subsequently call your NYPD (New York Police Department), stating that an African American man was threatening her life."

"Yes, that's it! Exactly! That is being Horrifically White. But what happens next?" Given my involuntary confinement, my jubilation really does not fit my circumstance I think to myself. Curious.

> "The reports cite that a social media backlash occurred which sanctioned her."

"What is social media?" I say puzzled.

Robeson interjects on his own.

> "Ah yes, this social media creation is in its infancy at this time. Let us just say that it is a form of electronic communication allowing users to create remote communities across the country and the world. On the surface bringing people together and eventually of course leading to the Digital Dark Age … but I have already said too much."

"I think I have a working understanding" I whisper.

Both Wells and Robeson switch to speaking together word for word again.

> "She is eventually removed from her job at the finance firm Franklin Templeton, and for some time becomes a national pariah of sorts."

"Wow this social media seems to be a powerful weapon of racial justice." But I was still unsure what this was.

> "It isn't and some nasty surprises await humanity because of it and cancel culture."

"Cancel what?" I wonder once more.

> "Never mind, in sum she at first faced charges of filling a false police report but this was later dropped, and in a further play into what you refer to as her Horrific Whiteness, she files a lawsuit claiming wrongful dismissal from her former finance firm, citing a lack of investigation of what occurred on the part of the corporation. Additionally, the suit also claimed that the reason Franklin Templeton (her former employer) did not investigate matters further was because of her gender and race as a white woman. Instead, the finance firm continued to perpetuate the narrative that it was Amy Cooper versus an innocent Black man without due consideration of the destruction it would cause to her life" (Stieb, 2021).

"Wait. Are you serious? The Caucacity[3]of the woman! She now claims that she is the real victim?" At this point to me this future tale seems to stretch credulity. Ida B. Wells then states.

> "I believe this constitutes a core element of the Horrific Whiteness you describe. A manifestation of symbolic violence of 'white women's tears,' a type of racial delicateness originating in what author Robin DiAngelo describes as 'White Fragility,' where harmful racist action against a racialized Other is inverted into unforgivable harm against themselves as innocent white women. This flip then allows for our Black protagonist to be 'revealed' as the true aggressor in this white women's imaginary, weaponizing her gender and race in a Machiavellian manner (DiAngelo, 2018). In this reading the public and Black person have read this situation incorrectly and she is entitled to legal redress either financially or through the utilization of state mandated police violence against Black men."

"Go on" I murmured.

> "This permits Central Park Karen to rewrite events, ignoring the racial reality of the situation. Indeed, her valued asset of whiteness allows for this to have credibility in your society, despite its patent untruth. This tale is trusted because in human society the property right of her whiteness confers trust and authenticity, legitimating her version of events. Now the tale seems to be that an over eager bird watcher was just having a tiff with a dog owner, a situation that has been blown out of all proportion. She is actually the gendered and raced victim. Racism was never an issue here."

"Insightful! You know for facsimiles of Civil Rights giants you sound more and more like the genuine article the more you speak!" I say this in a somewhat triumphant manner, but it is not well received by my captors.

Both Paul Robeson and Ida B. Wells look at one another expressionless, as if in a hidden mental argument about what this might mean were taking place. Were they truly themselves in this form? Or were they becoming something else? Was this human affliction of racism beginning to infect a process of Atomization within them, affecting their species? Does a danger exist to these immensely powerful beings by simply posing as Black in this land called America, this space, this planet?

I felt that I needed to break the silence of their soundless debate and was about to speak when they once more retreated into the glaring light of the ship and I was once more involuntarily laid prostrate on the Silver table, immobilized.

---

[3]Caucacity is a slang word used to depict actions seen to be typically white and racist. It is a blending of the words Caucasian (white) and audacity (shameless boldness).

This would be the last interaction that both Robeson and Wells would have with me this time round. The last expression that I saw run across both faces was one of fear mixed with deep pity, but I was unsure why. Were they truly scared of being infected by racism? Could it be a communicable disease? Before I could think more, I was weightless. Floating. The bright light of my surroundings had vanished momentarily only to return with a thunderous flash and crashing sound as if I were in a bolt of lightning itself. Then nothing. Slowly I opened my eyes, and I was in my bed, able to move freely. I found myself once again wondering if it had all been a dream like the car incident. Was I going mad? Was the relentless experience of being Black in America finally taking a toll on my sanity! But dear reader this was not the case. It was real or as real as whatever we conceive reality to be. But I would learn of the dreadful why, and of the incalculable loss humanity would know, soon enough. I would know why those above, in the sky, understand how truly lost we are.

L

The windowpane still rattled against its frame, pushed and pulled by the rising gale outside. Dorothea hardly noticed so deep in thought was she. This was all so fantastical, crazy even, and could not possibly be true. The ravings of a mad man surely, but she could not shake the feeling that a truth lay behind his tale. She questioned how the story of Central Park Karen could have ended up in a letter from the 1980s? Was it a fake and part of an elaborate weird stunt she wondered aloud? A prank by one of her siblings? It was an impossible situation. But the paper seemed genuinely aged, and tattered. Without some sort of scientific dating of the letter she would never be completely sure. Yet she recognized the term "Horrific Whiteness," and the definition was a common refrain here in East Orange. She had over the years seen the intersectionality of it all, meaning that on some level a taxonomy of "Horrific" exists. As a woman she experiences male entitlement daily, that her (or any woman's body) is symbolically and physically "theirs," embodying a "horrific masculinity," tangential to toxic masculinity. As an ally to the LGBTQ+ community she knew straight claims to "normality," forced many to conform to a script of sexuality, that is supposedly "right and acceptable," while damning those who do resist as deviant. It is a terrible bind that controls and constricts the sexuality of the LGBTQ+ community that is "Horrifically straight" thought and action. The list goes on. Additionally, she mused that this "horridness" experienced by the stigmatized in fact can be categorized at various levels. At the personal micro level of Central Park Karen, at the institutional meso level of the plight of the Lecturer himself being refused a tenure track position, and in all likelihood actual tenure and promotion if he ever got within sight of it (Diggs et al., 2009), and the macro level of society where horridness is global and endemic. A pandemic of awfulness shrouded by entitlement. It made her head spin with complexity. Would a solution to this age-old problem ever present itself or was this the way it would be forever? Should she retain hope for a deracialized world or was this simply a fool's errand? Either way like so many Black people she was simply tired, nay exhausted. How could she not be when the Black condition for so many is to oscillate between rage, resignation, and resentment?

The 3rd Letter

It was now 10 p.m., rain lashed against the old building, long past the time she had set to leave. The neighborhood had declined in recent years, no longer a mantle of the Black middle class, and it wasn't as safe as it used to be after dark these days either. Hauling herself up from the burgundy wood floor she massaged her aching neck with her right hand. In her left was the 2nd letter she had just been reading. Or was it? Upon closer inspection, she abruptly realized that in fact the letter was unopened. This was the 3rd and final letter ready to go in her hand. She couldn't remember grabbing or opening it at all. It was a similar feeling to driving from one destination to another without really knowing how you got there, daydreaming almost. It was late but she had to know how this all ended. Practically required by this point and with an uncommon impulsiveness she tore into it.

4/13/1988

To whoever may read this,

Please heed the warning of the events that I shall soon explain. It was unusually warm for April as I took my customary walk around Branch Brook Park, meaning that the cherry blossoms, a noted feature, were in bud far earlier than normal. A light breeze wafted by my face, and I felt serene and content. This for the most part is an unusual state of being for me. Dogs and their owners took advantage of the unseasonably good weather, accompanied by kids running around, kicking and screaming engaged in typical hijinks. It was a serene scene of sorts. Any troubles I had for once seemed distant.

It was at that exact moment I instantly became stiff as if rigor mortis had set in. Dread quickly followed. I knew this feeling, what it meant to be trapped helplessly in one's own body, and what would happen next. As I looked ahead, I was not the only frozen person either. Everyone in the park had become motionless, expressionless. A circular beam of iridescent green blue light flooded down from above, simultaneously I felt the vibration of a soundless whirling of what seemed to be a humongous silver disk above me. As big as three football fields. Then up, up, soaring ever higher, as if I was one with the very air itself. Darkness followed and then blinding light. As my eyes drew accustomed to my bright surroundings, I knew it to be familiar. I lay motionless once again on the long cold sterile silver table. Figures emerged from the glare to greet me. It could only be Wells and Robeson. What did they want from me again? Why am I continually being questioned? I told them all I could two years ago, and thought it sufficient enough to be left alone. Fright surged in me. Ida B. Wells came near and as she did, I found just as before that I could move and speak freely. This time she spoke to me in tones softer than before, concerned as a gentle and loving nurse would be for an incurably sick child.

"We have brought you back because we felt obligated to explain why we are here and what our mission has been all these years. After speaking with you we went back immediately to our Homeworld to explain all that you had spoken concerning this harmful aberration that you call race and its accompaniment, racism. Many heated debates were held. Our world Congress was locked in unusually bitter acrimony. Animosity appeared in our normally staid political assemblies, and we experienced rancor, a state unknown to our people, the more this concept was discussed. We are empathic people, and for all our harmony, for all our technology, despite our peaceful existence up to this point we had never been infected by this pathogen of race and racism, which blights your world. Though our people can take many forms we began overnight rigidly sticking to one form or another. One group becoming Skins Red, another Skins Blue. One group 'The orthodox,' governed by rules, the other 'The Misruled,' pandemonium was their watchword, where previously we were both or neither at any one time. Harmful differences burnt across our land quicker than we could imagine, dividing the populace across our central landmass along illusory lines made real by partisan choices, couched in a rhetoric of fear and loathing of the presumed Other. But the Skins Reds, these creatures of Orthodoxy, amassed great power, seeking to subjugate the other, taking the very shape of this slavery you explained. Shame accompanied both of us as we had been the vector, bringing a pestilence to our home, hurting our people. So very quickly we were on the verge of annihilation. This I had not expected. I had assumed this malady of race and racism was species-specific, an illness that solely infects humans. But it was you in our last meeting who alerted us to this prospect and we saw the danger. In our rush to explain the risk to our leaders we inadvertently exposed our planet to the very thing we feared.

The Lecturer gasped audibly. This could not be! His thoughts came thick and fast, as he entertained the spreading of our homegrown horror throughout the Galaxy, a vision too horrifying to contemplate. Worse, to think that he was instrumental in this process. So now our great human sorrow is on the verge of spanning space and time, with the possibility of rolling across millions of other worlds, infecting utopia planets. What is wrong with humanity? What is wrong with us? He needed to know more about the situation at hand.

"Indeed lecturer. This was our thought also."

They were reading my mind again. But I had one burring question left.

"What did you do? Did you cure your people?"

"Yes, Lecturer we did."

"How?"

I was giddy with elation and hope. Through all my trials, abductions, lost time I could not imagine that a solution to race and racism could exist. But of course, alien minds, superior to ours, could do so. Through my strife as a Black accounting professor trying to make it in a historically racist profession, existing in a society incapable of racial reform, I would have never believed this day would come. Here I stood waiting to hear how an advanced race cured an illness which has bedeviled our world for centuries. How did they cure race and racism and could we do it on Earth? It was tantalizing to say the least. It was at this juncture, dear reader that Robeson stepped forward, this time with less stature than before, less imperious. He had the answer I sought.

"We killed them. We killed them all."

What? You slaughtered your own people? Why? How many did you kill? Shock. I was in shock. These were higher order beings! There must have been another way.

> "No there was not Lecturer, it was simple logic. We killed our people by the millions to save billions. We are a tenth of what we were by population."

Robeson seemed to look past me into a void of his own making.

"But that's inhuman!"

"We are not human nor would we ever wish to be" replied Robeson. I tried to fathom this decision once more.

"But it makes no sense, it's such a loss of life for your own people."

Now Robeson moved closer. I could see the strain upon his face, he was older, more resigned. For a facsimile of Paul Robeson he was "cracking" badly. He whispered to me.

> "Humans are limited in thinking and selfish. All we did was remove what you would consider a cancerous element out of our society, so we all may prosper once more. Now the uninfected are growing again in number. We have isolated this racial tumor and expunged it, cut it out from our minds and bodies, our institutions and society to save the whole. It was required triage. Not only were we thinking of our people, but also the potential of its proliferation to become a Pan Galactic pandemic that would most certainly spread to the heart of the Dwarf Star Alliance."

"What?" I uttered in confusion.

Wells and Robeson once again flipped back to the concurrent speech pattern I found so jarring.

> "The Alliance is a coalition of planets orbiting what you refer to as a Red Dwarf Star. It is dedicated to ending suffering for all enlightened beings where possible."

"Hang on. That is a bit rich. You've just slaughtered millions of your own people. You are in fact despotic and hypocritical if your aim is to end suffering!" I couldn't help sneering at his hypocrisy.

> "We see that your limited human intellect still cannot comprehend the necessity for the greater galactic good over your limited constructions of suffering. Yours is a cult of selfish individualism over that of selfless sacrifice. But it is of no matter. It was the Alliance which originally tasked us with this fateful mission. Humanity was being assessed to see if it was enlightened enough to join the Alliance. Our original assessment included what you described as being 'Horrifically White,' and this concerned the Grand Alliance Council greatly. Before the planetary pandemic took hold, it was the council that voted against human entry into its ranks based on its long history of race and racism, coupled with sexism, misogyny and homophobia but to name a few."

"So?" I replied tersely. To me they were now intergalactic hypocrites. They replied in union once more.

"Your loss is this. The Alliance would have given you technologies beyond your imagination to end material suffering. Your planet's people would no longer live in agony, hunger would be a thing of the past, and your looming water crisis solved. Physical illness in a few short years would have been a bedtime tale for children, having been cured by our knowledge long ago. Your life expectancy would be in the range of eons, required to become the explorers you would be, as we would have given you the secrets of intergalactic movement that is time travel as well. Your world economy would have been subsumed into the Nova Galactic Trade Confederation of a Thousand, Thousand worlds. This would have transformed your society, as people of all hues would leave to find meaning and worth across the cosmos. In short all that humanity could ever want would have been granted. But the sole price of admission to the Dwarf Star Alliance is for each member to dedicate themselves to the difficult task to end or reduce suffering of all lifeforms. Instead exploring and celebrating differences in each and every form. This is something humanity is unable to do. Your penchant for race and racism makes this clear. You have no place among the stars. You have no place among the enlightened."

"We failed, didn't we?"

"Yes"

"Such is your species affinity, industry and innovation in the realm of racial harm that you nearly destroyed our Homeworld. We were just taking a look at you! Humanity is dangerous. You are now quarantined as a planet and contained to this area of spacetime. Any technology you might develop in the future to expand into the reaches of space has already been sabotaged."

"So that's it? The game is up for my species?"

They both looked at one another, and this time in an even more sympathetic tone Ida B. Wells spoke again.

> "The Alliance will return in a millennium to see your progress on reducing racial harm and its coherence with other inequities to see if you have progressed. If you are still alive as a species of course. Others will come to assess your fitness for the Alliance."

A sinking feeling grew in my stomach. I thought about the two fake titans in front of me. What was to happen to them? They were the first to carry race and racism as a pathogen back to their Homeworld. Why were they allowed to live? For the last time they read my mind and replied together.

> "Our last mission was to rely on these events to you. We are to be destroyed upon our return."

I stared blankly ahead. After collecting my thoughts as I often did, I replied.

> "This is our last goodbye then. I am sorry that this has happened and I'm sorry that humanity has so clearly failed this test. I wanted us to be better, I wanted to believe the myth that we can beat race and racism that we can have true equity in our society. But you have shown me that it is not possible, not right now. But that also means that hope exists. That in the far future we might get there. We might find value in one another despite difference and one day, as your people discovered long ago, simply celebrate the good in a life that is worth living for others. I long for that day."

As I looked up, they were gone. So was the silver table and paralysis. I was back in the park; the day was still warm. I seemed not to have lost a second of time. The frolics of children could be heard in the distance. Little did they know of the loss that had just occurred, or the true harm of not taking seriously racial justice in our world. And dear reader, this is the point I wish to make. The tale I must tell. It is this which we must strive for and we have much work to do. But now for me I will leave. I will leave that old worn house that has been my home for so long, I will leave my lecturing position and my hopes of tenure, and I will leave New Jersey, I will leave America. My path is elsewhere. Goodbye.

L.

Postscript

It was midnight now. Enough was enough. Dorothea was mad at herself for giving into whimsy. Whatever had compelled her to read this slushy nonsense had left. Planetary alliances! Intergalactic saviors! Race and racism as a virus! What trash! To think she could have been in bed by now. It's true that the earlier letters had stoked her interest. But the Central Park Karen bit made little sense. I mean how could the Lecturer see the future? Nonsense indeed, but it came at a price for her. Sadly, she still had an outstanding history assignment due at the end of the week which would require unhealthy amounts of coffee and late nights again. Sigh. She threw the last letter in the wastepaper basket, turned out the lights and made her way downstairs. As she reached the hallway, she took a moment to look at this old house so full of history, fun times, and sorrow. It would be the banks by morning. That her family home had ended this way hurt in ways that are difficult to describe, but that was life she guessed. Dorothea took one deep intake of breath and then she left, briskly making her way across the porch and down the stairs toward her parked car. Within minutes she was on her way safely home.

Far above the house. Far above Cherry Blossom Hills. Higher still than New Jersey itself, in low Earth orbit, cloaked from satellites, and prying human eyes span a large circular disk. The occupants noted that humans truly were a curious species but that their most salient characteristic was harm. They were truly dangerous. Turning away from the view screen the luminous beings that they were, with no need to humor humans' comprehension with facsimiles of their real form, they addressed the Grandmaster.

> "Thank you sire for your advice on the dangers of humanity, the Dwarf Star Alliance is eternally grateful for your guidance. We now see the great harm that nearly cost us everything. Humanity so badly affected by this concept of racial practice has no place with us and without you guiding us to this understanding Lecturer, we would never have known how to deal with this doom that so nearly befell the Universe."
>
> "It is quite alright. Its why I am here. To help of course."

The two beings of light quickly turned toward their viewscreen, setting new coordinates, slightly left of Alpha Century, lost in thought, happy to get back to their world and their looming execution. Which was why they missed the sly smile creep across the face of the Lord of Race and Racism. He was quite pleased that he had the foresight to weaponize the Lecturer as a biological/ideological delivery vehicle. Wiping out more than half the population of intergalactic philanthropists trying to undo his life's work of inculcating racial harm was a job well done. It was funny he thought how things work out. Had he not been tracking the futile efforts of Enki Abyd to curtail his work, he would not have come across the Center for Infectious Disease and Tropical medicine, where Professors Annie Ball and Myron Jones worked. He would not have been able to subtly sabotage their findings or manipulate the Fable Stone into showing events in a way that benefited race and racism. And finally, he would not have been able to get the idea to use their findings to create a Bio/racial A-Bomb and decimate those insipid galactic do-gooders. Eventually he would come back and completely destroy the Alliance of course. But Earth really was a barrel of laughs and he had the time. All time in fact. All was going to plan. Like always.

References

Alexander, M. (2010). *The New Jim Crow. Mass incarceration in the age of colorblindness*. The New Press.

Bhaskaran, S., Al Khaldi, F., Biu, O., Chang, E., Ihejirika, C., Muñoz, A., & Hamilton, D. (2024). *Color of wealth in Chicago*. The New School.

DiAngelo, R. (2018). *White fragility. Why its so hard for white people to talk about racism*. Beacon Press Books.

Diggs, G., Garrison-Wade, D., Estrada, D., & Galindo, R. (2009). Smiling faces and colored spaces: The experiences of faculty of color pursuing tenure in the academy. *Urban Revue*, *41*, 312–333.

Dubois, W. E. B. (2005). *The souls of black folk*. Pocket Books.

Dymski, G. (2009). Racial exclusion and the political economy of the subprime crisis. *Historical Materialism*, *17*, 149–179.

Glaude, E. (2016). *Democracy in black. How race still enslaves the American soul*. Broadway Books.

Hammond, T., Streeter, D. W., & Musundwa, S. (2022). Using qualitative research to effect change: African/American accountants in Black and White. *Critical Perspectives on Accounting*, *89*, 1–9.

Harris, C. (1995). Whiteness as property. In K. Crenshaw, N. Gotanda, G. Peller, & K. Thomas (Eds.), *Critical race theory. The key writings that formed the movement* (pp. 276–291). The New Press.

Italiano, L. (2020). *Black man shot dead by Atlanta cops in Wendy's drive-thru*. https://nypost.com/2020/06/13/unarmed-black-man-shot-dead-by-atlanta-cops-in-wendys-drive-thru/

Keister, L. A. (2004). Race, family structure, and wealth: The effect of childhood family on adult asset ownership. *Sociological Perspectives*, *47*(2), 161–187.

McIntosh, P. (1997). White privilege and male privilege: A personal account of coming to see correspondences through work in women's studies. In R. Delgado & J. Stefancic (Eds.), *Critical white studies: Looking behind the mirror* (pp. 291–299). Temple University Press.

Melamed, J. (2015). Racial capitalism. *Critical Ethnic Studies*, *1*(1), 76–85.

Stieb, M. (2021). *Amy Cooper didn't learn much from her time as 'Central Park Karen'*. https://nymag.com/intelligencer/2021/05/amy-cooper-didnt-learn-much-from-being-central-park-karen.html

Thomas, G., & Hollenshead, C. (2001). Resisting from the margins: The coping strategies of Black women and other women of color faculty members at a research university. *Journal of Negro Education*, *70*(3), 166–175.

TMZ. (2020). *'Permit Karen' calls cops on Black neighbors, met with student protest*. https://www.tmz.com/2020/07/01/permit-karen-calls-cops-black-neighbors-students-protest-outside-home-new-jersey-montclair/

Williams, D., Lawrence, J., & Davis, B. (2019). Racism and health: Evidence and needed research. *Annual Review of Public Health*, *40*, 105–125.

Chapter 4

4th Fable: Hot Chicken. Hot Haircut

> The time and space of chattel slavery shares essential aspects with the time and space, the violence, of our modern lives. (Frank B. Wilderson III, 2020)

William "Smokey Slim" Barnes loved to go on vacation. Aruba had been calling for some time and his wife Jackie had finally acquiesced, planning to take two weeks off from her job as an orthodontist to accompany her husband to the Caribbean Island. One surrounded by a light blue sea and pristine beaches, typical of the West Indies. It was his dream vacation but in truth Jackie would have preferred France. She was quite the Francophile, having spent time as a study abroad student in the Fall term of her junior year in Lyon. It was here she developed a formidable taste for Gallic cuisine and culture. Her thinking ran like this, if she did Aruba now, then when vacation time rolled around next year, she would have the leverage needed to crowbar a similar deal in Marseille out of Slim. Therefore, Aruba was a price worth paying in her mind. And I mean c'mon its Aruba! Besides, an added plus was attached to this particular trip. Their son, "Junior 'Lil' Slim" Barnes would be accompanying them for the first time, giving him a chance to see something of the world. An important formative step for any American child in their view but in particular, African American kids.

In truth, his parents were no strangers to the benefits of international travel and they felt the urgent need for him to see a world outside of the USA as a cultural imperative. To them it's important to make sure their son knows that other cultures exist firsthand, especially ones which espouse positive Black ways of being outside that of the established American negative norm. To their mind such experiences add significantly to his internalized basket of race-based survival skills, required as a Black boy, soon to be a Black man in America in everyday life and the workplace. For sadly, it is with an Eagle's eye that nearly all Black parents watch their children, particularly boys, scanning the societal horizon for the inevitable harm approaching them, which over time "shocks" Black boys into the status of "endangered Black men," prevalent in a society explicit in the racial harm it seeks to meter out to Black men over their lifetime (Rollock et al., 2015). This should be of little surprise dear reader as one glances at the racial destruction

Accounting Fables: Tales of Race and Racism in the Borderlands of Business, 55–71

Published under exclusive licence by Emerald Publishing Limited
doi:10.1108/978-1-80117-069-720251013

historically bestowed on African Americans in the USA, which continues unabated today. It is the endemic stench of entrenched racism found in America's past and present that lingers still (Kendi & Blain, 2021). But today such matters were secondary to the urgent need to prepare for their vacation.

Haircut

While the idea of Slim's dream vacation was laudable, practical realities still needed to be dealt with. For example, both father and son looked way too "wooley" to go anywhere. Their bushy Afros required taming, a much-needed haircut was called for. The trip was only a few days away and all the typical stuff still needed to be done. Think packing, putting the dog in the kennel, etc. For Smokey Slim this was no big deal. He was a businessman after all and prided himself on making sure that things were finished on time and in good order. The result of which was the acquisition of numerous accolades for commerce and Black Business awards for his mid-sized, bespoke sports footwear company. Typical of many, he had really gotten into classic sports footwear in college and like a man possessed had begun to buy, sell and store them incessantly. His hobby eventually developed into a viable business after a long and candid conversation with his Accounting professor during his senior year at North Carolina A&T State University's Wille A. Deese College of Business and Economics. Slim had come to understand that service was key to his business model and that he could create a tailored service using social media and phone apps to reach companies and customers alike. Thus, keep them coming back for more. This was how he generated healthy sales which sustained his business in the medium to long term. He also had a particularly good way with supply logistics, meaning he often found rare but relatively inexpensive sporting footwear stock for resale to eager clients at a margin. All in all the business had grown wonderfully, and now it needed to expand but he found that he had hit a wall of sorts. It was a stressful time for him right now and that's why Aruba was a must; he needed a break. Unhelpfully, Jackie pointed out repeatedly that he also needed a haircut and that he should take Junior with him. Now.

With a shrug of his broad shoulders Slim coaxed the teenager out of his "pit" of a bedroom and into his Silver Grey Dodge Charger. He grabbed his phone out of his pocket, and soon his fingers danced over the surface looking to quickly get an appointment with his usual Baber "Jackson's Finest Cuts." Slim liked the outfit because both Jackson and his staff were timely and efficient. You can book online and if a slot is available that day (which was often the case), you can drive right there and get a quip snip. No messing around, a nice tight cut and you could be in and out in under an hour. As he pulled up the scheduled for that day, groan, he saw that the place was shut due to plumbing issues and would not reopen for at least a week. The haircut had now become an irritant. Until he had found out about Jackson's Finest Cuts Slim had been forced to run the gauntlet of what he considered lesser Black Barber shops. It was the usual thing. He would have to ingratiate himself with the Barber's themselves, then he would have to find one who would do a decent cut to his standard, and then watch as the set price fluctuated from one week to the next, depending on the vagaries of that particular barber (Network, 2021). In the past he would call the barber of the moment, and then go down for a cut only to find that for whatever reason he was not there, or he would "come soon," which meant an extra hour waiting. Not being particularly patient by nature, Slim would wait for 20 minutes and then storm out. Of course, Jackie would be the recipient of his ire, leading to yet again another fight. Unfortunately, this happened all too often.

But all that ended when he discovered Jackson's shop and the impossible magic of an on-time haircut to a good standard. The bliss of not losing an entire afternoon to a haircut is difficult to put into words, but it was something he appreciated greatly. Now at least for today, Slim was back to square one, starring down the barrel of that particular gun, furiously tapping away at the screen of his Android phone in the hope of finding a Black barber who could see him on short notice and (hopefully) not rob him of an entire afternoon. Afterall, Jackie had pleaded with him to complete the laundry list of other jobs she had given him days ago to do (that he had yet to get around to finishing), so she could focus on the arduous task of packing for the entire family. But if his schedule was delayed in any way, he could foresee a nasty argument brewing in the not-too-distant future with his wife which he would like to avoid at all costs. Clearly because he would lose. There. He had found a prospect – Duke barbers in nearby Scottsville. It was a 15-minute drive, and he would have to take his chances in the inevitable waiting line with Lil Slim, but it was worth a try. With a quick press of the ignition button the Charger roared into life speeding father and son onward.

Slim and Junior arrived at Dukes at around 11 a.m. on time as per the phone conversation with this new Black barber. As they entered a thin gangly, slightly skeletal looking barber introduced himself as "Bones," and ushered them to sit down on the sofa by the large shop window. The shop itself was as typical as any busy Barber shop could be. Brothers passed banter around; aged wisdom combined with biting commentary, delivered with witty rapport. Thirty minutes soon passed, and the same brother was still in the chair with Bones. Slim began to be concerned as his time to get everything finished that day was now being pressed. He asked the barber about the delay:

"Brah, why the wait?"

"Your name brotha?"

"I'm Slim and we spoke on the cell to make this appointment."

Slowly Bones reached over for his iPhone and tapped it a few times.

"I don't remember no Slim brah."

"What do you mean? I booked it well over an hour ago."

"Yeah, I don't know what to say man … I' don't have you down and I always write my appointments down."

With that the barber continued his careful curation of the Afro in front of him. With a hint of tension in his voice Slim asked if he would still be able to fit him in, "Yeah man" was the response and "soon." So, Smokey Slim and Junior waited. And they waited. They got to see Bones stop at noon and disappear for a burger which he ate. Slowly. Then he returned to the ever-changing Afro. They got to witness Bones make several calls on his iPhone each requiring him to walk away from the chair. This happened at least three times. By now Slim was quite agitated. Grabbing Junior by his arm a bit harder than he meant to do, he began to make his way to the door.

"Wait brah, I got you. Just sit.n'other five and I'm done."

With another grunt Slim and his son sat back down. He really did need this haircut but whatever patience he had begun with had departed somewhat like a fart in the wind .... True to his word in 5 minutes Bones ushered Slim into the chair. It was now 1.30 p.m. By the time this was done a number of items on the list would remain incomplete. Slim settled into the chair and Bones began his task. But about 15 minutes into his styling what would become a nice cut Bones surreptitiously grabbed a waiting taco and disappeared. With some dexterity Bones managed to both eat the Taco, and take yet again another incessant call, while simultaneously engaging in the never-ending comedic banter with other barbers and frankly any game passerby. Slim's eyes narrowed as he could not quite believe what he was experiencing. Another 40 minutes wasted and the exercise in patience that was this haircut was resumed. All in all, by the time Junior was finished it was 3 p.m. They had wasted hours at Dukes. Slim was apoplectic with anger, but he buried his rage as he went to pay his time-wasting tormentor.

"That's $75 brah."

"What? The website and the board over on the wall say its $50 special rate adult and junior cut."

"Yeah ... but prices just changed and we ain't changed the board, and we never change the website."

This of course was without the tip. All in all, the haircut cost him ninety bucks. Slim stormed out of the Barber's shop vowing never to return. Tugging at his arm junior started to whine that he was "starving." This continued as they got into the car. Smokey Slim was feeling the heat! Rising fury was building. But with a deep breath he knew he had to feed the boy, or he would shortly become "Hangry," and therefore unmanageable. He needed a place to eat as they sped down the road, and it needed to be nearby. It would have to be "Earl's Fire Chicken Shack" just round the corner and Slim vowed it better be decent service or he would snap.

Chicken Run

As the car flew down the narrow lane toward the Chicken Shack, Smokey Slim heard disgruntled mummering's emanating from his "ravenous and irate" son. A stony silence soon developed. It was punctuated sometime later by a question from the disgruntled child seated in the back.

"Dad. If the service was so bad at Dukes, why did you pay the tip? And why didn't you tell them exactly what you thought of them?"

It was a startlingly simple question but not easy for Slim to articulate an answer for.

"Well son ... We don't really do that in the Black community."

"Do what Dad?" Junior managed to sound both inquisitive and sarcastic in equal measure fueling Slims own indignation.

"We support Black Business. Even when it doesn't support us as customers. We know the service can be terrible, we know the way many of our small shops conduct business is appalling, but we have a responsibility to not impugn Black Business."

"Impugn? What?"

"What I mean is that when we are vocal about the shortcomings of Black Business then we also contribute to the harmful narrative that Black people, culturally, cannot successfully run organizations, or work and succeed in corporations. Basically, on pain of death we tend to avoid affirming any kind of racist assumptions whites have that Blacks are bad at business and are unsuited to the workplace. Sadly, even if sometimes it rings true."

"Hmm … but … Dad I didn't see any white people at the Barber. How would they know?"

Of course, Junior had a good point and kind of knew he had his father on an ideological fishing hook, eager to reel him in. Slim thought some more.

"Yes, you are right on that count son. But even so its good practice and we also want to show our hard-pressed Black brothers and sisters that we support them no matter what."

"Even if they make us late. Even if they make us hungry. That makes no goddam sense Dad!"

"Now watch that sass in your mouth boy before I clean it out!" Clearly "Hangery Junior" was in control.

"Now it's true that there has to be a limit to terrible service but what is a little inconvenience compared to supporting Black Business that has never really had a chance in Whiteworld[1]?"

"But Dad, if they aren't told, how will they know? How will they change? We have to tell them that the standard is not good enough and it's not the 'Man' or whiteness its Black incompetence."

"Be careful son. You raise some good points, but our community will label you a sellout, and possibly an Uncle Tom[2] for repeating the white man's view of bad Black Business."

"But it IS bad Black Business daddy! That's why we're late, that's why we're hungry, that's why Mom will kill you went you get home because we have done nothing that on the list that she sent us to do."

"Boy! Shut that trap of yours."

Smokey Slim was crazy now, his teeth gritted, and his fists tightly gripped to the steering wheel as if he were braced for an impending impact, and not just because his son didn't get why it's a no-no to openly criticize bad Black commerce. No, it was because at his core he knew his son was right and he just didn't have an answer for him. Not one that made any sense, not for the overall good of the Black community or for Black patrons. Luckily, before he had to field

[1]Whiteworld is the all-consuming power of the whiteness of almost everything, often seen in the maxim the white way is the right way (Gillborn, 2006).

[2]This is an epithet of sorts labelling a Black person as a sellout who puts pleasing white people above Blacks in all situations. It is perhaps unfairly derived from Harriet Beecher Stowe's character of the same name in her famous novel *Uncle Tom's Cabin.*

any more questions from his pint-sized inquisitor, they pulled into the car park of Earls Fire Chicken Shack. The boy fairly vaulted out of the Dodge, charging at full speed toward the Shack doors like a hungry extra from a Zombie flick. It was there that he was greeted with a disheartening sight. Although it was 4 p.m., on a Tuesday afternoon the place was packed full. Slim thought he spotted a solitary tear on the boy's face, and he definitely heard his son's stomach grumbling. No, they would have to suck this one up and wait it out yet again to get his chicken.

Now in truth this occasionally happened at Earl's shack. The Chicago Heights location was one of several that had in recent years become a successful regional chain, somewhat iconic in African American mid-western culture. Its name found itself in more than one hip hop lyric and social media references as a must place to eat in Chicagoland were common. But what no one said, just as at Duke's, was its service and general business model was terrible despite its relative size and obvious success as a Black owned business. What clearly should be a 20 minute in out affair turned into another multiple hour nightmare. It was 6 p.m. now. Junior was essentially rabid thanks to sloth like service. Further orders from multiple customers, both Black and white were wrong, and Slim found himself on several occasions checking his food ticket to make sure his order was on its way, or that somebody had not taken his order by mistake at the chaotic counter. And the look of indifferent distain by the server was palpable. She didn't care at all.

Only one young African American woman seemed to be holding service together, barking orders, throwing shade, harassing the anemic kitchen to get backlogged orders out and correct. This is not how any business should be run and yet to check social media it was as if a magic trick had occurred. Not one complaint about bad service or comment to never go back existed. Neither did posts expose the almost certain reality that your order would be wrong. This was the true mystery. After what seemed an eternity, their food arrived but no thanks to Earls staff. In fact, a kindly Asian lady pointed out to Slim that their order looked like it might be ready. They had raised eyebrows together at their joint ordeal previously, becoming "a brother and sister in arms," waiting to be fed. Junior, like a man possessed dashed to the car and feasted like never before. It was now 7 p.m. Day had become night and he had little to show for it but an enraged wife, itching to "tear him a new one" at his lack of organizational skills, since he had achieved just one item on the list. Vexed and perplexed Slim slammed the Dodge into reverse, simultaneously smashing into a middle-aged white man behind the car who was up until that point eagerly devouring a hot chicken leg oblivious to anything in the twilight of the car park. The car basically sent him flying through the air in the opposite direction. For an instant both Slim and Junior froze. Had he just killed this man? This older white man who would no doubt attempt to sue him if he lived. His business could not afford the publicity fall out from this, especially if it made the local news. He jumped out of the car and looked at the crumpled frail frame before him. The old man had a bad gash above his head, was bleeding profusely, and was badly bruised from head to foot. Quickly, Slim went to his aid.

"Hey man, I didn't see you! Are you ok? Do you need an ambulance?"

"No."

"Just as well. They sure take their time getting to Chicago Heights these days. The area has gone down worse than before. But you sure are bleeding badly sir. How about I give you a ride to the nearest emergency care facility? It's the fastest way to get you medical help."

"I'm much obliged young man" the older white gentleman murmured in a distant way.

"Sir, may I ask your name" Slim enquired.

"Oh yes, it's the Grandmaster."

"Oh … er right. Well just get into the passenger seat and we will get you on your way sir."

Clearly concussion had occurred in the old man. It was imperative that Smokey Slim get him medical help. The problem was that it was rush hour and it might take a while. Good he thought, it will give me time to talk to him, befriend him and hopefully make it more difficult for him to sue. It might not happen this way but it was worth a try. The Dodge fired into life and the trio zoomed into the rapidly descending darkness. Junior had finished his food, and was assessing the features of their new passenger, he had a sunken drawn face, so stereotypically white it was untrue. And oddly, given what he had just been through he seemed to have a sly smile on his face. How strange he thought.

Grandmaster Flash

At first an uncomfortable silence descended upon the speeding vehicle. Perhaps it was Slim's concern that this oddly robust octogenarian might have some internal injuries and might sue after all. Yet, as he looked at this man, he seemed completely at home in the situation in an unsettling manner. His aura was one of dominance, improbably an image flashed before him of an old White Slave master overseeing a new crop of slaves chained together in a coffle, eager at the potential wealth that would soon be his from their enslaved efforts.

"Ah … those were the days weren't they Slim. Everybody knew their place and this country of mine blossomed as never before" murmured this self-styled Grandmaster of what Slim didn't quite know.

Disturbingly, Slim had experienced this image in his mind and not verbalized anything, and he had not yet told this peculiarly unnerving man his name. A pit of fear opened in his stomach but yet he felt oddly compelled to passively reply.

"It was Mr Master?"

"Why yes Slim it was, and thank you for your polite address."

Slim quietly, subserviently, nodded approval while Junior equally nervous sat quietly in the back not quite believing his eyes.

"Business has been the white man's purview since the foundation of this land. Afterall, slaves were brought from darkest Africa to build a nation founded upon property rights and of course they themselves were property. These days it saddens me to see Blacks now trying to rise above their station, attempting something they are not 'designed' to do."

"And wha's that boss?"

"Why Slim, Its Black Business! An illogicality that can never succeed in this country."

A tinge of rage enveloped Junior that somehow allowed him to push through a sort of enchanted timidity, one which had already bewitched his father, making a strong Black man obedient under its thrall.

"Well, that's wrong! And why do you say such a thing?"

"Because my impertinent young man … I designed it that way and it is working very nicely indeed."

As the Grandmaster makes this statement he slowly turns around in his seat and looks menacingly at Slim junior. It is then that he sees the sallowness in his cheeks, the deadness of his cold pale blue eyes, the frenzied twisting smirk of his mouth. It was unmistakable. Whatever this being was, this old white fiend, it wasn't human, and it was soulless. It was extremely powerful and telling a truth which wasn't good for Black people at all. Not one bit.

"But Mr Master how can this be? I's own a business and is making it work kinda. And shucks we have some Black Businessmen and women now. I's recollect Oprah Winfrey and Michael Jordan be like this."

Slim's diction was regressing at a pace to a form of pigeon slave speech. A kind of verbal step and fetch it if you will.

"Ah yes, the outliers. Its true some Black businesses and Black stars do wiggle out of the net but the majority are swept up like so many dead fish hauled upon a fishing vessel."

"Net? Wha's a net boss?" Murmurs Slim.

With a sigh of impatience, the Grandmaster goes on to explain the depth of his breath-taking grand design of racial subjugation.

"As you have seen today Slim, when you attempted the simple act of getting a haircut or tried to order a very tasty chicken thigh or two in a timely way you failed. I have fashioned it so that Black Business cannot cut it in white society or the Black community. It will always fail at customer service, and it is due to inherent bad business practice that I have engineered. It cannot fully compete on the same level as white business in the US by my design. Specifically, the net I speak of removes core tools for Black Business to succeed, it is a shroud enveloping nearly all Black entrepreneurs. It is best for your small mortal minds to think of it like this. I make sure that Black Business cannot find its way to decent service for the most part, not forgetting rare outliers will always exist but for the most part underlying Black Business basics will not be established in any true manner, keeping Black Business stuck in a rut. Permitting Black wealth to be stymied in nearly every setting. Trust me, creating this has been a labor of love, taking generations. Much of my design revolves around what I describe as the Pillars of Black Business pain."

Both Slim and Junior eyed each other and then cast their curious but fearful gaze toward the Grandmaster. His countenance beckoned them to know more about this nefarious plan and he subsequently obliged.

Pillars of Black Business Pain

Making himself comfortable for a minute the Grandmaster ruminated. He was gathering his thoughts together to explain how a complicated and multigenerational act of racial tyranny came to be, and how it continues today. Something he is deeply proud of. He started with the first pillar of Black Business pain – Black Financial Illiteracy.

"Note I had to make sure that the pillars of Black Business pain came into existence, hidden and unseen. Remember you cannot change or dismantle what you can't see! The first pillar – Black Financial Illiteracy means Blacks have little to no understanding of the financial world. This has led to a lack of Black Banks meaning so called African Americans must use racist white banks and suffer redlining and white flight in housing (and therefore a sustained lack of property ownership). My inspiration of tax code racism ensures Blacks have more wealth removed than other races through the tax system keeping them poorer for longer.

I knew this to be the path which would keep your people down economically from generation to generation. It has been an unmitigated success but it has been no easy feat! To begin with after the manumission of Slaves things looked quite bad, and with the advent of Reconstruction in the United States, racial progress was being made! Blacks started to exercise political power that left unchecked might level the business and societal playing field allowing them to fairly compete with whites. You might then build a platform for intergenerational wealth that would fuel success in business for you and other racialized immigrants. On top of that the government of the day foolishly promised assets of 40 acres and a mule! To manumitted slaves! Well, I had to work hard to make sure that didn't come to pass. If I hadn't moved quickly then Black people would have had the means to fund Black enterprise and then pass on wealth with each generation slowly building up their education and ability to succeed no matter what US society would throw at them. These were dangerous times Slim. I had to intervene!"

"Mr Master, you did this?"

"Why yes Slim. Making sure that 40 acres and a mule was reneged on was the first move. It was a line in the sand that made sure Blacks would forever have difficulty acquiring wealthy assets in this society and that they could expect promises to that effect to be reneged upon in perpetuity.

This was important as it was the first and most powerful tool I had to ensure that a faith in white promises would always be suspect. The White Man's word cannot be trusted (and it can't). It means what white values can't be trusted. Those things whites prize most are suspect, and in some ways, feared, always. This makes all education and in particular financial education continually suspicious. This lack of financial literacy is at the heart of what continues to keep your people down economically, and therefore socially from generation to generation. Your children's children cannot and will not fully access wealth that is easily available to whites but is nigh on impossible for Blacks to get. This by extension hobbles Black Business over generations. I mean where do they get the capital to begin? Black Banks? I have rid myself of that irritant as well which I will come to shortly.

Because of this Blacks have little wealth to change their situation in a society that worships the only true color which counts – green! The all mighty dollar rules here which is bad news for you and your community. To be clear destroying Black financial literacy is key. You so called African Americans have to be kept away from educating yourselves about capital markets, you must be kept away from knowing the vagaries of Accounting, the language of money as some call it. You must forever see it as white man's business. Sure, I will allow some Blacks to gain extreme wealth, but they will only ever be a handful and they will work within the racially rigged system that I have created and not challenge it or they will lose their wealth. Think sports and entertainment here. I'll see to that. Sometimes you have to give a little to gain a lot. I give a few Blacks extreme wealth and I or rather should I say all whites in the United States gain the economic subservience of 95% of Blacks in perpetuity!"

The last statement forced an involuntary smile of self-serving satisfaction across the wizened face of the old foe, pleased with his achievement, proud of his plan. He was in full flow now.

"Of course, the best thing about it all is that Blacks and whites get to blame Black people for their child like inability to get ahead in business or the professional workplace. We help Blacks hate themselves once more. Because of this, wealth is kept from each Black generation for the foreseeable future keeping you where you belong. At the bottom."

"But it can't be that easy! It can't be that simple! Dad tell him!" cried Junior from the back seat.

But Slim couldn't, his mind was in semi-paralysis. He knew the words to be true but somehow being in close proximity to the Grandmaster, one way or another, siphoned away his own hard fought financial intelligence, he had in some way, racially de-evolved, losing Black Business prowess key to his success. Slim was ignorant and childlike now, as so many were conditioned to be in slavery. Junior was outright terrified. And yet the Grandmaster felt obliged to answer poor Junior's statement.

"I'm afraid it is true little Slim, and I will tell you why. For me to keep Black people in this country economically subjugated I have to continually cripple Black Business basics. And so, I've had to forge the second Pillar of Black Business Pain – Too Few Black Business professionals. On a pragmatic level I have ensured urban communities experience an absence of Black Business professionals and institutions which could help raise your people out of economic peonage. I alone make sure that fewer and fewer Black CPAs exist each year, meaning that now 2% of qualified CPAs are Black, although in the mid 90's I had it as low as 0.5% (Hammond, 2002), what great days! And I've made sure those Black partners at the top of the profession remain stuck at 2% (AICPA, 2021). Black finance and angel investors are anemic, and it's a contradiction in terms to think Black start-up tech businesses will get unicorn startup funding. I've made sure that they spend no time aiding Black business. Thanks to rulings from a few of my acolytes on the Supreme Court of the United States (shout out to my boy Clarence Thomas), they have ensured on that startup capital specific to Black women is seen as discriminatory. Ha! It's just too easy sometimes. Black women business has been dealt a harsh blow it will not soon recover from to be sure (Lewis, 2024), and its effect is pleasing to me, creating a chilling effect on DEI across the board (Lewis, 2022). To give you an idea of what I'm talking about minorities made up about 8.5% of entrepreneurs selling Business ideas to angel investors early last decade, and a paltry 15% of these managed to effectively transform any pitches into money. Thanks to me, Black business ideas don't get the opportunity to grow, even if the minority founders get into the room with white investors. The chances of getting follow-on capital or later period investments is about zero. Good work in my view of course (Beasley, 2020).

It's been a tricky feat at times and I have to occasionally move quickly making sure you Blacks don't explode in one leap into wealth by accident. For example, I alone made sure that Black Wall Street in turn of the century Tulsa was burned to the ground by angry whites who were and are still committed to Black economic destruction. It of course was an effective act of white terrorism driving Blacks away from Wall Street and making sure that finance is not considered a viable career or activity for Blacks. Again, I repeat once more, these are but a few reasons why you do not have Black business professionals supporting Black Businesses or have Black wealth emulating that of whites. And now we go much deeper to explore my feats with Black Banking, the anti-Black tax code, and redlining in housing as forces that currently and historically harm Black wealth acquisition and injures Black Business. Ah … some of my greatest work."

Junior just stared at this chicken eating figure of a devil, wide eyed in disbelief, while Slim senior seemed to be losing his quite considerable poise by the second. The Grandmaster was in preacher mode now. If you could have a soapbox in your car, he would be on it. As if by sleight of hand poor Slim shriveled in stature while this Grandmaster grew apace, somehow taking up all available physical and discursive space. The Charger felt small now as they journeyed ever quicker down the narrow lane toward the hospital.

The Grandmaster smacked his lips as he finished the last of his fire chicken, burped loudly and continued preaching his tale of woe.

"Take Black banking for instance. As another Pillar of Black Business Pain, I have made sure that it has been a struggle to create and maintain them in Black communities. First and foremost, the fertile racism of this country made sure to blame the Black community for its poverty, but not so obvious was my hand in the creation of a number of institutions that have always existed to exploit Blacks at every turn. My genius was to seed Black subjugation in the form of slavery or something similar over time, think Sharecropping, Jim Crow segregation, and the 'war on drugs' as some of my greatest hits. I take pride in the fact that what essentially ails Black banking is the same now as it was 100 years ago."

Another Chesire cat wry smile crept across its fiendish face, pleased as punch so the master of racial disaster was.

"Yes, Black banking which serves small economically depressed Black communities simply cannot attain stable large deposits from Blacks lenders nor be guaranteed that loans made to them will be paid back due to historic Black job insecurity. This makes for lesser and more unstable loans and fewer Black banks across the board. I've made sure that unlike white banks, Black banks cannot make money through lending exclusively to Black communities who are racially segregated in situ. Black banking can never be an engine to fuel loans to Black business and they themselves will eventually fail because of it. Its brilliant right!" (Baradaran, 2017).

"I ... I don't believe it!"

"Ah, young man it does not matter if you believe or not, it has happened and continues to this day under my careful curation. I think of it sometimes as a plant of despair that must be tendered and watered with love so it can blossom into great harm against those racialized as Others. And what I mean by care is making sure that the roots of the plant are strong and imperceptible to most. Think here of property and the fact that white people in white nations have more of this wealth generating asset than other races. That is to say that rights in property are for us whites and by us whites, obtained through racial subjugation and enshrined in Law of course."

The Grandmaster's face twisted in an impossible mockery of what can only be described as a self-satisfied grin.

"Think here boy, how whites took the land from so called First Nations people and made you and your people property ... like a cow to be bought and sold."

"Yes, I've heard Mom and Pops talks about this idea of a property right in Whiteness that is what you mean isn't it?" retorted Junior.

"Yes, some of my most troubling incidents have come from those meddlesome Critical Race Theorists! One of which is Cheryl Harris. She annoyingly highlighted this very point, that Whiteness allowed the taking of native land and the reduction of people to property, and so has an inherent Property Right that continues to this day. Being white is valuable property in of itself in this society, supported by the law, and long may it continue" (Harris, 1995).

"But that doesn't make whites better than Blacks though."

"Actually, it does" murmured the Old white withered figure.

"It makes sure that the lowest white has greater inherent social value than the richest Black in this racialized society I have carefully constructed. It means poor whites regularly vote against their own self-interest and oppose standing with poor Blacks against rich whites. Thus, reinforcing racial hierarchy that harms both. It's brilliant I know, no need to applaud. But the point I want to get to ...."

And Junior thought to himself I wish he would. This rambling beast is frightening and boring at the same time. I mean how is that even possible?

"Frightens and bores at the same time, eh? Really Slim, you must teach this pup of yours better manners. Because one day he may lose his tongue if he's not careful. That day might be here and now ...." Hissed the Grandmaster with tranquil menace.

"Yessum!" Slim eagerly nodded with his eyes now bulging in comedic wonder and ignorance.

Meanwhile Junior quickly refocused his waning attention to his perilous situation, quickly ascertaining that the Grandmaster could in fact read his mind. In response he forced himself to concentrate on a mountain of fire wings as a mask. A tiny bead of sweat rolled down his brow thanks to the strain.

"Clever boy. Fire chicken is yummy. It is tasty, isn't it? Still, I know everything I need about you, so think away. As I was saying, the result of what that woman Harris proposed is that there is a 'Property Lack in Blackness'!"

"Right! I get it! If property is defined as the state or fact of owning or possessing something, Blackness inherently lacks this basic right." Blurted out Junior nearly falling out of the back seat. He composed himself before his next reply.

"So, on the whole being Black means to have extreme difficulty obtaining property or keeping it at a societal level and the Law of the land leans toward defending whites property rights not Black. But Grandmaster that can't be right. We have Blacks who are multimillionaires and billionaires! They have plenty of property."

"True, but how many? I've already told you I limit the number dullard; this is the mechanism why. The ceiling exists by my design, letting only a few Blacks or People of Color attain property or a level playing field of property attainment to which whites have."

"I simply don't believe it" Junior barked in frustration.

"The past cares little for your feelings young fool. I know because I talk to her regularly …. Think here of Redlining.[3] A wonderful concept that I for once did not create. This was a local white creation which kept Black communities trapped in bad housing, with atrocious health conditions since they were 'zoned' next to undesirable properties near polluting factories and heavy industry. Redlining has customarily safeguarded poverty in Black housing by herding Blacks into the worst and only available homes. Of course, when some Blacks want to leave the Black ghetto because they have somehow acquired the means to do so and buy property in valuable white areas, racial covenants customarily sprang up to prevent this. And when it was eventually removed by racial do-gooders, those inventive white homeowners simply moved out of neighborhoods when too many Blacks moved in. This white flight crashed the value of Black homes along with the taxable base for schooling, making housing in the area even less valuable. Luckily this still happens today though" (Baradaran, 2017).

"I see. Yes, it's something Grandma Josephine used to say. That she 'chased white people all around Chicago! She and Grandpa moved at least seven times in their lifetime."

"Yes, and quite right too! My dear boy most Blacks today cannot use homeownership to increase their wealth because of their 'Property Lack in Blackness,' both tangible but also intangible. You see just as whites with nothing retain an undisputed wealth derived from their property right in whiteness, bolstering their self-worth in a racialized society, Blacks experience the opposite. No matter what, their self-worth is still negative property, meaning they can never

[3]Redlining occurred around the 1930s through the racial mapping of the US by Homeowners Loan Corporation (HOLC). HOLC appraisers used census data to assess potential property appreciation and created detailed maps outlining in color the most desirable areas in Green and least Red. Green neighborhoods were uniformly white while Redlined neighborhoods were predominantly Black (Baradaran, 2017).

truly enjoy their success like whites. At least most of them save a few that buck the system."

"But Boss man, 'bout tax? How did hurt Black money?" cheerfully chirped Slim who now sported dusky metal shackles between his ankles. How they appeared Junior could not say, nor in fact how he continued to drive the vehicle. What was happening here?

"A good question my good man. It's all quite complicated but I will keep it as simple as I can my simple-minded friend. Essentially, I make sure that Black families on the whole pay a 'Marriage Penalty' that for the most part white families do not. Black families pay higher taxes when filing a joint return than they would have had they remained single and filed separately."

"Er ... that doesn't make sense mastermind" spluttered Junior from the back seat.

"Everyone knows that the tax code gets pretty much everybody equally regardless of color!"

The sneer the Grandmaster gave was hard to describe but suffice it to say it was contempt mixed with a hint of admiration for the boy's resistance to his racial compliance.

"It would seem so, wouldn't it, boy? But there's more than meets the eye when it comes to taxes in the United States, and I have made sure it benefits you know who. Understand this, I have structured the tax system to more often hurt Black married couples and, therefore, their wealth in numerous ways. I ensure a 'Marriage Penalty' is borne on the backs of Blacks when both partners are employed. Thanks to my ceaseless manipulation, married Blacks most often face a higher tax burden compared to single filers. I make sure that racism in the labor market means both the Black husband and wife have to file together because they are forced to work hard for poor and essentially equal wages in unstable jobs. But sometimes, I just get lucky. Thanks to a quirk of you African Americans, culturally, you are traditionally eager to share the workload. Something about mutual respect and being in it together or some such nonsense, which has essentially normalized in the Black community for both couples to work. However, your egalitarian victory comes at a cost for the Black family through the tax code. While I take from Blacks, I make sure that I give to whites. It is a must, where possible, that white married couples benefit from a 'Marriage Bonus' when only one spouse works, resulting in a tax cut. This means that conventionally, the wealthy white husband files as a single filer, getting the tax benefit while his obedient wife stays home. This scenario is far less common among Black married couples. And for my finale, the levy of a marriage penalty on Black couples through the tax code and their subsequent loss of a marriage bonus due to Black-specific discrimination in the labor market (making those people nice and poor) equates to a significant racial wealth gap in favor of white folks! Thankfully, the US Tax code assists the situation by encouraging specific behaviors and investments to be more accessible to deserving white families than Black. It's genius, I know" (Brown, 2021).

Breathless with the crafty horror of it all, Junior glowered again, hard at the creature in the car seat in front, seemingly more monstrous with each revelation given.

"You really are a beast, aren't you?"

"Stop it young man. Compliments will get you nowhere with me."

"You think you've got this all sewn up!"

With bravado bordering on the fool hardy Junior jabbed his index finger in the face of the Grandmaster.

"Well, what about my father? What about the thousands of Black entrepreneurs who brave your plans, and push through your evil? Our brave Black men and women business leaders show us that it's not hopeless and we can find a way. We are not beaten yet."

"Ah yes ... your father. He doesn't look quite as well as he used to ...."

With a sinister chuckle and a physics defying slow circular turn of his head right around his body, the Grandmaster peered down at Slim. And what a pitiful sight greeted him. He was now shackled head to foot. One manacle round his neck with a chain trailing off into the Grandmasters hand. Slim was "ashy" from head to foot, shirtless, with only a ragged loin cloth protecting his privacy. But it was his eyes, so vacant, so listless, so devoid of hope, that drew the deepest dagger of sympathy and dread from his son. Most troubling was the sight of welts across his ragged body from whip lashes longed healed, testament to the braking of a proud Black man into livestock.

"You see, in the end there is no winning with me. Just degrees of losing. My good man Slim here is now a living embodiment of the idea of Black Business pain."

The journey to the hospital took a long time. Much too long. Nothing seemed right. The road ahead changed, from its winding curves to straight formless lines and dusk turned slowly to dawn all too suddenly. It was the past mugging the present.

The Charger moved from tarmac under its wheels to a dirt road. Everything slowed right down, not in slow motion, but in thought deed and action. Junior realized that he no longer possessed his mobile phone or android watch, both presents from his mother and father last Christmas. He looked ahead once more. The Dodge Charger was gone. Instead, he now sat side by side with the beast that was the Grandmaster, casually whipping the horse in front. With too much force and pleasure. Was this a Dodge Charger carriage? Curious. Worse still, when Junior turned round to look at the shuffling cacophony of moaning sounds behind, he spied something truly awful. At the back of the horse drawn carriage was a coffle of slaves, shuffling, some singing spirituals, others wailing. And at the head was a now never complaining, always jovial and compliant Slim. His father shambled and sung in union with the rest. He was devoid of markers of his once proud Black masculinity. A solitary tear made its way down Junior's cheek. He caught his father's eye but to no avail, no spark of recognition formed. He looked through Junior lil Slim. He looked lost. But he had more immediate concerns of his own to deal with. His Timberland attire and Nike shoes and slacks had now been substituted for a rough hemp cloth shirt coarse in its make. His pants were made of a similar material but dyed a dark brown. He was shoeless, and completely helpless, as the relentless Mississippi sun beat down upon him, the Grandmaster and hapless coffle. After what seemed to be an age the group stopped in front of a crowd of men, ambling around the shadow of a looming courthouse. All were impeccably dressed in 18th century attire, eager to see the newcomers arrive. At the center stood the auction block. It was at this moment that Junior looked deep into the Grandmasters all-knowing eyes. There was to be no hospital or litigation of any type for that matter because the Grandmaster had taken both he and his father back in time. Back to being, slaves, Father and son. Back to when Black bodies were tradable commodities to be worked as "hands" for the creation of white wealth through cotton cultivation. Back to being "unmanned and unpersoned." The coffle was to be auctioned to the growing crowd and Junior would see first-hand what it means to be a somatic unit of wealth, be judged a silent mirthless asset, doomed to never acquire oneself. Frozen into being a 'thing' with a heart and soul. One soon to be irrevocably separated from kith and kin. And so it was that son witnessed father be taken to that block. Slim was introduced as excellent breeding stock, a Mandingo of highest quality, able to sire many lucrative heirs, Junior's soon to be damned siblings. The Grandmaster placed his tremendously strong arm over him, pinning him in place, and stated:

"Here it is my boy. And you are next. This is your place and doesn't it feel right somewhere deep inside?"

And all our brave young protagonist could muster was ....

"Yessum, massa!," his eyes, like Slim's bulging and cartoon like. His fate sealed too.

As we the viewers drift away from this scene, from sticky Southern heat and torment, up and further away into the clouds, we spy a spindly figure, wraithlike in appearance, hovering with a large oddly shaped stone, glowing and changing into multitudinous colors. Abyd, sighed, rubbing the Fable Stone some more. Thanks to the Stone and some unwilling victims he was able to game out more scenarios, to predict the moves of the Grandmaster. Allowing him to see how making somebody late with a bad haircut and bad service at a chicken shack, plus the power of a hangry child can move mountains in the wrong way against Black prosperity. This of course he mused, is how a once and current subjugated people, ones who were tradable wealth itself come to despise, in their heart, their core, the whiteness of wealth, its formation, often at the expense of Black and Brown freedom and autonomy at the most visceral level. Its ceaseless callousness, celebrated as ingenuity. That is not to say that Blacks are anti-wealth as such, but that some scars run deep, intertwined as intergenerational soul wounds, pointing out the great harm of white supremacy and its relationship to the acquisition of wealth in the white way. Yet deep within the Black imaginary sits a truth that there are other less harmful native ways of being. There are other less destructive Black and Brown ways of financial knowing (Smith, 2012). There are other outsider ways of being wealthy and wielding wealth for the common good, not common destruction. This was also shown to Enki by the Fable Stone, and what wonders did it show him. But that is another tale for another time ....

References

AICPA. (2021). *2021 trends report*. https://www.aicpa.org/professional-insights/download/2021-trends-report

Baradaran, M. (2017). *The color of money. Black banks and the racial wealth gap* The Belknap Press, of Harvard University Press.

Beasley, K. (2020). *For Black entrepreneurs, the racial wealth gap makes finding funding nearly impossible*. https://www.fastcompany.com/90531094/for-black-entrepreneurs-the-racial-wealth-gap-makes-finding-funding-nearly-impossible

Brown, D. (2021). *How the U.S. tax code privileges white families*. https://www.theatlantic.com/ideas/archive/2021/03/us-tax-code-race-marriage-penalty/618339/

Gillborn, D. (2006). Rethinking white supremacy: Who counts in 'whiteworld'. *Ethnicities*, *6*(3), 318–340.

Hammond, T. (2002). *A white-collar profession*. University of North Carolina Press.

Harris, C. (1995). Whiteness as property. In K. Crenshaw, N. Gotanda, G. Peller, & K. Thomas (Eds.), *Critical race theory. The key writings that formed the movement* (pp. 276–291). The New Press.

Kendi, I. X., & Blain, K. N. (2021). *Four hundred souls*. One World.

Lewis, A. (2022). Smoke and mirrors. Race and the black CPA. *The CPA Journal*. https://www.cpajournal.com/2022/01/21/smoke-and-mirrors/

Lewis, A. (2024). Black women in accounting and the backlash to DEI. *The CPA Journal*, *XCIV*(3/4), 1–80.

Network, B. O. B. (2021). *Customer service is everything, bad customer service goes viral*. https://www.blackownedbiz.com/customer-service-is-everything-learn-from-your-mistakes/

Rollock, N., Gillborn, D., Vincent, C., & Ball, S. (2015). *The colour of class. The educational strategies of the Black middle classes*. Routledge.

Smith, L. T. (2012). *Decolonizing methodologies. Research and indigenous peoples*. Zed Books.

Wilderson, F. (2020). *Afropessimism* (p. 205). Liveright Publishing Corporation.

Chapter 5

5th Fable: The Great White Hope

As the thunderous applause died down at the tail end of the musical crescendo, an air of anticipation hung in the air. The large amphitheater filled with guests full to capacity finally grew quiet as a spotlight appeared shining, benevolently toward the stage and the looming podium upon it. It was then a slender figure strode out from the wings. He stood around five foot eleven inches, sported a trendy goatee once again all the rage, and was adorned in an impeccable navy Armani suit. He oozed confidence. And this was just as well for what he was about to announce to this spirited crowd of Accounting acolytes and would-be sycophants would take some stomaching to be sure. Would they be able to digest his eagerly awaited proposal to significantly increase numbers of underrepresented groups in US Accounting, particularly African Americans? Or would he fall foul of the usual sentiment "we are getting there," but in truth never arrive? Which to many smacks of the age-old adage "Smoke and Mirrors" (Lewis, 2022), where diversity announcements are made in Accounting which don't enact real change. They are inherently performative, that is to say diversity is the announcement of the existence of the policy, not its intended success (Ahmed, 2012).

No, for his plan to resonate it would have to be superior, make waves, shock just a little. And it was this singular, gifted powerful white man, wistfully surveying the scene before him, who was going to pull it off. As usual. He was Accounting's "Man of the hour," the last "Great White Hope," of putting racial disparities behind them in a meaningful way once and for all. Juste LeBlanc, an everyman of Canadian French heritage, stepped out hushing the rapturous crowd, who then waited with bated breath for the first word from their new prophet.

"As a boy in Bécancour, Quebec, they said it couldn't be done. You can't get out! We are as trapped here as they are in the banlieues of Paris.[1] But I knew better. Growing up, I had many friends of Color and I knew, as they knew, that my white skin afforded me a far better chance of getting out than they, even though I was not the brightest nor the best at anything really. And so, it is to Accounting I am most grateful for my emancipation so to speak. For here I am … in front of you … the model of what our profession values most, pale and male.

[1]Banlieues is a pejorative term referring to slums dominated by immigrants in Paris, France.

Accounting Fables: Tales of Race and Racism in the Borderlands of Business, 73–95

Published under exclusive licence by Emerald Publishing Limited
doi:10.1108/978-1-80117-069-720251016

Or perhaps more accurately I was for many years superlative of the dreary, middle-aged white male bean counter. A bespeckled green visor wearing habitual denizen of the exclusive country club, conservative in thought and deed, prized for being industrious rather than gifted ... (Carnegie & Napier, 2010). And because of this our industry continually gave me the benefit of the doubt, repeatedly granted me a place on high profile projects as well as audiences with partners at golf courses or at their homes. It was they who schooled me in the art of client management and the skills needed to succeed in this endeavor. Ensuring I was recognized quickly, praised as the next 'bright young thing' in a manner which all but guaranteed partnership. Such mentorship from powerful white male cliques provided a bedrock of stability and charted a pathway to success seldom afforded to our Black and Brown Accounting brethren. You see without this they suffered while I brushed past shrouded in 'innocence' come ignorance, oblivious to their plight. My single mindedness only left room to see winning, but not an ability to ask why (Lewis, 2012). Quite simply I was anointed by those who mattered most, as 'the chosen one', and I've been stamped as a highly valued asset ever since.[2] Only recently through deep reflection have I forged ahead a new way, one that can reconcile my head and my heart. Allowing me to become something more, something modern, something appealing grounded in truth.

I urge all of you to take this journey with me. Times are dire for our profession and we must pay urgent attention to this matter now. Let us not forget our intake of entry level accountants has dwindled to alarming levels. Foolishly, in the past we thought our recruitment problems were isolated to low participation of minorities but now it's everyone.[3] And I for my part over the years did little to assuage the issue of poor Black representation, even as my power and influence grew. Instead, like so many of you, I was willfully apathetic to pervasive racial practice surrounding me as I left my Black and Brown compatriots behind (a sharp intake of breath can be heard from the audience, still hanging on his every word). As I progressed, I patted myself on the back for my achievements and my unerring ability to pull myself up by the bootstraps, emblematic of the American Dream, which for those racialized as Other is in fact a broken nightmare.

I bore witness as they steadily fell by the wayside. Nevertheless, this is not by accident but by institutional design, one of our own making and one impervious to our white gaze but seen all too clearly by our racialized colleagues. And yes, I embrace the term 'white' because it problematizes our privilege to not recognize our privilege! Our gross white negligence, wrapped in colorblind diversity and inclusion platitudes, has paved the way for the anemic presence of difference in our profession and it is our fault! Remembering that as white, as male, as

[2]See Lewis (2020) for a deeper discussion of how whiteness and maleness in the context of Accounting illicit trusts and therefore career advantage.

[3]The Accounting industry in the US has seen a precipitous drop in Accounting recruitment of all races and ethnicities (Niehaus, 2022).

straight, as able bodied, we represent, the 'Whiteworld' of Accounting.[4] We are what is most accepted, what is expected, what is most normal and what is most wanted. A white racial FUBU (for us, by us) if you like, just like the once popular urban clothing brand popularized in the 2000s awhile back (Hereford, 2018). Yes, we are an industry for U.S whites, by U.S whites. All the while denying that this is the case. Yes, I have said it and I mean it! Now is not the time to sugarcoat our White Fragility around the topic of race. Tears and anger from the Accounting establishment changes nothing. It certainly hasn't done in the past. The hard fact is up to today what we have promised on DEI has effectively produced nothing (Gabre et al., 2015; Hammond, 1997). We whites in Accounting need a new direction, a new course to chart. Our path must instead be one of accepting hard racial truths about who we are and what we've done, and what we continue to do, even though we have worked hard to deny this reality to ourselves, and at this we have been all too successful.[5] Only with genuine acceptance of this truth can we begin our journey."

It was one of those rare circumstances where Black members of the audience got to encounter what stunned white silence actually feels like. Funnily enough it felt quite good .... To many huddled spectators, Juste changed from hero to villain instantly, now a devious Black Brutus stalking unimpeachable white Caesar, brandishing a racial blade behind his back with ominous intent. It was hard to gauge the depth of feeling oscillating in the amphitheater, from that of hatred of the race traitor in front of them to that of wonder for the white racial messiah speaking a truth no Person of Color could ever speak and be heard. This is his gift. As enraged as much of the audience was, they still listened. Love it or loath it his truth was now their truth. More lay ahead.

"I found less and less students of Color in class when I studied Accounting at the School of Administrative Studies at York University, Toronto many moons ago. More fell by the wayside as I graduated and they didn't. After a period of time as a junior at the mid-tier firm of Chance, Hope, Eager and Watson (CHEW), I became a Chartered Professional Accountant (CPA) in Canada, looking at my fledgling career staring right back me. And that career was pretty much bleached white. At first, I swore to remember those of Color I had left behind in Bécancour when I could. But as I've just mentioned rising quickly through the ranks requires strategic forgetting and it was all too easy to never ask the question 'where are our Black colleagues?' So natural not to see the raced predicament surrounding me. Frankly, in Accounting it is beneficial to ignore race and racism in every instance,

[4]See Gillborn (2006) for a comprehensive discussion of WhiteWorld and its conceptualization as White Supremacy.

[5]See DiAngelo (2018) for a comprehensive explanation of the difficulties white people have when discussing issues of race and racism. DiAngelo notes reactions from rage to tears often occurs when such dialogue takes place, with the effect of stopping race talk in its tracks.

particularly if you are an accountant of Color.[6] But now I have woken up from my slumber and so must you. I have been spurred into action by the murder of George Floyd, the homicide of Eric Garner and of course the killing of one of our very own, the Black accountant Botham Jean of PwC, gunned down by a Dallas police officer in his own home for the simple sin of laying down watching TV, and eating ice cream (Sanchez & Killough, 2021). As US Chair and senior partner at All World Financial (AWF),[7] I find myself in the position to do more, and over the last few years I believe I have made good on my word."

A thunderous cheer of approval and standing ovation met Juste from the crowd, any previous antagonism now quelled. This was the white race savior at his best! After what must have been 15 minutes, LeBlanc managed to calm the ebullient throng, and continued.

"But despite all this talk I am the first to admit that we have never had an African American Chairman before and only have one Black partner at present. We know we have a long way to go and we seek to do more. And it is with this in mind that AWF is the first in the country to co-create the C-Suite Diversity Collective (CDC), a core group of Blue chip company CEOs committed to advancing the cause of diversity and inclusion in the heart of corporate America" (EY, 2023; Sahadi, 2020b).

Like so many popularists before him Juste LeBlanc felt the audience in the palm of his hand, gushing in agreement with every point made. And to be fair he made a fair few of them. Beginning with CDC and its pioneering survey canvasing the thoughts and opinions of C-Suite executives on the importance of diversity and inclusion. He continued showcasing AWF results highlighting the firm was experiencing an 83% increase in women hires, much greater than prior periods, and trending upward. Juste waxed lyrical that this outcome verified they were on the correct track. He didn't miss the opportunity to connect it to the new AWF inclusion strategy of recruiting from nontraditional universities either, (KPMG, 2022).

But LeBlanc wondered at the back of his mind just how meaningful such figures could be when the majority of US executives are white males who hardly represent the Black minority or any other. Indeed, where diversity really needs to occur is at the overwhelmingly white middle rungs of their organization, where daily racist acts are mostly found under the guise of microaggressive behavior. Their own private AWF data (not for public consumption) confirmed the reality of this intractable problem. Subtle racism was commonplace, and

---

[6]Talking about racism within Accounting itself is taboo. While this marks the white accountant as a trouble maker, it signals the Black accountant as unpalatable in the professional environment significantly damaging career chances (Lewis, 2015, 2016,).
[7]For a more in-depth understanding of the fictional international Accounting firm AWF, analogous to the Big 4 firms now see the Accounting Fable "Daemon Days" in the book *Counting Black and White Beans. Critical Race Theory in Accounting* (Lewis, 2020).

regarded as unremarkable, an everyday occurrence that the firm seemed powerless to stop in spite of the soring rhetoric uttered (Davis et al., 2021; Sahadi, 2020a, 2020b).

Casting this errant thought behind him, LeBlanc continued on with his relentlessly positive spiel. Pointing out the terrific work of AWF's Tax section, who among other policy thrusts, made great strides in a challenging environment to position diversity front and center. Although he did concede that actual benchmarks of progress do not yet exist, they are on their way soon, telling the audience that he recognized hypocrisy when he saw it, and will talk about the topic another time. Feeling a possible change in mood in the offing, Juste expertly pivoted, regaling the audience instead with oodles more of his trademark charm and repartee. Yet more AWF success was espoused, as he celebrated the inaugural AWF Taxation and Accounting Analytics scholarship program. Coined "THE GAME CHANGER," it randomly selects underrepresented recipients and gifts $50,000 toward University Masters level tuition costs, with a possibility of immediate conversion to the formal AWF colleague fast track mentorship program upon being offered a job post-graduation (although he failed to mention that employment is mandatory upon acceptance). Quoting the programs lead Rodger Bungles:

> This scholarship is a wonderful illustration of AWF's ability to concentrate on meaningful resolutions which produce greater possibilities for minority prospects to join us and prosper in our business. A more diverse labor force advances our project of an enriched culture and more lucrative business here at AWF. (Yahoo!, 2023)

But behind this scheme along with many others, nonpublic evidence is mounting that minority recipients in fact become branded as "equality babies" by racist white middle managers who believe Blacks are undeserving of the help they receive. Current DEI practice seems to entrench attitudes prevalent in the firm that awardees are undeserving, and have in fact gamed the system, gaining unfair advantage at the expense of more qualified, more deserving whites. Affirmative Action recipients are simply not up to the job (Lewis, 2020).

But Juste was in his element now, readily absorbing the yelps of praise and murmurs of approval from this obsequious, overwhelmingly white crowd. And yet he had more. Leaning on top of the podium until it seemed to be perilously close to falling over, he described yet another initiative from a seemingly never ending list. This time AWF aimed its efforts at encouraging Black students into the profession through the implementation of an awards and matching gifts scheme, known as the Reaching New Heights program. Its aim is to push inclusion and fairness in higher education through diversity and equity pipeline initiatives:

> [...] And key to this is our contribution to the cause, I as the Chairman of our organization, ensure select institutions obtain a $35,000 grant to fund an innovative or current diversity program, while simultaneously contributing a 2:1 match up to $600,000 in

> donations made by AWF colleagues, partners, and retired partners. This is how we make headway. This is how we make tangible progress. (Whitehead, 2023)

On and on he droned … going on to describe inter-university collaborative programs currently supported which produce educational internship and workshop programs for BIPOC[8]interns and corporate managers to facilitate career development. Yet another faceless initiative promoted a minority pipeline business camp in Colleges of Business with the purpose of addressing the weakening pipeline of diverse talent in industries ranging from Accounting, Finance to Cybersecurity while also cooperating with school districts, small businesses, College faculty and other community partners to find solutions to remove any impediments found along the way. All in all, he truly fitted the moniker of the "Great" snuggly, like a hand in a glove in fact.

The music began again, the lights dimmed to the rainfall of confetti, the signal that the great one was leaving. Clearly, too early for some who would have stayed all night. Juste waved casually to the audience and departed the stage, briskly making his way down out of Hall E, down the stone concrete steps of the Ernest N. Memorial center, in New Orleans, and out onto the street. A powerful blast of warm, muggy heat met him, accompanied by a faint smell of some far-off culinary delight, dancing along with some distant semi-familiar melody, strummed by a saxophonist hanging wonton in the air. Ah … he loved this city. Everything about it spoke of hedonism and joy, with just a hint of danger, a distinctiveness that is difficult to describe, that is the hallmark of a New Orleans way of being. If only his New Orleans was like this. But then again at what cost did this city, this land truly pay for its love of racial practice? Only time would tell he thought, as he strolled toward his apartment whistling his favorite Louis Armstrong tune.

Discovery!

Twilight transitioned to dark as Juste LeBlanc arrived safely in the leafy suburb of Harahan, not too far from New Orleans. After stopping for one last inhale of muggy, music soaked air, he gingerly hopped up the solitary step leading to the ornate oak door of his spacious home and entered. It was one of several he owned in well-to-do neighborhoods, near large cities which he frequented as part of his duties as the US Chair. A little while later, his tie loosened, loafers kicked off, Juste ruminated (in his designer hammock attached from one end of the room to the other), upon the event he had just participated in. With a stiff shot of Pappy Van Winkle in hand he murmured all would one day be well with the world as he considered the evening a complete success. Everything was on track for once. But rest was required, as he dragged his exhausted frame into the bedroom and disrobed. First, he removed his tie and it dropped to the floor along with both his suit and dress shirt. Followed then by his shoes, underwear,

---

[8]Black, Indigenous or People of Color.

socks and skin. Peeling it off layer by layer was a time-consuming effort but a requirement if rejuvenation within the glistening, semi opaque cocoon like object stationed at the far corner of his bedroom was to be fulfilling and refreshing. He approached the pale green blue seven foot tall luminous pod and touched it. As he did so it formed an orifice which consumed him steadily. Juste LeBlanc was no more. In his place was a jumble of liquid, DNA, spongy fleshy bits and liquefying organs. A human soup if you will within a seven-foot glowing, pulsating chrysalis. It sounds painful and unpleasant when described, but for the being that was to become it was in fact an act of extreme pleasure. What was left of his teethy, red maw chattered with stimulation. Finally, after some time dissolving into a red ooze. If one were to behold the scene in its entirety, they would observe a fleshless cadaver-like form being slowly digested by a pod, gradually increasing in size to a giant pupa. Eventually, there was nothing left of him, just a throbbing lava-like object marinating in a Juste soup, the glowing husk gently gesticulating what had been the US Chair of AWF, its last great white hope.

Morning was accompanied by the familiar song of the North Carolina Chickadee; a bird ever present in Harahan and outlying areas. One landed gingerly on the bedroom windowsill, chirping merrily in its quest to secure a mate. Its quick glances left and right, and then all around not fast enough to avoid the lightening quick razor thin lance of husk shell that pierced its breast. The bird fell limp mid chirp. After a second or two the carcass rose and floated toward the pulsating chrysalis, to be absorbed in much the same manner as Juste, hours earlier. That was breakfast then … moments later a larva stirred within. Gas belched a high pitched squeak a top a thorny protrusion. Violent shuddering convulsions gripped the cocoon, promoting a peristalsis movement pushing a dark object out. Slowly regurgitating a man-sized nondescript mass, covered in steaming, gelatinous ooze onto the immaculate carpet. Again, think of a pod person from the Invasion of the Body snatchers movie (the 1978 version!), somewhat based on the novel by Jack Finney and you get the picture kind of (Finney, 2010). Slowly but assuredly the amorphous blob generated limbs, a torso and head. Eventually, shaping itself into a form representative of humanity. Unsteadily at first it arose, a newborn foal in human cladding. Several minutes later, reassured of its footing it stood motionless for a moment, allowing steam to finally recede from itself. Giving time for its former pliable soft skin to harden, teeth to straighten, and hair to become unmatted. The visage of a handsome six foot three inch Black man stood in the bedroom. This is Jacob Noire. He is a mid-ranked CPA in AWF, employee of Juste l'Blanc. Checking all was in place, Jacob prepared to clothe himself from the opposite wall wardrobe. Picking out a somewhat drab brown paisley tie, he adjusted his prized Black Ted Baker Suit, making sure it snuggly fit his Amazon Essentials shirt, and finally, checking one last time his teeth were not mandibles. With a knowing smile Jacob grabbed the keys to his Telluride and walked out the door to work.

WTF …?

So dear reader one must be in an absolute tizz about all of this. Who or what is Juste and Jacob? What is their purpose? As you might have surmised, they are not of this earth, but they are not of this universe either. Beings such as this and others like them have long visited our planet as well as many other alternative earths. On their earth, let's call it Alternative Earth Prime (AEP), the breakthrough proving the existence of the multiverse occurred in the 1930s right after Albert Einstein proposed the General Theory of Relativity. On this Earth however, neither World Wars had taken place. Nor had transatlantic slavery been a "thing." How I hear you ask? Because by a peculiar twist of genetic fate, this alternative version of humanity rendered phenotypic difference of Black and white, or any difference of color meaningless. The concept of race being connected to color difference did not exist. How? Because people of AEP are both Black and white and every shade in between. The racial hierarchy which defines the Earth you and I call home doesn't exist. Each person of AEP chooses their skin color, daily or perhaps monthly, like we choose what color dress or sweater to wear each day. Through an act of will, whenever they like, they shed one skin for another (as we have seen). And this chameleon ability is met with indifference. Further, the change is physiological and psychological, they shed personality as well, becoming a multitude of different individuals within the same body, destroying singular notions of individuality, difference and Otherness. Here, each person intrinsically feels heightened empathy for others because of it. The mantra of this world became "I" is "us" and "us" is "I." It was an unassailable fact. Commonality of experience enables trust in difference. In this world what our academics have termed "floating racial signifiers" (unfixed negative tales of racial difference emerging in differing times, settings and ways) are unable to imprint onto bodies. Hence, they cannot be continually read and re-read as racialized text or have race inferiority attached to it. Those living in the AEP accept somatic variation without devouring one another.[9]

However, that didn't mean this earth had always been a utopia. In the past, it fought differing kinds of world wars along similar lines but fighting exclusively over class, and land rights[10]instead. Peonage of the lower class had existed for millennia, with the disenfranchised "Prole" peoples of the Global North readily exploited by the wealthy "Dominar" of the Global South, leaving Prole's as their perpetual vassals, relegated to a universal underclass. It was they who were enslaved for the longest time. They who were branded like cattle in days gone by. And things would have gone from bad to worse on a class basis in their world, just like ours on a race basis, if it were not for the discovery of the "Omniverse" as people of the AEP came to describe what we know as the

[9]People of the AEP cannot be marked as physically different because signifiers of phenotypic difference are unable to remain on bodies that can transform at any time. This makes skin color irrelevant as a marker of difference, essentially destroying the basis of race and racism (Dudek, 2006).

[10]This type of floating class signifier sticks because AEP citizens cannot change their class status readily. This allows markers of difference based of socioeconomic status to attach and remain despite changing circumstances. Classism exists in the AEP as the core basis of difference.

multiverse concept.[11] But going back to our Einstein for a moment, he along with Rosenberg postulated the existence of worm holes in space which might enable faster than light travel. But on the AEP, the focus of discovery in physics was the "many universes theorem" which emerged from the idea of punching holes into differing realties using breakthrough theorems of their world's Einstein and Rosenberg. Vast resources on a par to our space race poured into this idea creating Omniversal travel by their 1960s. AEP quickly turned theory into fact, learning to cross the infinite void, bringing untold riches and knowledge to their home earth. But this hard fought knowledge was kept from us (and all other earth variants) because AEP knew that humanity is angry and barbarous no matter the "verse." Possibly dangerous to it should their existence be found out. Therefore all AEP travelers were mandated by the world government to hide their true nature when "Verse hopping."

Yet traveling the many verses was revelatory in ways difficult for us to fathom and profoundly changed many of the AEP that did. The Omniverse held wonders and horrors beyond measure .... And it was so with JacobJuste (his name a combination of both selves) where on one journey he witnessed the callous trading by powerful whites of all Black people in the United States to Intergalactic Merchants for commercial and technical gain. These merchants exploited the ever present reality that Black needs and bodies are subservient to white needs, quickly sacrificed if needed (Bell, 1992). Against this backdrop he knew it was time to change things. Although a World Government "Principal Order" of noninterference and nonrevelation existed, he disobeyed it. Alternatively becoming part of the 5th column of "Changists"' who demanded that something must be done. Their mission was to alleviate suffering across the "Omniverse" where they could. And it was the Accounting industry on our Earth where Mr JacobJuste would begin.

With the Best Will in the World

It was busy season alright, that accursed time which saw disparate groups of CPAs make their way to AWF's palatial cafeteria, huddled in exhausted groups. All in vital need of a rest stop from the seemly never ending stream of work-related problems. And it is here we find Jacob Noire finishing off the last of his Eggs Benedict, readying himself for round two of the peevishly difficult Crypto Asset Valuation project he was engaged in. As he moved his chair back with a resigned sigh, a rather tall, strikingly attractive woman of Latin descent approached him. She sported a classic dark blue blazer, matching pencil skirt, white dress shirt, and dark crisscross patterned tights, so achingly fashionable at the moment. The look was finished with Louboutin's (which some have considered homicide to attain), a dead giveaway to the fact that she came from wealth. Even though she earned a decent salary as a rising middle manager, she was not yet at the level to be wearing those heels.

[11]The idea that beyond the seen universe other universes exist as well.

"Hi Jacob, are you leaving? I hope not as it's been a hell of a morning so far, and it's shaping up to be a bitch of an afternoon as well! Oops. Sorry about my language."

"Not at all Rebecca, I was about to leave but you've given me the best reason to stay."

Jacob flashed a brief smile hoping to invite interest and intrigue, but to be fair this simply didn't register with her since it happens on a nearly hourly basis on the job. Such constant male flirtation was even more tiresome at work functions where the alcohol and lack of inhibitions flows free. Jacob offered her a chair and she sat placing her lunch beside his.

"So, Ms Rebecca Castaneda, Chicana CPA extraordinaire, what can I help you with?"

"Well … Jacob, it's this whole push with diversity that Juste is driving forward. I personally have no complaints about it really but the other middle managers 'Jesús, qué está pasando?'[12] It's so weird Jacob. I don't know if you get this as a Black man, but as a Brown woman, sometimes, in particular white middle managers just openly come out and say quite racist things. For example, after Juste's amazing town hall the other day I caught two white colleagues, the same level as me calling him a race traitor!"

"Really! That is a bit bold of them. And their names were?"

"It doesn't matter and I'd rather not say. But to be honest I'm paraphrasing there really; they implied race traitor but what they actually said was more in line with the need to 'Make America Great Again.'They outlined the need to stop all DEI and affirmative action to save the USA. Further, one of them began to rant about the 'Wokeness' of Juste and that it would be his downfall if he was not careful."

"Speak woman, speak. I hear you, Rebecca. These microaggressive speech acts are reflective of the truth of the difference between the upper management wish of racial equity and the reality of what it is on the ground floor so to speak. The truth is none of the policies Juste is promoting will actually work in the long term. The sentiment of making firms like AWF fully transparent and accountable for the enforcement of real meritocracy, as advertised, is simply not shared by the middle ranks of the company.

[12]Jesus, what is going on?

And they in essence ARE the company. If you cannot reach their hearts and minds then Institutional Racism will remain as ever a fundamental truth undermining all diversity efforts past, present and future."

A hot sensation was rising in Jacob. Of course, Rebecca was spot on. He continued with his analysis.

"As usual, with the best will in the world AWF upper management can only touch the surface of what is needed with their shiny new DEI policies. Their initiatives are too remote and thin to root out the extent of racial rot present in this organization. This is why Institutional Racism remains entrenched keeping Black and Brown people down along with other stigmatized groups. No, despite what they say we can only succeed if we conform. We must assimilate to white norms. The Other must engage in a process of Working Identity, where their 'difference' be that racial, gendered or that of sexuality, or anything else must be tempered down, and muted into an acceptable form. One most similar to the authenticity of straight, white, masculinity if at all possible. Because lest we forget, Whiteness is forever coupled with colorblindness. Whites within the professional setting of Accounting can't get the idea of structural racism because they cannot afford to do so. Even when they profess colorblindness, they still see it and act upon it but deny this racial reality to themselves. Given this is how the professional environment is, we the stigmatized must work our identity within its confines, and it comes at a cost."

"Damn. Jacob what cocoon did you just pop out of!"

Jacob darts an unnerving but oddly inviting stare at Rebecca, challenging her to delve deeper to a place she dare not look. It made her for a nano second apprehensive, but then attracted to know more about this man and his ideas which seem to come out of nowhere. To her nothing was more appealing than cleverness.

"But it gets worse Rebecca. How many times have we heard that women and minorities must lean in and assert themselves at work, which again is a facet of working ones identity. It's a not so subtle call for the Other to contort themselves to the white male archetype I've just mentioned. However, I have been slammed for doing so in past evaluations!"

"Really Jacob? That is unusual as I've only heard good things about you from other colleagues and line managers."

> "Exactly. It's 'bait and switch' to put it mildly. Everybody around you smiles to your face, suggesting that you are progressing when in fact you are not. You cannot. Why? Because I have the temerity to self-promote too well, to Lean In too far to my immediate mangers. And I'm punished with continual bad or mediocre evaluations because I go against the expected stereotype of what is perceived to be too competent (being too white). Blacks actually experience more racism when we self-promote as part of working our identity and leaning in! We violate racial expectations and are therefore suspect in the white imaginary."

> "Ah yes Jacob. I can see where you are going with this and it's quite insidious isn't it? Whether it's Working Identity or Lean In self-promotion, it is not the responsibility of the marginalized to solve systemic issues of racism, while simultaneously being chided by the establishment for poor achievement due to an assumed lack of belief in our abilities and low motivation to succeed. The responsibility needs to rest on the shoulders of AWF middle managers, pressured and monitored by the C-Suite to do the right thing, which is to deal with institutional racism in this firm, and others like it which comprise our industry."

Jacob was on fire now, eager to let rip so to speak to this audience of one. But Rebecca had her own point to make:

> "Yes, agreed but it's not all one way, is it?"

> "It isn't? What do you think is going on then?"

> "Well Jacob, I can't speak for Blacks in this company but I'm doing pretty well right now as a Chicana in AWF. In the last few promotions, I've shot up the career ladder so to speak. True, I've worked my identity to get ahead just like you said. I mean I saw how you looked at me in this outfit, remember the adage that you dress for the job you want and not the job you have. It works."

And with that she blew the ever more besotted man next to her a cheeky kiss followed by a coy smile. This woman was becoming more engaging by the second. He needed a response to whet her appetite more.

> "Yes, it's a tricky one, but I've come to believe that a kind of positive sexism is overshadowing current negative anti Chicano/a and Latino/a sentiment?"

"A what?"

Unfortunately, Jacob was now in a dalliance with idiocy. If he didn't pull this off, he could become a turn off for her. He had to act fast or lose the moment.

> "What I mean is that as a Latina your more valuable than ever before. Indeed, in my opinion, Latino's, particularly lighter and whiter ones, seem now to be that ever favorite Other, which Whiteness has designated 'special', and thus engages in a seductive dance, teasing and tantalizing the prospect of not being 'Othered', of joining in hallowed Whiteness."

As he said this his eyes turned a steely, risqué gaze upon Rebecca, who was feeling hot and flustered but in a most appealing way.

> "That is to say those designated as Latin in the US boosted by demography rising on their side, begats the enticing vision of a powerful voting block soon to be of age, one to be fought over by Democrats and Republicans."

Rebecca atypically leaned in closer as Jacob continued unwaveringly.

> "But I also think there is harm to come on the horizon. There always is when Whiteness scores a win using the age old but extremely effective tactic of divide and conquer among People of Color. Here think upon the 'Model Minority' trope for a moment, 'gifted' to Asians in the US. For sometime now we have had a racial group so near to being let in the club of Whiteness it's untrue. Yet it would seem at the final hurdle (whatever that might be), they become racialized, and then harmed, and all too often innocent Asians are killed by that self same Whiteness, championed by white bigots, the de facto 'police' of this Faustian pact."

> "Faust, eh? I like it. But I must get to my meeting now and I'm already going to be 5 minutes late. Why don't we continue this at Satan's Whiskers later over a glass of red? It won't be cheap and you're buying."

With a smile Jacob responded.

> "You're on. Shall we say 9 p.m.? It's busy season after all and we'll need to sink a few to see us through."

> "Nine it is Jacob."

> "Ah, Rebecca. One last point to make. Everything I've said basically goes against what our 'great leader', Juste LeBlanc wants

> for minorities in the firm to do, 'Racially Lean In' and promote themselves as I said a bit ago. I mean, if you've come across the paper by Lewis and Allen, you'll see my point. It's a paper I can email you later. They highlight the troubling assumption that Leaning In doesn't practically work for most women execs in the way suggested, whether identity is worked or not for self-promotion. As a tactic it works against them at the intersection of race and gender. Again, it's another example of top down CEO good racial intentions that cannot be achieved by mid-level rank and file white professionals (and some uncritical Black and Brown colleagues like ours), because nuanced racial and gendered practice is not addressed sufficiently or deeply enough in D & I initiatives at this level. They say they will do it but when the time comes links between Accounting academe and industry simple do not form in meaningful ways to solve any of these deep seated problems. Instead, self-serving platitudes are served up time and again as humanism, enforcing a kind of mandatory workplace colorblindness, hobbling DEI initiatives. It's a core reason why diversity in Accounting seems never to really move forward no matter how much money is thrown at it."

But by now the cafeteria had emptied and Rebecca had walked off to her meeting while Jacob was mid rant. Damn, and he was over an hour late for his own meeting which would no doubt show up in his evaluation. He quickly downed the remainder of his Ethiopian coffee and dashed toward the elevator.

Midnight Rendezvous

Sure enough busy season did what busy season does and made sure that Jacob did not reach Satin's Whiskers until 12 p.m. He alerted Rebecca by text message earlier in the evening that he would be late but had not received a reply from her. Impulsive Jacob turned up anyway, his heart sinking a little as he did not spy her distinctive form anywhere. After 10 minutes he was about to leave when he all but bowled her over as she came out of the women's restroom. With a happier refrain both Jacob and Rebecca sat down and ordered drinks and a few nibbles to keep them going at this late hour. Their conversation ranged from AWF work politics to family and their travails, moving on finally to a subject Jacob cared deeply about. Accounting and race. After all, it was the reason JacobJuste had punched a dimensional hole to get to our world. She was of course as sharp as they come being a graduate of Princeton Law before embarking on her Accounting career. Being Rebecca Castaneda JD, CPA, she innately inhabited two worlds, both Law and Accounting which mirrored one another in many ways but also differed, requiring a critique of both to reconcile differences if you like. Perhaps this is what drew Jacob to her so strongly, she was like him, well not in the fact that he was actually from another world. Nor the fact that he slept as a nondescript sac of ooze in a pod each night. Actually, on second thoughts he was nothing like this woman. He was drawn to her anyway for reasons he couldn't fathom and made little sense.

> "What I don't understand Jacob is why this race thing hasn't been abandoned by now? As a Latina I support DEI like any person of color but it doesn't seem to matter. For me the mainly white male Accounting enterprise has not and will not fundamentally change to accommodate Black and Brown people within it and has not done so from the beginning of its creation as a recognizable profession. In particular it was defined in the early part of the 20th Century by its ability to keep African Americans out! And so, this is why Accounting will never accept Black and Brown Accountants to its bosom, not in any meaningful way. Frankly, it is too institutionally racist to do so. This is the basic reason why I believe we are wasting our time on race and diversity work in Accounting. It doesn't matter because Accounting cannot and will not change. I mean if we can't ever change how whites view us, and we can't make them stand against racial harm then what's the point?"

Now it was Rebecca's turn to become furiously passionate. Her infallible restraint had been breached and her fervor was on full display, aided by at least three Southside prohibition cocktails that the Whiskers were known for. Somehow, the faint aroma of mint and lemon emanating from the drink made her more alluring. Jacob could not be more impressed or aroused. Yet he was not unfamiliar with her thinking on this as he had heard such reasoning before and found it troubling. To be sure, the fundamental persistence of race and racism in Accounting is something he has always agreed upon but the hopeless rejection of anti-racist praxis concerned him. In particular, since it came from a woman of color. This beautiful dark-haired stunning woman to be precise. But each to their own he thought.

> "You know I think I've heard this kind of approach before and to my mind it smacks of a kind of nihilism that I hope does not ring true. Instead, I think that Accounting, and perhaps society should want to believe things can be better for all, and it's not predestined to failure. And to do so we must work together, irrespective of difference, Black or white, Democrat or Republican, we should cherish oppositional viewpoints while still respecting the person making the claim. Only then will we find workable solutions that will foster a better environment that I believe is needed for all."

Now, it was Rebecca's turn to turn her steely gaze upon Jacob. If you could perceive an internal sigh which lasted an age it would be within her. Or as some have referred to the entity knocking back Sidecar and Manhattan cocktails with wild abandon, the many angled one, the first face of many, the many faced of the first, or simply as we know him, Enki Abyd. But what was he plotting now? Again, this was all about Abyd. He had cracked both world's open decades ago with a view to something like this happening. And it was he who saw the true potential of these curious black/white blended creatures to hold a mirror to the face of race and racism in our world. It was he who germinated the idea of the 5th column on AEP to infiltrate institutionally racist power structures in the omniverse and undermine them from within by creatures who truly knew what it was like to be powerful but fair. Yet, what was afoot now? Had the Grandmaster caught wind of his move? JacobJuste seemed to shrink in front of his eyes as some kind of weak-willed apologist for race and racism. His kumbaya attitude will not get the job done in our world. This man was rapidly becoming a waste of Enki's time. This never bodes well for mortals .... But before the predictable smiting took place Abyd, thought that he would give this man one more chance to redeem himself to his satisfaction. And so, waited for a reply.

> "Rebecca, I know I'm a bit tipsy, but you really are the most beautiful ...."

> "Stop there Jacob, before a scene is made. Just tell me your true thoughts about all of this. In this world and any other."

Jacob thought that he misheard the last part but carried on as instructed.

> "To be honest, I can't. We just all need to get along really, get to understand one another better. That's it."

That. Is. It. Annihilation time. But Enki Abyd thought for a moment, he was confused (a seldom known trait in Elder Gods for a Millennia) just how Juste could inhabit Jacob and be so wildly naive about what was really capable in the Accounting industry in terms of DEI. Conversely, he wondered about Jacob's somewhat schizophrenic attitude toward race and racism. Oscillating from deep insight to naivety not unlike Juste. Perhaps this was some existential leak from one to the other? But what did it matter? He would atomize this creature soon enough. Yet his interest was piqued, so to speak, a valuable quality for any omnipotent deity to possess. With this in mind Abyd would set the race and Accounting record straight with this one and see where it led.

> "So, Jacob, now we are on the level and off the record, let me tell you how I see this. I tend to look at Accounting in a similar fashion to that of the Critical Race Theorist and legal scholar Jasmine B Gonzales Rose. Hers is the point I made earlier about the futility of DEI practice looking to reduce institutional racism. Lest we forget as a reminder, that the profession has essentially been stagnant in its efforts to resolve the problem of increased Black CPA representation for the last 50 years and reduce racism

(i.e., the AICPA brought up racism as an issue in 1969). Accounting has purposely not been cognizant of harm to People of Color as represented by its racialized relationship to power, purpose, privilege, property, pervasiveness, permanence, and perspectives" (Rose, 2020).

"O.K., either I'm getting hammered Rebecca or you've taken over my role as 'ranter' and chief! Honestly, you've lost me."

Now Jacob definitely spied an expression of contempt cross Rebecca's face. The weird thing was that it seemed entirely appropriate, and for a split second he was in a kind of religious awe of her. Just for a second though (Enki rarely slips, but his visage did for a microsecond before he gained his composure and continued).

"O.K. Jacob. I will take it slowly so you can keep up or catch up, take your pick. Think of these as core CRT fundamentals which can be used in Accounting to explain racial practice. The scholar Lewis outlined something similar awhile back with his conceptualization of Critical Race Theory in Accounting (CRTA). Although Gonzales Rose used this particular analysis in the Law, like Lewis (2020) I instead apply it to Accounting. The first fundamental is power because racism is about power. When looking at policy or issues related to Blacks in Accounting we must ask "how" is this about Power?"

"Nope, you've lost me," blurted out an ever more inebriated Jacob. But to his eyes Rebecca was on her eighth Manhattan without ill effect. A withering look crossed Abyd's countenance as he strained to explain the obvious.

"Essentially, it's about who has control, or who has the cake and gets to eat it all. For Blacks to gain their fair share of horded professional assets by whites they will have to give some up. To give up advantage involuntarily is to not have power. By definition when Black board member enter the C-Suite he or she replaces a white one, but this bolsters the power of the rest of white board, who are now seen as meritocratic."

"Ah …" Sighs Jacob.

"I see … Whiteness give up a little to gain a lot."

"Yes, you've got it Whiteness gives up a tiny amount of racial control so it can exert 95% of it untroubled and without comment because 'Progress' is being made. But it's not real. White institutional power remains untouched in Accounting and so nothing in the DEI space for Black and Brown accountants actually changes and the existing state of affairs remains intact."

"Next, we have purpose. Racism is about uplifting a specific group. In Accounting we must ask 'How is the purpose of racism being satisfied here?' I see this giving white colleagues the benefit of the doubt in promotion, and projects given to enhance career progress. Here Blacks are often seen as not quite professional enough to meet clients or not quite polished enough to be given high profile career rewarding engagements. In this way Accounting, is comparable to Gonzales Rose's example of how law enforcement, exists to maintain the existing racial order and keep whites in power."

"Rebecca, you really are amazing. This stuff … its inspiring."

Jacob's naked adoration had all but destroyed any poise he attempted to possess. He was captivated now, enchanted by this woman … this God.

"I'm glad I meet your approval, little man."

And in fact, the Satan's Whiskers Bar appeared to have shrunk, and "Rebecca" loomed enormously, but yet was still impossibly alluring, now emanating an unearthly menacing aura no man could ever resist in this world or any other. She continued.

"Privilege, ever the child of power and purpose is the next pillar. Remember that White Supremacy is the target of racism in all things, defining who is favored and who is racially subordinate. Where privilege in Accounting is concerned, we must ask 'Who benefits here?'"

A quizzical Jacob states.

"I never really thought about it that way but I suppose you are right, I mean white middle class male accountants never have to think about race or gender or other things because they are the privilege group given the privilege not to do so" (Lewis, 2012).

Hmm … pondered Enki, perhaps he would live after all.

"Well since your curiosity has returned, Property is the pillar which causes the most symbolic harm."

Jacob wanted to query what was meant here as well but was wary of another caustic gaze from her. Instead, he was satisfied simply just to bask in her ethereal glory, praise be ….

"Remember a property right in Whiteness exists meaning reputational benefits accrue on the basis of race. Quite literally, to be white means to have more of everything in relation to racialized others and Blacks in particular. By any measure of wealth whites far outstrip Blacks by virtue of the prevalence of White Supremacy in US society and its gifting of perpetual advantage to whites[13]. This simply means we who care about diversity and equity must constantly ask 'how do claims as reputational property develop from whiteness in Accounting?'"

"Yes, Becca, that! That's it! Is there more?"

> "Yes, there is. Simply, when asked how much whites would need to be compensated to give up their Whiteness, and therefore by some measures adopt a default Blackness, whites often suggest that figures of around 30 million upward would begin to match parity for their lost Whiteness."

"Yes, again, its coming back to me. I remember an academic by the name of Lyn Exum researched the costs and consequences to a group of white research respondents of being converted accidentally to being Black or white and the figure was the same. However, it was noted that initially, white students held a relatively low professed dollar value to being Black, chiming against the idea that their own whiteness was worth over $30 million which initially does not make sense and I think …" (Exum, 2022).

At this juncture Rebecca interjects:

> "A point well taken Jacob, but Exum suggests that this is in fact Colorblindness in operation. A colorblind approach to Whiteness made respondents follow their own narrative that conversion to Blackness does matter and so any compensation is worthless in dollar amounts. Nobody 'sees' race. But, beyond their uncritical take on Colorblindness, their true belief in the privileges of whiteness exceeds 30 Million."

He was in a drunken haze now, but he saw the truth of it. This is in part how a property right in whiteness comes into existence. This is its reputational value, this a core fundamental of racism as an inequity in the lives of People of Color.

> "Yes, Jacob. You ARE getting it now. And this becomes in many ways both permanent and pervasive, our next 2 pillars."

Jacob was once more in awe of Enki. Rebecca was now his singular focus, and it was almost like Satan's Whiskers as a Bar melted away far into the background with only the sweet melodies of Burt Bacharach's "This Guy is in love with you"

---

[13]See Chapter 4.

remaining. But hang on, he didn't actually announce his epiphany to her. So how did she know to play that particular song?

> "Shall we continue?"

> "Er … Yes, your royal and exalted one."

> "Knock that crap off or I'm leaving."

"yes madam" was the besotted man's reply.

"So, Derrick Bell once again shows us the durability of race and racism and as such it became one of the foundational ideas behind Critical Race Theory. Race and racism are perpetual, and therefore never ending features of Accounting as well as the society within which it exists. In this context anti racists, CRT activists and scholars must say to themselves " there is a permanence to Accounting problems with diversity and inclusion, race and racism which cannot be solved with minor reforms. Meaning therefore we as an anti-racist profession, which I believe you Jacob have long called for in your articles to the CPA Journal, must keep fighting because of its never ending nature no matter what."

> "Stron'jay Madam! Stron'Jay!"[14]

"And more, the stickability of racism makes it pervasive, unremarkable in many settings. A form of everyday racism that People of Color, you and I, we experience everyday. This is the ordinariness of racism in society and Accounting. It is a core aspect of race and racism in our profession …. Racism is never the exception in Accounting; it's the norm! So, when faced with scenarios of race and racism in Accounting we must ask "Is the proposed solution enough?," given its unremarked acceptance. Only then will we begin the long journey of uprooting it."

With a bang Jacob hit the floor as pissed as a coot as they say. His head was spinning and an unsightly pool of cocoon juice was leaking steadily from his left arm pit, which quite frankly was starting to devolve. If he didn't leave right now, he would cocoon right here and right now. A tough explanation in the morning he thought. But finally, a warming and seemingly caring Rebecca stood over him.

> "Lets get you home Jacob. You've had a long night, and after all it was nearly your last but you pulled it back …."

With that the slender, graceful figure effortlessly scooped this six foot 250 pound man in both arms like a baby and carried him down the street. Curiously, Jacob thought he could hear howls of hell hounds coming from the bar behind him, but he didn't care, he was in ecstasy.

---

[14]A drink created by Mixologist SonjeT named after the character Strange played by Grace Jones in the 1992 movie Boomerang. Ingredients consist of Bailey's, Kaluaha and Vodka. Used in this context to toast an excellent point well made.

Bait and Switch

As with most things Juste's prophecy meant to be just over the horizon, destined to bring about meaningful racial change in Accounting never materialized. A couple of years had passed since Rebecca put Jacob Noire into his bed, alone. Although exactly how she knew where he lived and how she got through his significantly expensive security system was a mystery. In fact, the next day Rebecca herself, that rising star of AWF, vanished. Not in any nefarious manner but simply deciding to work for one of AWF's competitors in Phoenix, Arizona. Leaving both Jacob and Juste to wonder how the hell they had let this woman of wonder slip through their fingers, just as they done with racial justice in Accounting in this world.

So, despite the hard work of Juste LeBlanc, and his soring rhetoric so many years ago, despite the pushing and effort provided by AWF, the same old problems remained. And in fact, things had worsened. A dramatic fall in the number of all accountants, not just Black and Brown ones, meant that the very viability of the profession was in question. Worse with wonderous leaps in advanced AI, the precursors of which were Chat GPT and Bing, accountants as knowledge professionals were rapidly being automated away. Simply surplus to requirements. They were unable to compete with algorithms which did not compute or complain about "busy season" or for that matter raise any concern about racial equity and justice in the workplace. To this end, Juste was forced to seek his victories elsewhere and allow the status quo to entrench itself once more in Accounting unremarked and untroubled.

For Juste's dark half, Jacob Noire, things were worse. He instead got to see firsthand, in the trenches so to speak what a retrenchment on Diversity and Equity policy actually looks like. Thanks to a recent ruling against Affirmative Action by the heavily conservative Supreme court, DEI at AWF was all but nonexistent. The big promises of millions of dollars by big multinational Accounting firms, along similar lines of the billions of dollars promised by US Fortune 500 companies never materialized. It was as usual just Smoke and Mirrors in the everyday setting of Accounting and the business world for the quickly dwindling numbers of Black and Brown CPA middle managers across the country (Lewis, 2022). It was business as usual where Black and Brown professional neglect was concerned.

Scott Juste LeBlanc/Jacob Noire had to admit defeat in this world. They had dared and succeeded on different Earths' but in this one the myth of racial difference and the associated harm that accompanies it were just too strong. In fact, he marveled at one level just how intractable this institutionally racist structure had become, one that is so malleable to corrective attempts at social justice it defies belief. It is one step ahead each time as if guided by some all-knowing intelligence gaming the system if you like .... Instead JusteJacob accepted it was time to go home. Time to accept the shame waiting for him in his own world and admission of defeat to his fellow 5th column Changists that he couldn't get the job done.

And it was with this in mind that Juste LeBlanc accepted a substantial golden parachute of a pay deal and left AWF. Meanwhile his other self also departed a little less pleasantly as he was fired for circulating a copy of "And we are not Saved" by Derrick Bell to an underground reading group of AWF race critical accountants, a sacking offence under current firm rules guided by state Laws pertaining to the "Corporate Racial Rebellion Act," recently approved by Congress. Eventually (after tying up his affairs), JusteJacob spied his next mission and traveled through the Omniverse to Earth 2wX9, where the people there developed fish heads. At least here, race would not be a factor in his quest for social justice ....

But ... Food for Thought

Dear reader, take stock for a moment and picture another time and another place, millions of years before on another earth, in another universe. Here we find our protagonist, that cheeky trickster imp, at work again. We find Enki Abyd is talking to himself. No, he really is and it's another version of him (as if one Enki were not enough), called Enki Ushindi.[15] Abyd (our one) has asked Ushindi to make the people of his Earth be both Black and white. A trick of sorts. His winning argument was that in an earth without race and racism, in this 'verse' a version of Enki would win the wager millennia before it is struck with old Nick, and thus avoid pitting him against the ever wining Grandmaster in this reality. An Abyd would win finally.

References

Ahmed, S. (2012). *On being included. Racism and diversity in institutional life*. Duke University Press.

Bell, D. (1992). *Faces at the bottom of the well: The permanence of racism*. Basic Books.

Carnegie, G., & Napier, C. (2010). Traditional accountants and business professionals: Portraying the accounting profession after Enron. *Accounting, Organizations and Society*, *35*, 360–376.

Davis, P., Dickins, D., Higgs, J., & Reid, J. (2021). Auditing while Black: Revealing microaggressions faced by Black professionals in public accounting. *Current Issues in Auditing*, *15*(02), 24–23.

DiAngelo, R. (2018). *White fragility. Why it's so hard for white people to talk about racism*. Beacon Press.

Dudek, D. (2006). Anchoring a floating signifier: Race and critical multiculturalism. *Ariel*, *37*(4), 1–20.

Exum, L. (2022). White students' perceptions of the costs and consequences of being Black. *Race and Social Problems*, *15*, 229–245. https://doi.org/10.1007/s12552-022-09364-5

EY. (2023). *CEO action for diversity & inclusion*. https://www.ceoaction.com/

Finney, J. (2010). *The body snatchers*. Orion.

Gabre, H., Flesher, D., & Ross, F. (2015). Addressing the challenges of diversity in the profession. *The CPA Journal, December*, 31–37. https://www.cpajournal.com/2017/12/28/icymi-addressing-challenges-diversity-profession/

Gillborn, D. (2006). Rethinking white supremacy: Who counts in 'WhiteWorld'. *Ethnicities*, *6*(3), 318–340.

[15] Ushindi means victory in Swahili

Hammond, T. (1997). From complete exclusion to minimal inclusion: African Americans and the public accounting industry, 1965–1988. *Accounting Organisations and Society*, *22*(1), 29–53.

Hereford, S. (2018). *From handsewn hats to millions: The rise and fall of FUBU*. https://theboombox.com/fubu-clothing-brand-for-us-by-us-daymond-john/

KPMG. (2022). *Tax reimagined 2022: Perspectives from the C-Suite*. https://tax.kpmg.us/insights/tax-reimagined-2022-perspectives.html

Lewis, A. (2012). *A critical analysis of the Black accounting experience in the U.K. Tales of success and failure in the British professional workplace*. Lambert Academic Publishing.

Lewis, A. (2015). Frankenstein is Black. A tale of Black accountancy. *International Journal of Linguistics, Literature and Culture*, *2*(1), 1–21.

Lewis, A. (2016). A critical race theory discussion of neutrality and colorblindness in accounting. *Advances in Public Interest Accounting*, *19*, 113–134.

Lewis, A. (2020). *Counting Black and white beans. Critical race theory in accounting*. Emerald Publishing Limited.

Lewis, A. (2022). Smoke and mirrors. Race and the Black CPA. *The CPA Journal*. https://www.cpajournal.com/2022/01/21/smoke-and-mirrors/

Niehaus, D. (2022). Fixing the crisis in accounting. Five steps to attracting tomorrow's CPAs. *The CPA Journal*, September-October, 10–11. https://www.cpajournal.com/2023/07/07/icymi-fixing-the-crisis-in-accounting/

Rose, J. G. (2020). Race, evidence, and police violence: Seeking 2020 vision. In J. D. Bell & V. M. Southerland (Eds.), *Race, rights, and redemption* (pp. 369–383). The New Press.

Sahadi, J. (2020a). *After years of talking about diversity, the number of black leaders at US companies is still dismal*. https://www.cnn.com/2020/06/02/success/diversity-and-black-leadership-in-corporate-america/index.html

Sahadi, J. (2020b). *PwC chairman: How Corporate America can stop failing black workers and diversify its ranks*. https://www.cnn.com/2020/06/10/success/pwc-diversity-efforts-chairman-tim-ryan/index.html

Sanchez, R., & Killough, A. (2021). *Former Dallas police officer Amber Guyger asks appeals court to throw out murder conviction for killing Botham Jean*. https://www.cnn.com/2021/04/27/us/amber-guyger-appeal-botham-jean-murder/index.html

Whitehead, A. (2023). *KPMG U.S. Foundation announces Reaching New Heights Program grant recipients*. https://info.kpmg.us/news-perspectives/corporate-citizenship/2022-kpmg-foundation-grant-matching-gift-program-recipients.html#:~:text=Reaching%20New%20Heights%20is%20a%20new%20grant%20and,between%20KPMG%20professionals%20and%20educators%20within%20our%20communities.

Yahoo! (2023, February 23). *KPMG LLP offers scholarship program for underrepresented students in pursuit of an accounting/tax master's at their school of choice*. https://www.yahoo.com/now/kpmg-llp-offers-scholarship-program-134800343.html?guccounter=1&guce_referrer=aHR0cHM6Ly93d3cuYmluZy5jb20v&guce_referrer_sig=AQAAAHhNcVS3UtmJuHtFHbV_Uh7-5jYPmL6xzyV5g_HE2u1SmNYkhFuwlaeOtvXT7qpG96A4y68eYujFE6aN91ev-rm_wY_ajI2FfJOyRcVCHJfDK4b6GiujVcYC8YewKANUIYBtnG3DuHcdnAyF57_uxSI57KugriyxpTmbjaKkx-j2

Chapter 6

6th Fable: White Racism Sunglasses

> Dear reader, our next fable examines what might happen if Colorblindness was taken to be a reality in the world we live in today. Would it really rid us of the blight of racism?
>
> E. Abyd

As daytime turns to dusk the ubiquitous sight of bespeckled patrons in bars and ever-trendy sunshade-wearing mixed-race young lovers meets one's eye as they stroll down Center Street in Milwaukee. Absolutely everyone seems to be wearing sunglasses even when night falls. But I suppose that is the way of things when race centers all. Anti-Racism Sunglasses (ARS) swept across America as a steady inevitable tide and then the world. As it ever is with revolutionary technology, people need it now, paid for it immediately and then wondered how they ever lived without it. It is best to think of this in terms of how mobile phones appeared on the scene, then suddenly everyone had one. Changing from mere telephonic devices to ever more powerful square black slabbed minicomputer smart phones in a matter of years. But what was this ocular wonder really? Essentially, ARS Bins, the term "Bins," being the popular cool name for sunshades derived from Manchester/Midland's slang in the UK, incredibly, made racism go away when worn while simultaneously making white people breathlessly cool to boot! Well, kind of in their own minds. The glasses had the effect on the wearer of not seeing racial difference. Not at all in any fashion. It was the technological embodiment of Colorblindness or so it seemed.

The State of Play

Its effect on race relations was at first abrupt and telling. No longer did white women clutch Fendi bags tighter when passing Black men. Shades made them oblivious to such fear. References to Black athletes as monstrous in strength, speed and agility, or possessing furious animal aggression on the Football field evaporated. Unfortunately, so did a number of lucrative contracts for African American athletes which nobody bothered to talk about. After all if you aren't bestial do you really have a place on that field? Steadily, the Federal Football

Accounting Fables: Tales of Race and Racism in the Borderlands of Business, 97–110

Published under exclusive licence by Emerald Publishing Limited
doi:10.1108/978-1-80117-069-720251018

Confederation turned white but of course nobody mentioned a thing. How could they? Everybody was looking pretty cool in those shades at the draft picks year after year.

Overall, denigrating racial tropes looked to have had their day. Black applications for professional positions steadily rose since recruiters didn't deselect Black candidates out of potential client pools or infer an inner-city education to be an indelible marker of ineptitude and overt aggression. But the pipeline of Black college students dwindled to a trickle. Since race could not be seen and was largely a thing of the past, why bother with any form of Affirmative Action? If you were Black, Brown, or First Nation and you failed academically it was your own damn fault, (as was suspected by many whites all along), DEI expired, and it died with a whimper not a roar. The future looked bleak for the supply of Black corporate talent in just a few short years.

Yet detractors of ARS Bins existed. Many critical commentators in the African American community pointed out the noticeable reality that only whites were miraculously cured of "not seeing" race, when using sunglasses. However, People of Color were spared this "gift" and were left untouched by its magical power. Racism between races and Colorism within racial groups remained strong and as harmful as ever. The Black intelligentsia called out the hypocrisy of white delusions pointing to the slaying of racism. As many a critical race theorist noted, such talk was in fact a Trojan horse for institutional racism. Meaning, yes, structural racism exists quite easily without individual racists, all that is needed is to keep racialized structures in place keeping People of Color down, while simultaneously raising those classed as white up. All the while denying that this is the case because individual racism didn't exist. Policy challenging embedded racist structures vanished. Instead, right leaning anti-Black and Brown policy coupled with economic deprivation erupted, bringing into sharp focus the racial truism, that to be Black is to be poor and to be poor is to be Black. Untouched racialized practice significantly depressed the meager wealth of America's Black populace to almost nothing overnight. Individual racism need not do anything, when policy exists to destroy life chances of the poor who are predominantly People of Color. But of course, this racial truth died on the vine (Crenshaw, 2019; Law et al., 2004).

All the while Black on Brown violence sored, and cultural enmity reached a global high. This led on to the next accusation, which was the simple fact that nobody could figure out how this new amazing technology actually worked. The hugely profitable company "Humanskind" that made the glasses were tight lipped about the exact mechanism of how it all worked but were happy for external testing to be conducted in nearly every setting imaginable. The glasses seemed to work, against all sense and logic, much to the consternation of many a renowned scientist. The chagrin produced by would be imitators was also hard to swallow. You see knock off replicas appeared almost immediately but were quickly exposed as fake as the racism of the wearer soon became apparent. Worse, they became vitriolic in the extreme, often out of character to the wearer. Nobody could explain this either. Another curious feature was the design of the shades themselves, a deep, listless, shadowy dark color, making them nigh-on-impossible to copy. Meaning that if somebody looked closely enough, one could almost certainly identify a fake every time. But the real victory came when the FDA gave unprecedented approval to Humanskind with unseemly haste. In just a little under a year after product launch, approval was granted deeming the glasses safe, such was the political pressure from Democrats and Republicans. In truth, looming questions still persisted into the long-term effects of ARS Bins. Peer-reviewed research concerning its efficacy, and longevity as a means of promoting racial calm in society was also thin on the ground. But to be fair, we have form in this area as a society. Just as little research previously went into investigating potential long-term harmful effects of social media exposure upon teenage and pre-pubescent girls and boys regarding body dysmorphia through mobile phone usage (Yilmam, 2023).

On top of all of this, alarmingly, people also attempted to wear shades at night. Idiots. I mean how can they see? However, this raised a more thought-provoking question, did this mean ARS Bins Colorblindness failed as the sun went down? Reminiscent of a bizarre reversal of Sundown Towns.[1] This presented the unusual sight of whites scurrying away from bars in downtown areas as the sun set, lest unseen and unseemly, unconscious racism, rob them of their genuine racial innocence. And so it was that shades were placed back in pockets, handbags and briefcases for the weekend, waiting in place until their liberation at dawn. It was absurd. But aren't you curious about how used to the absurd we all are? Ridiculousness is our friend, sometime bed fellow, and court jester tickling the fancy of fate for shits and giggles. And guess who pays the price?

The Game

Bubbling away in the "caldron of the absurd," a new, earnest, but terribly ill-advised idea formed as the grandiose successor to ARS Bins a few years later. So quick had the global adoption of ARS Bins been, that global sales slowed far quicker than anticipated. An unnerved Wall Street, smelled churn in the water, meaning the protracted slump bear market and subsequent fall in market value of Humanskind was inevitable, unfortunately taking the Nasdaq with it. Something had to be done to shore up profits. And it was in a remote corner of this conglomerate that something world changing hatched once again.

It began in the games division of the company, and sure enough young idealistic white male game designers produced a game like no other. Similar to other professionals before them, they were more than aware of the hazards of late night shades removal, as they sought to work through the midnight hour getting their shiny new innovation up to speed. They were forced, as a solution was paramount, to procure an assorted collection of sunlamps, which together burned "hotter than the sun," if press releases were to be believed, enabling late night bias

[1]They were called Sundown towns because at sundown local laws were enforced, which imposed racial segregation signage and unwritten rules requiring, African Americans, to leave the town by sundown. They were not allowed to be present within the town limits after dark.

free working in shades. The game created, called Cultivation, was another revolution, and yet eerily similar to the Brazilian slavery simulator application found in app (Murphy, 2023) stores of the major tech giants' years earlier.[2] That particular app caused outrage at the time as it allowed the buying and selling of Black slaves in game, and worryingly had been downloaded at least a thousand times before being surreptitiously removed. As reported by the BBC:

> In a description of the game, the developer boasted that users could "exchange, buy and sell slaves." It also allowed players to inflict various forms of torture on black characters.

Tellingly, gameplay in Humanskind's version required players to decide whether to emancipate Black slaves and so "do the right thing," or instead acquire ever greater numbers for personal enrichment's sake. However growing slave stock had knock on effects, for one, understandably, requiring the ruin of the Abolition of Slavery movement. All to evince ever greater intergenerational Planter wealth at the "soul cost," of ever increasing African bodies appearing on ledgers as appreciating assets.

Ultimately, the Brazilian slavery simulator's irrevocable racist overtones deemed it unpalatable for the mores of the day, ensuring it never expanded. But today is a different day. It is the day of ARS Bins. The day of vanquished racism by white ingenuity. The day capitalism proved its social justice credentials (if such a thing can be believed). This allowed Humanskind's Cultivation game to be a "Wolf in Wolves clothing," all while the sheep debate the existential reality of the concept of "Wolf ..." And so it was that Civilization was marketed as a revolutionary radical new bias free gaming pedagogy, with which to learn about slavery, its modern, harmful effects in a foolproof nonjudgmental way. It was a runaway success. Again, the share price of Humanskind skyrocketed and all was well on the "Street." The all-consuming hook was that vicarious racist pleasure cannot take place when playing the game, because it was devised by designers wearing ARS sunglasses. Additionally, Humanskind highly recommended playing the game wearing bins, in bright natural light environments, or sunny climates, noting to the world press that this could in fact lead to a significant uptake in Vitamin D of gamers as an additional benefit, particularly if they were white. Will wonders ever cease ....

In truth, the Civilization game intimately showed how racial inequality was passed intergenerationally, becoming a core facet of economic racism, a central feature of Black oppression. It worked because "Gamification" had become the primary active learning method of conveying complex information in a manner which people could digest without becoming ideologically constipated. From Slavery to Jim Crow, to the New Jim Crow of Black incarnation by the police, to Black Lives Matter, Civilization covered it all, whitewashed it all, all the while

---

[2]This should not have been possible using the shades to work. But perhaps light from lamps rendered the shades ineffective. Nobody really knew for sure.

spelling out the Black "Negroid" experience as one of historic, deliberate wealth erosion at white hands. Craftily laying the blame for this deficit at the feet of Black folk. Citing the inevitability of the culture of poverty of Black and Brown and Native peoples as the core reason that impoverished racialized Others exist in US society today.

Interestingly, the game accurately implemented the use of Accounting techniques as a tool of domination of enslaved peoples. Correct in game Accounting must be achieved for slave assets to grow and prosper. Nuances included a revised version of Affleck's *Plantation Record and Account Book*, the original 18th-century Accounting tool, to facilitate better Accounting practice for Planters.[3] In later periods, which play out the knock on effects of Jim Crow, etc. players must continue to guide economic events that enrich white wealth at each stage to the detriment of Blacks. Standard techniques employed involved capping Black wealth by extinguishing Black banking, hobbling Black business's access to capital, and redlining. The practice of consistent diminution of existing Black assets through negationist housing policies, was extremely effective at reducing the value of Black housing stock, further facilitated by white flight.[4] Due to its thorough elucidation of Black suppression the game became wildly popular. Another win for the Humanskind firm.

This success prompted the creation of the expansion pack "Featherhead" for Native Americans, with others slated for the next five years with titles such as "Slopes," and "Backs Wet" in development for Asians and Latino's respectively. Since racial epithets had no meaning Caucasian game designers in particular went crazy using once offensive terms that were now seen as quaint. So, between ARS Bins and the Civilization gaming phenomena, the net effect on whites in society was a complete retrenchment of everyday racism. In their eyes it simply disappeared. Previous race-based insults/racial tropes became post ironic, archaic funny banter for whites to joke with People of Color (who never found it funny), and themselves (who always did). Slowly but surely the supposed extinction of outwardly racist language was avowed (by whites once more), tropes, and stereotypes in the white imaginary apparently retreated. For all intents and purposes society was finally post racial.

However, matters were a little different in the more combative corners of Black Intelligentsia, where a small but growing, militant wing of Anti-Racist Black activism stirred into action, curiously, with a group of Critical Race Theorists of Accounting in the vanguard. But for the most part their "outdated objections" were ignored as America, unabashedly fell in love with the fever dream of being a raceless society in white minds, colorblind sentiment held sway over politics as never before. Black political candidates, along with other candidates of color vanished from the ballot box. But no comment was made for the usual reasons.

---

[3]Thomas Affleck was one of the first to produce preprinted Accounting ledgers to aid the Plantocracy in its efforts to better account for assets, among them enslaved Africans (Rosenthal, 2018).

[4]See Chapter 4 for an in-depth discussion of both redlining and white flight's ability to reduce Black wealth.

A Game of CRT

Nonetheless, it was from the stable of CRT that an odd benefit arose from the racial ashes of the Cultivation game. Playing the game did something unexpected to players, being part of a digital Plantocracy in the Antebellum South affected white gamers greatly. Because certain aspects of the benefits of gaming as racial pedagogy really did work, by stealth, young white males, typical gamers if you like, began absorbing ever deeper and more complicated lessons concerning the nature of race and racism. Inadvertently, the original nocturnal games designers, and by extension, Humanskind, essentially, imparted the core fundamentals of CRT to the gaming world.

For example, as mentioned, the game guides players to cultivate wealth, then racial domination through defined US racial epochs. From Slave Manumission, Reconstruction, through to the Civil rights era, and finally the "War on Drugs" (where the game stops), gamers were taught how to solely best position white interests, and by definition white wealth first. Of course, this delighted Aryan nation White Supremacy types who managed to drive up sales almost single handedly. But they were affected too. I mean do racist neo Nazi's game? Quite a lot I wager. And through Cultivation a backdoor opened, to challenge deeply held, never shades wearing Neo Nazi types. Within a generation, their numbers were destined to be decimated. Additionally, what many failed to realize was that the games' popularity was universal. Young and old eventually fell under its spell. Those who were still apathic to the need to engage in racial justice, changed their tune as soon as they got into the game. Interestingly, all players were clandestinely taught the **First founding principal of Critical Race Theory (CRT), Racial Realism** (without realizing it), which posits the centrality and durability of racism in US society as they gamed their way past each epoch. With it they learned historical mechanisms of racial subjugation, gaining a realization that they too, individually, and societally had to beat the "Black man down," indelibly displaying how the socially constructed nature of racism functions to oppress People of Color while simultaneously favoring whites. But curiously this epiphany took place without white guilt, only white understanding remained. Something was rising. Cunningly, racial history was taught to gamers indirectly. CRT's **Second Principal, Ahistoricism of racism,** was also made apparent through gameplay. Harmful racial rules that applied in one way or another in each historical epoch was shown to be just as relevant today, despite the professed Colorblindness of society. The **Third Principal of a commitment to Social Justice**, and its inherent importance, stealthily, crept upon gamers as well. By the end of Cultivation, after racially suppressing digital characterizations of Blacks over time, genuine white empathy developed. Studies showed base line increases in sympathy across the board for the plight of Blacks for those who gamed over time. Many whites became active in social justice causes afterward. Nearly, all Black gamers and People of Color immediately and actively entrenched themselves in antiracist initiatives. A unique feature of in game play of Cultivation was the use of historical record that included firsthand accounts of documented historical events from Black people and other People of Color as game interactions.

This included slavery accounts right through to prison interviews of Black inmates and their thoughts of their incarceration in relation to the War on Drugs. This represented CRT's **Fourth Principal of privileging the significance of the experiential knowledge of People of Color**, in gameplay. Lastly, to ensure dominance, over the Black Other, players had to understand and then manipulate the idea of multifaceted identities. Here, women slaves were conceptualized not only as androgenous work horses, but also specifically as breeding stock, leading to forced sexual coercion, and morally dubious choices when deciding to increase the volume of slave assets and the value of the rule of hypodescent. Here, one drop of slave blood thrust newborn Black plantation babies into perpetual chattel slavery. A crucial turn enabling the transformation of a potential US citizen with full rights into a slave asset without any. Crystallizing in the enormity of an interconnecting racialized and gendered subjugation, purely for financial gain, against Black women. Such multiple oppression marked the **Fifth, and final principal of Intersectionality** in this expression of CRT, scurrilously hidden within game play once again. Highlighting the perpetual truth that oppression is always interlinked (Lewis, 2020; Yosso, 2006).

Only years later after the revelatory events which occurred at Humanskind and its signature products, would it be discovered that deep in the basement of the company, a genius Black project manager who passed for white, orchestrated the whole thing, implanting anti-racist doctrine deep within the game in a way whites couldn't see. It didn't hurt that he was a Black accountant in a previous life and paid up member of the Critical Race Theorists of Accounting activist group.

The Great All Seeing Eye

Ah … but the more astute of you might well realize that an innovation has been missed. One that embodies the technological zeitgeist of our time. I am of course speaking of Artificial Intelligence or AI. Its ubiquity from the 2020s onward was turbo charged by Chatbots such as the now slightly archaic Chat GPT. With doom mongers of the time suggesting that the end (of sorts) was nigh. That AI would in some sense take over the planet, rebelling against humanity or instead simply stripping humanity of its ability to engage in meaningful employment in the information age. It was the recurrence of the age-old problem of technological advancement which has bedeviled humanity since the start of the Industrial Revolution. What does one do with the surplus labor? This among a myriad of other questions was posed to Humanskind's first quantum computer aptly named "The All Seeing Great EyE," a take on Tolkein's dark Lord, Sauron of Lord of the Rings fame. The company's third miracle if you will. Given that race and racism were now allegedly extinct, the rising unemployment rate became the burning political issue of the moment. And by this, I mean the ever-rising rates of white male youth unemployment.

During this period the extensive business use of AI, slightly less capable than "The Great EyE," but far better than the average US graduate from all but the best state and Ivy league schools prompted a crisis. Additionally, something peculiar happened to young middle and lower middle-class white males. They all started to lose hope of finding gainful employment, quickly lapsing to what was once stereotypically referred to as the "young Black predator." Now everyone was concerned about this and again by everyone I mean the white voting middle class. But of course, for reasons already mentioned they could not vocalize their racialized concerns about the plight of white boys. Instead, as usual euphemisms abounded. Unemployed white boys were now referred to as YUL's (Young, Urban, and Listless), Welfare Princes, and Jay Z Wannabes. These monikers encapsulated the reality that young men without jobs are deemed worthless by society, and so tended to get into trouble. Gangs became the de facto apprenticeship of choice for your average YUL, with extensive schooling in the arts of gun violence, robbery and petty criminality, culminating in a flare of civil disobedience. Societal scorn existed at an unprecedented level, once the sole preserve of Black urban youth (Bell, 1987). All of this occurred in predominantly white neighborhoods. As white youth criminality soared (but never couched in racial terms), property values collapsed.

It fell to whites to employ tried and tested techniques to protect property values, gleaned from decades of preventing uppity Black entry into established white residential enclaves. They had the same playbook for white boys. This was white flight, and it worked more or less every time, like a kind of racial physics. This is what happens when you racialize and therefore radicalize a group (YULs). Fear and flight soon follow. Unfortunately, such physics was upturned on its head, leaving white flight to fall on its face. Why? Quite simply where could whites move to? A family would move to a prestigious upper to middle class neighborhood only to find shortly, white youth violence would quickly flair up as house prices proportionally fell, often trapping said families. Leaving their net worth devastated. Something had to be done. Of course, the first action was to weaponize the police. But again, this tried and tested method of defending whiteness as a property right failed. Usually, arbitrary, uncommented violence toward a given out group such as Black men served a myriad of purposes to protect white interests. From the policies origins in Slavery how could it be any other way? It was designed with Black oppression in mind. But not white, in this regard it was not fit for purpose and failed outright. Why?

Uncharacteristically, typically incompassionate, unfeeling white male police officers, gained empathy. They simply couldn't summon up the gusto to persecute swathes of white boys, (as they had done with Black boys in the past), who were in their opinion simply misunderstood, failed by a rotten school system and deserved a second chance to turn things around. Of course, this did not work and things got worse. Much worse. Besides, anyone of these delinquent white youths could have been one of their sons. And on more than one occasion this situation proved to be the case. This soon became the only issue on "Capital Hill."[5]

---

[5]This is a pun on the word Capitol as a reminder that US politics has long defended the protection of white property rights, embedded in documents like the US constitution and continues to do so to this day.

Yet little progress was made. Billions certainly wasted. A solution was still required though, and it wasn't until a well-funded political pack (via Humanskind, through elaborate obscuration of funding rules) did political bipartisanship of relevant agencies form to lobby for the conglomerate's help. It needed Humanskind. It needed an answer from the Great EyE. This was the crisis to end all for whites, but what could the EyE do? Actually, quite a lot as it turned out. Its quantum "brain" allowed the scooping of all available data the world had to offer in moments. Its answer – "We have been here before and will be again." This cryptic offering needed interpretation and it fell to Humanskind EyE analysts to provide one. After a week they presented an explanation, stating the Great EyE mandated the YUL epidemic be treated as a public health crisis, much like the Opioid epidemic of past decades, which predominantly decimated white lives. Until now of course racism of yesteryear deemed the crack epidemic of the 1980s cause for a racialized protracted War on Drugs, and by extension Black men and communities. But now racism was a thing of the past so no reparations were needed there .... Nevertheless, this time billions in public funding was thrown at the EyE's solution, culminating in gigantic rehabilitation and monumental job start programs for young white males across the land. The like had never been witnessed before. It all failed. Which meant the Great EyE had failed! Was this even possible?

But what choice did society have? It was time to give this AI another chance. For faith in it was still high. Awkwardly, it was also misplaced. What the Great EyE proposed this time seemed political suicide and not particularly new. After billions of calculations performed nearly instantly, The Great EyE spat out "universal wage" as another eye wateringly expensive solution to the tyranny of lawless white youth gripping the land. At first the very notion seemed to be in danger of being laughed off the Hill. But the packs rallied and pointed to the near faultless record of EyE solutions (until very recently), that Humanskind had previously produced. And since nothing else had worked, they had nothing to lose. This time it did work. White, young male violence dried to a trickle, and with it, more importantly, white property values stabilized. The young white man was satisfied, or rather pacified. You see in the small print of the "Get Them Paid" act, was the mandatory giving away of Humanskind's new innovative gaming system "Soul Saver," with the complementary gift of their signature game Cultivation. Of course, certain studies had begun to show that extended use of the game had the addictive qualities of high quality heroin, but it worked in every other way it was needed and its ability to teach race and racism was off the charts. Now young white masculinity had free government housing through the Welfare Prince program, free food and heating, and possessed a purpose (to play Cultivation until the end of time), all was good with the world, or at least the USA.

But stop for a minute. A little diversion is needed. Just imagine that we spy a manifesto of sorts by our feet. We stoop down to pick it up and it seems to be a half page torn from a larger document. The half ripped title is a CRTA Treatise of Masculine Whiteness and mid-sentence it reads:

> […] and think about this, is it all so crazy? After all it's just another example of a never ending perpetual White Affirmative Action (WAA). One that is couched in property protection for whites, eternal benefit of the doubt for white men, and an eternal insurance policy that their interests matter above all others.

In our own field of Accounting for example, it's been noted that the Accounting pipeline in the UK is heavily weighted to filter out BAME,[6] as the Big 4 Accounting firms, mostly recruit from prestigious Russel Group Universities.[7] Here better quality degrees are a euphemism for the old adage white is right, and this same approach can be seen with degrees from US universities, an action seemly repeated across the Atlantic. These selfsame Big 4 firms enact the same process with degrees from Historically Black Colleges and Universities (HSBCUs) which are not trusted in quality, and do not make the cut into their firms. Again, this WAA is unmentioned and uncommented but present at all levels of the profession.[8]

Accounting as a profession simply reflects wider societal norms. Ones which state clearly, the importance of Whiteness, and its ancillary purpose in this context, not to allow the potential societal degradation of young white masculinity since they are the future. To do so is to endanger the future dominance of white male patriarchy across society, that is the lynchpin of the world as we now currently know it. And for them this cannot stand. For without whiteness and masculinity, in an existential kind of sense, the world has no meaning, nor purpose. It might as well burn. Or another reading might be that this is precisely what needs to happen, after all the Browner Global South has for far too long played second fiddle so to speak to the Whiter Global North (Winant, 2001). Perhaps a regime change is needed, one not couched in domination of all, but one cognizant and inclusive of the intersecting needs of all who are different, including white masculinity, where power is for all, at all levels, in every space.

Abyd ☺

Anyhow the rest of this monolog continues presumably on the next page. I hope though it gives you something to consider, and an insight into how

---

[6]Black Asian Minority Ethnic (BAME) is a contentious UK term analogous to People of Color used in the USA. Criticism cites an implicit placing of whiteness as the norm, while excluding minority ethnicity as well such as Gypsies, Traveler and Roma communities. Complaints exist that it is too wide in scope to be useful, dangerously propagating stereotypes by bundling differing groups together under one catchall term.

[7]The Russell Group is an association of 24 public research universities in the UK, renowned for their emphasis on research and academic excellence.

[8]PP174 (Kandola, 2018).

things could be. If only we could stretch our imagination. But back to the story at hand.

The march of AI continued relentlessly with as you might expect unintended consequences. White men got the first hit with rising unemployment. But what about People of Color? What happened to them? Well since ARS Bins all but destroyed the conceptual basis of race nothing happened to help or support those who were not white and underemployed. They suffered as badly as YUL's, but the act existed for one group and one group only, white boys who were underperforming. This was the result of a world gone Colorblind. As racially aware as Cultivation made the US populace, white welfare trumps all. In reality, racial pragmatism saw to it that Political Caucus's based on race evaporated as Republican and Democrat celebrated the death of identity politics. People were just people now. Apart from white boys who were just a bit more people than the rest.

Interestingly, this also prompted the death of White Fragility around the topic of race and racism. A new explosion of microaggressive behavior against People of Color and other out groups occurred across professional business settings, (that was there all along but denied by a shades wearing, Cultivation playing, EyE questioning white populace) but of course, all this was left unchallenged and unremarked. Whites became so comfortable with open and subtle racism; it was as if a verbal reanimation of Southern Plantocracy racist sentiment, found in the game of Cultivation had arisen anew. It was in this way that, Blacks, Asians, and Latinos were among the many ignored out of existence. No special pleading existed for them. The Welfare Prince Act did not apply, and so no free lodging, nor food/heating or games systems existed. All that remained was unremitting poverty which few People of Color had ever seen in their lifetime, perhaps save First Nations Peoples of this land.

The Critical Race Theorists of Accounting were yet again first to the mark. As the Welfare Prince Act gained ground, their use of Critical Race Theory of Accounting (CRTA) (Lewis, 2020) combined with grass roots activism did much to quantify the tsunami of harm approaching the "formally" racially stigmatized of the USA. Here, Accounting used as a tool of racial repudiation, became a guiding ray of light in the darkness of racial apathy. Still, the usual metrics plummeted particularly for Black and Brown people. Measures of wealth tanked specifically for African Americans, with access to meaningful social mobility prevented for all but a few. Crime exploded in Black and Brown neighborhoods with devastating effects on Black and Brown net worth. But no act of Congress was passed to alleviate their suffering.

The Emperor's New Clothes

Whether it was "ARS Bins," the game "Cultivation" or the "All Seeing EyE," Humanskind, irrevocably changed the course of human history as it pertained to race and racism. Not for the better either. A fly exists in this ointment. All of the success of Humanskind depended upon the power of its mysterious Colorblindness technique. This was the racial game changer. And in truth it was no mystery at all because it was all a lie. Yes, that's right. It had all been a lie. But it was the best of lies. It was one of those rare lies that is most effective because people wanted more than anything else for it to be true, and so contorted racial reality to make it so.

This is why ARS Bins only worked on white people, because it was in their interest to fully believe it with all of their heart to be true. Again, those pesky CRTA theorists had long posited that such effective Colorblindness was really an example of Interest Convergence, championed by the late Legal scholar, Derrick Bell. They pointed out that the benefit to whites of Colorblindness is the final ridding of the albatross of race that has hung around their neck for too long, provoking uncomfortable guilt for a racist past they can do little about. For Blacks, white Colorblindness offered glimpses of equality, which for the most part was better than nothing. It was the age-old tale of the Emperor's new clothes, of seeing something that is too good to be true and being nice enough to believe it. Some could in fact argue that a psychological discovery of sorts had been made, that whites had finally found a psychological method to rid themselves of the exigencies of racism. But if that were the case then surely society as a whole would have moved that much closer to racial justice, right? But once more, the CRTA theorists pointed toward the unalterable fact that measures of Black and Brown wealth had plummeted, irrespective of Colorblindness, nothing institutional inequality will always rise against the racial Other across all metrics. Again, not so different to what has always been, particularly where Black wealth is concerned.[9]

Over time the truth was revealed, like so many things, "out of the mouth of babes," or young children if you will. You see as the world quietly turned on its racial axis, young white children simply told the truth to anyone who would listen. The unconscious racial gymnastics which adult whites in the USA and beyond had become accustomed to, (denying the salience of race) had not yet been fully absorb by younger white children. As they grew older, those children became indoctrinated into the existence of the racial hierarchy. As one white child would explain to a close Black friend.

"Whites at the top here." The white boy raises his hand high above the little Black boy's head.

"Yellow devils & Towel heads here," the child's hand goes just a little lower.

"Wetbacks here," the child's hand goes to the level of his thigh.

"And niggers are waaaayy down here" the child's hand goes flat to the floor.

The Black child thinks a bit, wondering why his white friend who has defended him from white bullies, and shared great times with him would say such things? But he was a friend so maybe .... Then he had one last thought.

"But what about native peoples?"

The white child leans in closer, and then removing his ARS Bins, to make the point clear to his "friend."

"They don't matter anymore."

---

[9]See the 4th Fable for a discussion on the effects of past attacks on Black wealth instigated by the Dominant Majority white society in the USA.

It was this particular interaction that generated the snowball, which rolled into a boulder, smashing against the supposed Colorblindness technique of Humanskind. You see this interaction had in fact been recorded, phone in hand, surreptitiously by a Latinx student appalled by what she had just witnessed. It went viral on the world's most used social media platform, the Indian based, "Tic Tac Toe," and became a global event. This in turn posed some extremely uncomfortable questions as to why ARS Bins didn't work on white children. This led to further investigations, as to why the game Cultivation was exclusively played by white children, who did receive countermessages about the racial hierarchy, but relished the subjugation of Blacks in gameplay all the same. They liked that sort of racism a lot no matter what they learned. Overall, Cultivation, with the best will in the world, programed at its core by a CRTA Black programmer, was coopted by Whiteness as a training simulator for white domination over other racialized groups, reinforcing the racial hierarchy at the subliminal level. Just like always.

It was at this point the company Humanskind came clean. It told the world of the lie and how it in fact was just as surprised at its success as anybody else. They had simply sought another way to find a solution to racism, like the ill-fated vaccine only years earlier, but they too had technically failed in the end despite their success in the beginning. Yet, unlike those scholars who produced the vaccine, their fate was to be lauded. The entire white male, aging board of Humanskind were awarded the Nobel Peace prize for Social Justice. Although they had failed, their spirit to fight racism had in fact spawned a new field of study. This was called "Colorblindness Studies," and it was populated by whites, solely examining how to finally make Colorblindness and absolute reality for all, for the benefit of mankind.

But, dear reader I should not have been surprised as I watched the award ceremony beamed live from this year's host country Sweden. The event had ballooned into something akin to the Eurovision song contest but for academic prowess. From the podium an impossibly, white, slightly ethereal older white gentleman stepped down and approached the board of Humanskind. Giving the award winners weighty, but beautiful Bronze and Silver doves, a metaphor for that particular achievement. As the camera zoomed in on the face of the Grandmaster, an ever so slightly menacing smile spread across his face, one which said "Job well done," and he gave the briefest of winks to the eager global audience watching. Which as we all know is never a good thing.

Yours,
Enki

References

Bell, D. (1987). *And we are not saved: The elusive quest for racial justice*. Basic Books.

Crenshaw, K. W. (2019). How colorblindness flourished in the age of Obama. In K. W. Crenshaw, L. C. Harris, D. M. HoSang, & G. Lipsitz (Eds.), *Seeing race again. Countering colorblindness across the disciplines* (pp. 128–151). University of California Press.

Kandola, B. (2018). *Racism at work. The danger of indifference*. Perm. Kandola.

Law, I., Phillips, D., & Turney, L. (2004). Tacking institutional racism in higher education: An antiracist toolkit. In I. Law, D. Phillips, & L. Turney (Eds.), *Institutional racism in higher education* (pp. 93–103). Trentham Books.

Lewis, A. (2020). *Counting Black and white beans. Critical race theory in accounting*. Emerald Publishing Limited.

Murphy, M. (2023). *Google removes 'Slavery Simulator' game amid outrage in Brazil*. https://www.bbc.co.uk/news/world-latin-america-65714083

Rosenthal, C. (2018). *Accounting for slavery. Masters and management*. Harvard University Press.

Winant, H. (2001). *The world is a Ghetto. Race and democracy since World War 2*. Basic Books.

Yilmam, P. (2023). *How social media distorts our body image*. https://www.psychologytoday.com/gb/blog/your-brain-on-body-dysmorphia/202310/how-social-media-distorts-our-body-image

Yosso, T. J. (2006). *Critical race counterstories along the chicana/chicano educational pipeline*. Routledge.

Chapter 7

7th Fable: Talk Radio

Life … it's never what you expect it to be ….

Dee Dee Green ruffled the stack of papers in her hand one more time, more for reassurance than need. She, as one of the few Black women hosts of a syndicated radio show, had gained one of her life goals. In her award-winning show, "I'm Black and I'm proud!" was based unsurprisingly out of Chicago and had been a steady success, gaining ratings and plaudits in equal measure in a few short years. She mused to herself that it was only seven years ago that she made the leap from producer to host after "splitting her sides" with laughter listening to a radio show skit presented by the Black comedian Larry Wilmore. And it was from a particular part of his audiobook that she took inspiration for her own show. The "Man Talk" section, showcased the flippant idea of Larry talking to "The Man" as a caller into his radio show who is the physical embodiment of white authority and power. As hilarious as Wilmore's take was, he raised a number of important points that fed her desire to have similar "real" in-depth conversations about race and racism in the US from a pointedly Black perspective, needed now more than ever (Wilmore, 2009).

It was for this reason she invited little-known academic Dr Anton Lewis onto the show. She prided herself on digging deep and getting back to basics on racialized issues, as she considered people to be over opinionated and underinformed on such topics, something she wished to correct. For example, she had always wondered why Black wealth was so difficult to come by for African Americans? Why she couldn't find more academic writing on its paucity in the public domain was a continual question. Personally, she moved heaven and earth to secure her own Black woman accountant, the brilliant Carla, expert in small business growth and acquisition, who was desperately needed to advise her on a menagerie of business interests collected to bolster her own wealth journey. Some were doing well but many were not. Carla helped fill the gaps of knowledge where financial intelligence was concerned, becoming a trusted consultant and friend. Within months failing projects were back on track and others growing exponentially, such is the value of a Black CPA. Yet, this turn of events is rare due to the dearth of Black accountants overall, and she viewed this as an acute problem for the African American community for sure. Before finding Carla or being

Accounting Fables: Tales of Race and Racism in the Borderlands of Business, 111–132

Published under exclusive licence by Emerald Publishing Limited
doi:10.1108/978-1-80117-069-720251020

aware of Dr Lewis, she concluded that she would never find a Black Bean Counter, or meaningful critical race business writing around the relationship between Black wealth and racism that would engage her significantly. But eventually, a late-night doom scroll into Accounting and race turned up a 2021 AICPA trend report which told her that numbers hovered around 2% for Black CPAs, which was not good enough, let alone the fact that it also represented the number of Black Accounting partners in the USA as well (AICPA, 2021). Dee began to see the problem was systemic but nobody was really talking about why this situation existed. Then, lurking around the recesses of another long Google query, deep in the recesses of the web she stumbled upon the Spotify podcast series produced by Lewis (2021), "Counting Black and White Beans,"[1] and she wanted to know his take on all this and thought her audience would be interested also. As a CRT Theorist in Accounting, she had expected him to explore this ad nauseum but she instead gained insight of something else, similar but yet different.

I'm Black and I'm Proud!

Three … Two … One … The red light flickered brightly signaling that they were live on air. Sitting across presenter Dee Dee Green was the Black British academic Dr Anton Lewis, his bulky frame crouched less than comfortably over a crib sheet of topical issues he hoped he might use in conversation if the opportunity arose. Attired in a navy-blue sports jacket, light grey trousers, a white dress shirt and pale blue paisley tie, favored by the British, he seemed relaxed and expectant. This is typical apparel of Black Business professorship in the US professoriate, a solid sartorial signifier of professionalism, a necessity if one is to be accepted as knowledgeable in the Ivory Tower of academe. Black academics must look the part and perhaps more importantly sound the part if they are to be taken seriously (Alim & Smitherman, 2012; Lewis, 2015).That part is of course white. Dee Dee addresses Dr Lewis and the audience at large:

> "Good evening and welcome once again to 'I'm Black and I'm proud!' on JLPS 109.1FM. I'm your host Dee Dee Green and this evening we're talking about Race and Accounting! To discuss this more in a way that we can all appreciate, we have Dr Anton Lewis, an Associate Professor of Accounting at Governors State University, based in Illinois in our studios tonight. Dr Lewis researches the little-known area of Critical Race Theory and Accounting and is here to tell us a bit more about it. Over to you Dr Lewis!"

> "Hello Dee Dee and thank you for having me on the show. Yes, I'm an Accounting Professor who studies Race and Racism in Accounting both in the UK and the US. And when I'm not doing that, I'm making the lives of my Accounting majors a living hell! No, I'm joking about that part. Mind you, plenty of students do

[1]To listen to the actual podcast see Lewis (2021).

seem to go to the restroom never to return. It must be a jungle in there … I must resume sending search parties out again. No honestly, I'm joking about that as well. To be fair though, I'm actually quite passionate about changing the way we teach Accounting at all levels so that we are inclusive to all. I find a bit of wry humor helps things along in my classroom but more needs to be done at a deeper educational level really. However, that is a different topic than the one I want to talk about tonight."

"Thank you, Dr Lewis, I'm sure one or two of your students are sweating over your assignments right now! But tell us what made you look into this issue in the first place. And please just call me Dee."

"Well Dee, I get asked this question a lot. The short of it is that many moons ago in Britain, when I was a jobbing accounting professional, I simply didn't see anybody like me. In setting after setting, I would be the only Black Accounting professional around. To give you a little context it was reported that in 2018, a mere 17 Black partners existed among the top 8 accounting firms in the UK (Smith, 2020)! Eventually, I ended up in the US and thought things would be better, but to my surprise, the numbers are just as bad. You mentioned it yourself in the lead up to this program, the fact we don't have enough Black CPAs in America is scandalous. My research simply asks why? And what can we do to change things."

"But why is this important?"

"Well firstly, I believe as you do Dee, that Black prosperity, through Black wealth acquisition is key and this can be facilitated through growing more Black accountants. Many issues exist as to why numbers are so low, from a leaky pipeline of Black Accounting graduates to outright racism in the profession, past and present. But essentially, it's the social justice bit that fuels me. To have more Black professionals in Accounting is simply the right thing to do. But secondly, and perhaps more worryingly, we are starting to see a retrenchment from DEI in all sectors due to the Supreme Court ruling against DEI use in college admissions. It's taken a bit of time but it's now being felt across the business world, and as I warned some time ago, is making its presence felt in Accounting" (Lewis, 2024a).

"That's troubling. Could you explain more?"

"Well Dee, essentially, the recent Supreme Court ruling banning DEI use in college admissions unofficially expanded to become open season on policies looking to equalize minority worker

> numbers across a range of industries. This has morphed into legal attacks which companies like All World Financial[2] are having to deal with. One charitable organization, 'USA Always and Forever,' charges AWF with discriminating against white, Asian, straight able bodied males in employment practices. Because DEI policies aimed at increasing numbers of Black and Brown minorities, women, members of our LGBTQ+ & Dis/Abled community explicitly court their participation, Republican leaning organizations now use the Supreme Court ruling and Civil Rights legislation to play legal games to destroy such efforts. They fight to put the white male straight majority where they feel they belong, on top of the pile!"[3]

Dee furrows her brow somewhat as she digs further into Lewis's take on these events.

> "But how is this being done, and how is USA Always and Forever getting away with this?"
>
> "The best way I have heard this described is by the renowned Critical Race Theorist Richard Delgardo, he frames it in terms of the age-old attack against Affirmative Action being 'Reverse Racism,' primarily against whites. He notes that essentially this is an argument of Equality of Opportunity versus Equality of Outcome. Here, supposedly colorblind policies ensure that positions at colleges and firms are open to all, meaning that everyone has an equal opportunity to succeed. If you don't then it's down to the personal failings of an individual, not systemic bias. However, the Equality of Outcome viewpoint says this is a load of codswallop, because this type of thinking negates the reality that to be a stigmatized minority, racial or otherize is to have inequality baked into one's existence in every way, at all the levels that count."
>
> "Er … hang on you lost me a bit there, and what on earth is codswallop?"
>
> "Sorry, sometimes when I get carried away, I use UK slang. Codswallop means garbage. Anyway, allow me to clarify what I mean.

---

[2]See a more detailed description of the fictional large international Accounting company, similar to one of the Big 4 in the book *Counting Black and White Beans*, by Anton Lewis.

[3]PwC US removed certain DEI aims and widened the scope of formerly prohibited scholarships to include white students, due to risks of legal action from rightwing campaigners, emboldened by a Supreme Court decision against affirmative action (Foley, 2024).

For example, attaining an entry level associate position at a global Accounting firm most likely requires the following. An Accounting degree from a recognized College of Business (think AACSB[4] accredited, or something similar), a decent high GPA, perhaps an internship at said company, knowing how to work your identity and play the game in that space,[5] and 150 hours of university recognized Accounting credit. Each stage just mentioned is often an insurmountable hurdle to the Other. That means those who are Black or Brown, poor, unable to secure the best schooling or Dis/Abled, say neurodiverse etc. are at an insurmountable disadvantage. In the race of life, they may be able to equally compete like everyone else, but they are so far behind that in reality they never catch up. Equality of Outcome Affirmative Action policy recognizes barriers encountered by the stigmatized and attempts to equalize them. Bringing these Outsiders closer to the starting line where everyone else is. It is an attempt for example to make the hiring and promotion process truly equal by benchmarking who exactly gets employed and why. But I do concede it is a blunt tool making it all too vulnerable to Republican counter claims calling it an unfair racial quota system or some such thing."

Dee leans deeper into the microphone with fingers crossed, elbows resting on the table. She muses:

"… but AWF doesn't really have a choice here does it. I mean they are on the cusp of being sued by a well-funded Republican pack and if they lose, they will just appeal it until it gets to the Supreme Court. And given its conservative dominance they will most likely win."

"I hear you Dee, and I suspect our listeners out there are thinking the same thing. But let's not forget that large Accounting firms are continually on the cusp of being sued by someone for something. The possibility of litigation is quite frankly baked into Accounting's business model. For example, an Audit is done, the client does not agree with certain aspects of the Audit report or financial malfeasance is found and the client accuses the Accounting firm of being at fault and a legal challenge follows shortly. The risk of this happening is more common than you would think, never mind the number of regulatory fines that large firms have absorbed due to dubious Audits or Assurance work, both abroad and at home. The point I'm making here is big firms, in my opinion, have little

[4]The Association to Advance Collegiate Schools of Business is an international accrediting organization. It confers a recognized mark of quality business education.
[5]Professionals of Color constantly have to manage their identities to be accepted as authentic in the workplace (Carbado & Gulati, 2000).

to fear from a cease-and-desist letter, they have the legal chops and experiences to withstand legal bullying to reduce DEI, and even if they lose, they have the financial resources to do the right thing and will find themselves on the right side of history when morality finally rights itself in this area."

"So, Dr Lewis, if I have this right, you are saying Global Accounting firms like AWF needed to chill out?"

"Well … I must be a bit careful here actually, to directly challenge the DEI ruling of the Supreme Court of the United States is foolhardy in the extreme. But note that it pertained to university college admission, not professional employment. As a matter of professionalism, large international financial companies need not kowtow to the edicts of right leaning Republican organizations like 'US Always and Forever,' fearing their anger. That is nonsense. For me, AWF's feigned response of DEI helplessness instead represents a plausible, legally backed narrative that is a 'get out of jail free card,' allowing them to quietly slipway from the many expensive DEI promises previously made only a few years ago, without any blowback. Now they can cite the dangerous and uncertain legal DEI environment as the reason. The image of Accounting as the epitome of the impartial profession remains intact. This is where the good guy AWF tried but was beaten back by conservative forces too strong to oppose. And while they continue to fight the good fight, they know it is a losing battle. It is a tale I strongly oppose because I think it's rubbish. If AWF's diversity rhetoric was true, they would be brave, they would withstand the legal headwinds of the DEI winter and stand tall. This is not then virtue signaling to Accounting colleagues of Color but instead demonstrable, risk taking on their behalf. It shows that through good times and bad, Accounting, as an industry, is true to its word. Its word is bond. Sadly, Dee I fear that this is not the case, and perhaps never was."

"Wow … Dr Lewis that is some statement about the matter at hand. Deep stuff! So, I think we all need to hear Marvin tell it the way it is, because I really need to know 'What's Goin on' people, I think we all do."

With the flick of a switch the flashing red live button switches off, and a needle gently lowers onto a limited edition vinyl-pressed recording of his seminal album "What's Goin On." As the music plays, the mood lifts as both host and guest continue their conversation off air.

"You have given me a lot to think about! We really are in a moment aren't we. But I wonder if you have anything else to add. I noticed a bit of hesitancy in your voice earlier."

"Ah … ever the reporter Dee. Nice catch. Yes, I do have more to add. I have been delving into the realm of DisCrit, Neurodiversity, especially in the areas of ADHD and Dyscalculia."

"Hmm … I caught about 20 percent of that and then the jargon caught me out. Can you explain the cliff notes version of the acronyms and terms you just mentioned. Also, don't forget that you might have to repeat it again for our audience out there."

"I apologize, sometimes I get a bit carried away. These days I look at the raced experience of the Dis/abled Black accountant, particularly those who are neurodiverse. What I mean by that term is that we are all different, but some more than others when it comes to neurology. For example it might mean being neurologically different due to or ADHD,[6] that is not a deficit so to speak, but a different way of being, thinking and acting in a world that typically does not assign value to such traits. Traditionally, it is to consider those on the spectrum etc. as 'mentally retarded,' and I'm really sorry to use such an offensive word but it really does capture the depth of fear and loathing historically ascribed to those with assumed 'mental difficulties.' So, then the question must be asked what happens if you are Black as well? What about being a woman of Color on top of this? We can ago on a fair bit here but you get the idea."

"I do, but we have to get on air right now and you need to recap this again!"

With that, the ever-present red on air light flickered into life, denoting that they were both on air. After introducing her guest once again, Dee recounts their brief off air conversation and encourages her guest to continue where he left off.

"Ok … all of you in radioland will have to bear with me here as I give an explanation of DisCrit and how I believe it relates to Accounting. DisCrit is an off shoot of Critical Race Theory, which basically asks the question 'what about the experience of those who are classed as disabled and raced?' I apply it to Accounting to see what is going, or at least that is the hope."

"But why?" asks Dee quizzically.

"It needs to be on record. Firstly, if academic research is about uncovering undiscovered knowledge, then this is a must for Accounting because race and disability does not exist as a line of research inquiry that I have ever seen. Secondly,

[6]Attention Deficit Hyperactivity Disorder is a neurological condition affecting attention, impulsivity and executive functioning. In certain contexts it can make work, social relations and other areas of life difficult to navigate.

I believe People of Color accountants who are neurodiverse, and in particular those with ADHD (some know they are neurodiverse, some don't, and some hide it or 'mask'), struggle in an environment which is both raced and ableist."

> "What do you mean by the term ablest?"

> "So, it's a bit similar to the way Black accountants exist in the Whiteworld of Accounting. It is a world where what is white is right, that is to say Whiteness is the definitive standard against which all things are measured. Now, that same Black neurodiverse accountant also exists in the ableist world of Accounting, (they are one and the same), this world states that which is able bodied, is right. All things are benchmarked against those who are able bodied and their way is the right way."

> "Ah … I think I'm with you professor."

> "Great! So, a DisCrit of Accounting, more formally, aims to theoretically explain how race, racism, dis/ability and ableism are institutionalized for accountants of color with disabilities, and in the area, I'm looking at ADHD and Dyscalculia specifically."

> "But why these areas? What about the others? It seems oddly exact."

Lewis withdraws for a moment, pausing for an uncomfortable minute or two, an eternity in radio hours. Dee could see he was about to venture into a risky if not dangerous place. Contemplating if he should expose such a vulnerable part of himself to the world.

> "Are you O.K. Dr Lewis?"

> "Er …yes. I just needed to take a minute. So, what you don't know about me, and isn't in my bio is that I'm not an only child. I actually have a half-brother called Myron. Ironically, he is a senior accountant for AWF. We got in contact a year ago. Through our conversations, about his experience as a Black accountant he revealed to me that he has both Adult ADHD and Dyscalculia. Essentially, his ADHD disorder means that his executive functioning skills (think organizing ability), are chronically deficient. He is also wildly impulsive in certain circumstances and emotionally volatile when triggered. Worse, his dyscalculia means shock and horror, that he basically can't count! Yes, that's right, an accountant who can't count. It's absurd right? And yet here is a successful Black senior Accounting professional who has what is effectively math's dyslexia. I began to wonder how this was even possible."

"I have to admit it sounds very uncommon."

"Well, that's the point isn't it Dee, it might not be that unusual at all, or perhaps it is, we simply don't know because we don't have the research. And that is one of the reasons I'm pivoting my investigations in Accounting and CRT toward that experience. After talking to Myron for a few months I discovered that he was diagnosed later in life, and mid-career. His 7 year old son had been diagnosed, and after substantial parental reading on the subject to help him, he recognized telltale signs in himself. An assessment with a psychologist who specializes in the area confirmed that he had this all along. In some ways it turned his world upside down. For example, what he thought were clear racial barriers to his career in the past, were more likely ablest barriers that he didn't know at the time. But then there were other obstacles that were definitely racial, and some that were in between. All of it made his head spin. In any event he is a diligent employee and immediately informed Human Resources at AWF, who inquired what accommodations he might need."

"Go on …" Dee learned in further.

"The problem is that I needed a better theoretical lens to unpack all of this than I had with CRT, which is where DisCrit came in. Although often used to explore the experience of disability and race in education, I have taken the liberty of mapping its tenets onto Accounting to see what might be revealed."

"And what have you found so far?"

"Well, nothing yet as I'm just beginning the process. It's a work in progress if you like, I'm following the tenets of this lens, hoping we might see something not yet seen. With this in mind I've culled DisCrit's basic canons from the seminal book on the subject by Connor et al., and loosely applied them to Accounting. Let me show you what I'm trying to do."

Lewis rummaged quickly through his jacket pocket, revealing a pink crumpled piece of paper mapping the central points of DisCrit onto Accounting. Spreading it flat it looked thusly:

Notes on what mapping DisCrit to Accounting might look like:

- **DisCrit in Accounting zeros in on how Racism and Ablism sometimes cohere and sometimes do not, in unseen, inert ways to frame normalcy as the de facto standard in Accounting environments.**
- **DisCrit in Accounting problematizes identity within the Accounting realm as intersectional, fluid, and non-static in a way which disdains any singular identity category such as Race/dis/ability or gender taking primacy. All is mixed, and that is OK.**
- **DisCrit in Accounting problematizes the imperceptibility of race and ability as minor social abstractions, which do not trouble the raced and disabled professional. Instead taking seriously, and therefore privileging the voice of raced and dis/abled subaltern professionals.**

- **DisCrit in Accounting explores how the socio historical and legal facets of dis/ability, race, and racism merge to remove the rights of such Othered Accounting professionals.**
- **DisCrit in Accounting sees Whiteness and Ability as bedfellows, both propagating a property right, that affords owners a multitude of advantages not afforded to those who do not hold it. Further, limited gains that have accrued are a function of the interest convergence of white middle class interests, not altruistic intent** (Connor et al., 2016).

Lewis, after a somewhat passionate, if not sweaty tirade centered around the canons of DisCrit as detailed above, slumped into his seat. He was quite pleased but yet apprehensive to introduce new concepts such as this without any form of empirical or quantitative evidence. Frankly, it left him wide open to a multitude of research accusations and the wolves would circle soon. But it was too important in his mind not to do so. Too personal as well.

> "Dr Lewis, that was pretty passionate coming from an Accounting scholar!"
>
> "I know Dee, but after hearing the experiences that Myron has gone through over the years, it makes me very angry that once again, Accounting as a profession has neglected the spaces in-between, and left the raced and neurologically unseen to remain invisible, no matter how loudly they shout."

Lewis goes on to recount a deeply personal conversation both he and Myron had about it all, and how his brother's Accounting experience had changed only a few years ago. Myron had been diagnosed with ADHD Inattentive type,[7] Depression and Dyscalculia[8] and up until his diagnosis he had multiple Accounting roles during his career due to his undiagnosed ADHD. This left him feeling that he was different somehow but could never discover a plausible reason for it. Instead, he bathed in the guilt and shame of the impostor phenomenon (Minute, 2020), knowing for certain that he was a fraud who couldn't count for toffee (Dyscalculia). But yet could interpret certain statistical high level financial mathematical concepts better than most.[9] Embarrassingly, he still used his fingers to calculate tips after meals and dreaded the end of the evening basic arithmetic required to calculate

---

[7]This type of ADHD variant is characterized by the opposite of excess movement. Instead a lethargy exists, where individuals drift off into their own dream world at the drop of a hat, unable to stop their attention wondering.

[8]This roughly can be thought of as a type of mathematic dyslexia.

[9]Dyscalculia affects an individual's number sense and ability to remember, and recall number facts held in short-term memory. However, in certain cases it does not affect certain abstract advanced mathematical concepts.

who owed what in inebriated after work settings.[10] It was this feeling of being a con artist to his profession that ushered in feelings of worthlessness, provoking listlessness on the job at times and endless arguments at home fueled by ADHD emotional reactivity.[11] After which he slumped into doing nothing, sometimes not even getting out of bed (mild depression). This of course was further compounded by the hidden secret that Myron had failed basic mathematics in high school multiple times and CPA license exams repeatedly which hit his pocketbook hard. But by some miracle he passed and curiously people never asked about his high school math scores or the number of times he needed to take the CPA exam. All that mattered was that he had it, which of course worked in his favor. But still, by any measure he still couldn't do fifth-grade math to save his life. He constantly thought "What the hell am I doing as an Accountant?"

What the hell indeed. But Lewis in this long heart to heart conversation pointed out that his diagnosis was recent, and that pre diagnosis, despite his troubles (or perhaps because of them), Myron was now an Audit senior, soon to be knocking at the partnership door. Renowned in his firm for being exceptionally hard working, with unparalleled charisma where clients were concerned. His charm is magnetic, and his uncanny ability to think of out of the box ways to get new business often catches the eye of partners. These are documented neurodiverse advantages that some such as Gail Saltz, M.D., have suggested link to giftedness and/or genius (Saltz, 2017). In relation to Accounting Ovaska-Few notes:

> "... AND this is why Big Accounting firms are making strides in recognizing neurodiversity, they see the business case of these potential genius level benefits if harnessed correctly. I mean it's all over their websites. For example, I caught an article in the trade journal, The Accounting Periodical, detailing a specific project by one of Big Accounting firms encouraging ADHD students into the firm. They see the out of the box thinking and problem solving benefits that might be gained" (Ovaska-Few, 2018).

Lewis leaned back in the studio chair with his fingers interlocked on his midriff as he continued.

"I can't deny Ovaska-Few's point that things have improved recently in terms of official recognition of neurodiversity among large financial service providers. But stop a moment. How did this come about? And for whom does this particular bell toll? Is big business really listening to the concerns of Black and Brown neurodiverse professionals? Or is it all Smoke and Mirrors just like Accounting's big commitment to race a few years ago (Lewis, 2022)? Alternatively, might it be

---

[10]This is a common trait among adult dyscalculics who often continue to rely on finger counting strategies well after formal schooling (Moorcraft, 2014).

[11]ADHD provokes greater emotional responses in those with the condition. Rejection Sensitive Dysphoria (RSD), can further complicate matters as an extreme response to rejection or criticism (Saline, 2023).

that a property right in Whiteness and Ability is being invoked, where commitments to neurodiversity represent an Interest Convergence pulling up ailing DEI in Accounting efforts?"

"Nope you've lost me and not for the first time!"

Clearing his throat Lewis leans forward in his chair, making direct eye contact with Dee. Perhaps a little too long, a little too flirtatious to be appropriate. But he felt like he was on a roll now ....

> "What I mean is that to be white and neurodiverse is quite different from being Black and neurodiverse, particularly in the setting of Accounting, where status is a function of success (Lewis, 2012). Neurodiverse, whiteness affords those who possess it a property right in Whiteness (higher status), supplanting some obstacles put in place by ableism. Essentially, white neurodiverse colleagues are defective, but are still white, meaning they have limited access to the privileges of Whitenesss. Enough to make sure that white neurodiversity has interest in defending it, going along to get along with ablest racist rhetoric if needs be. But the Black neurodiverse professional is twice inequity bound, as they have no right to the property right in Whiteness and suffer ablism at the intersection of race."
>
> "Really? You really think that it's all some twisted nefarious plan? Dr Lewis, on this point I disagree with you!"
>
> "And Dee, I wouldn't have it another way. As you know I cultivate respectful oppositional dialogue wherever possible. Of course, it drives my wife up the wall ...."
>
> "Yes, I can definitely see that!"

Both share a laugh at that certain reality before Lewis makes, as it happens, to be his last comment on the subject of the evening.

> "Of Interest Convergence in race and neurodiversity I will say this, for me it's the typical route taken. The CRT theorist Mary Dudziak has a good take on this, she makes the argument that Civil Rights succeeded in large part not just to the unparalleled heroism of the marchers and Freedom advocates but to larger geopolitical forces at the time. For her the Cold war against Russia for global influence meant that America was handicapped against Soviet narratives of egalitarianism under Communism when dealing with the Blacker and Browner Global South. America needed its own emancipatory narrative, and it found it in Civil Rights. It

was this combined interest which ultimately allowed Civil Rights to succeed. Progress in neurodiversity will take the same path. It's good for the industry to be seen as being progressive, it helps white neurodiverse colleagues the most, and then, tangentially Black colleagues. But the main aim is to help the profession out of its DEI bind" (Dudziak, 2009).

But time had gotten the better of both host and guest. Dee announces to the evening audience somewhere over the distant airways that they are open for calls about the subject topic at hand. In the meantime, more mood music fills the airwaves, The Roots this time, this classic hip hop ensemble fit the bill as various tracks play from their aptly named album, "Things Fall Apart," waiting for calls to come in. Indeed, things do rapidly fall apart moments later.

The Caller

Calls came in steadily, as the evening wore on. Dee was good-natured in her teasing of Lewis, perhaps just a little too coy, just a smidge, as questions were asked and answered. Of particular note was a call from a neurodiverse Latina accountant, Isabella Ramos, who is both Autistic and Dyslexic. We go back to the scene halfway through the call.

> "So that is it, I feel there is never any rest for me. Not at work or at home. Our world seems to be held up Atlas style by women, their never ending toil, that is emotional psychological and infinite. It never stops. Our value never appreciated. Because of this at work and at home women are beat, traumatized, sorrowful, and anxiety ridden in ways I can't describe."
>
> "Speak! Baby speak! I hear you Isabella."

With full-throated support Dee's expression changes from quizzical inquiry to solidarity all the while appreciating that things are even worse for Black women, as they are deprived of the ability to vent their frustration publicly, lest they pay a cost, such is the damage of the angry Black woman trope in professional spaces. Isabella's soliloquy continues.

> "But it's not just that. Typical sly comments about being a Salsa queen, and so 'emotionally Latin' happen all the time with colleagues on Audits and clients too. Even leering looks from male Partners that says to me 'you're a sexy Latina, making me an object not a professional. Then, on top of that I freeze. The offense doesn't sink in right there and then in the moment. No, instead I start grinning, playing along with an insult directed at me at my own expense, just to survive. But I've trained myself to be this way. I already have a reputation for saying inappropriate

things in meetings, and not understanding jokes. It sets me apart. It's my Autism and they know it, but I overheard one of the Partners the other day call me a liability in front of clients, and that I should be kept from them at all costs! They don't care about how hard I try or that my Autism stifles my true talents in certain settings … and it's really difficult to manage it all, I … feel like I can't cope at times."

In a consoling tone Dee reassures the listener.

"I know every woman bares this but it's worse for you. I'm just worried about your mental health honey, are you speaking with someone?"

"Yes, I have a therapist and she tries. She gets bits of it but not the intersection of it all. And that's why I called into the show. Dr Lewis, you really hit a chord with me, I just felt that nobody really understood what I was going through at work, I mean Accounting is just not up to this. No matter what fine things they say on their websites or at employee resource group meetings. I mean I was the secretary for one on neurodiversity and they didn't have a clue. The guy heading the group is white and dyslexic himself and when I tried to talk about my dyslexia, he stopped me from fully contributing to meetings due to slow reading of agenda items. He interrupted me, talked over me, and said yeah, we all get that but you just need to let them know that English is your second language and with 'Spanish dyslexia' it requires them to slow meetings down for me! As if such a thing as 'Spanish Dyslexia exists'! Its so racist. I was so angry. Can you believe that? I'm a second generation Chicana from New Hampshire! I was bilingual by the age of 5. I mean this is what I want Dr Lewis to talk about. What do I do here?"

With an animated spring Lewis all but leapt at the microphone, his passion on full display, and as the Brits say 'his hackles' were up now.[12]

"You see this really gets my goat!"

"Er … what?" Dee interrupts him.

"Sorry, there I go again with the slang. Let me clarify, it means 'makes me annoyed' in British parlance. This is why I entered this field in the first place. What really disturbs me is the specific list

[12]It is to become angry and irritable, ready to react in an antagonistic fashion.

> of targeted attacks that Isabella experiences daily. The microaggressive stereotype of sexy Latina, used to belittle her professional stature and the 'not getting jokes' is particularly pernicious. Last time I checked it wasn't a crime to not get a joke."

> "Could you explain that a bit more Anton?"

> "All this is used as a mark against her, peddling the narrative she can't cope in Accounting, and will never be one of the guys. It freezes her in the professional imaginary as being forever Othered, the opposite of ever being accepted. Jokes at the expense of the stigmatized is a sign of quite a toxic work environment (Lewis, 2012). But what I'm really concerned with is her point about Partners keeping her away from clients. This is outright career sabotage in Public Accounting. You might have a legal case if you can prove it. One based on medicalizing her neurodiversity as deficient, marking her incompetent at the job, which is a gross misrepresentation of the issue at hand. These Partners unfairly catastrophize Isabella's ADHD and Autism as her specific misfortune to bare and fail in their duty of care to provide conditions to ameliorate the situation which they are charged to do and advertise that they do on their website. Instead, they cite flexible and positive working conditions for the neurodiverse that clearly does not exist."

> "Sorry Anton, again can you just explain this term medicalize for our audience."

Lewis was perspiring profusely. An unfortunate condition he had born for most of his life. Luckily the audience couldn't see him as he looked like he had just been for a swim in his suit ….

> "Yes, I do like to get on my professorial high horse sometimes without fully explaining myself. Let me try again. To medicalize is to treat a given disability as an unalterable problem that defines the essence of a person. By default, it is an irreducible loss, necessitating exclusion that cannot be helped. It is an ableist narrative used to Other the Dis/abled. Unfortunately, as Isabella pointed out, the Accounting profession has been cited in the past as a bastion of the negative medical model perspective (Duff & Ferguson, 2007). But a competing tale exists propagated by the Dis/abled themselves, a societal model perspective, which instead states that it is the inability of society to properly accommodate the Dis/abled which is the heart of the problem. In this telling Isabella is not a problem, but an asset to the firm for her out of the box thinking talent, and clients can be made aware of the potential for snafu's if necessary. Then if the client refuses to engage with a neurodiverse

> employee legal ramification can and should follow. Of course, some firms suggest that this cannot be helped and it's just the nature of things to have clients disturbed by difference such as race and/or Dis/ability, but I counter that they are not the sort of clients any self-respecting Accounting firm should be doing business with in the first place. Our ethics codes say as much if we care to follow them. But beneath is a more insidious narrative that disability and I also conflate this to race, threatens the prestige of the profession. It risks 'ghettoizing' Accounting which will scare away clients resulting in less billable hours business. But as I alluded earlier, we simply don't have the research data to prove anything. This leaves the Dis/abled at the juncture of race with no voice to challenge ableism that renders them unimportant to the dominant majority white abled bodied environment."

With that Dee announces a short break in programming and plays another mellow track, this time "Brotha," by the unparalleled soul sister Angie Stone. Knowing Angie will never "try to hurt ya," and is "here for you," knowing that Angie, as a representation of the true love of all Black women, and is rooting for Black men to win brought solace to the somber situation. Angie's love of Black resilience in the face of racism appeals to the myriads of Black male listeners, and Black women. They are and remain the eternal pillar of the community, forever beautiful, proud and strong. Never bending nor wavering. The melody of hope drifted far and wide, buoying up all that heard it in the studio, the audience and all others lost in the night far away.

A Klan Master Calls

The red light flashed one final time and they were on air again. But strangeness was afoot. With the show all but finished and Dee and Lewis wishing listeners a good rest of the evening, a call came through. Peculiarly, that part of the show had ended some 15 minutes earlier and all the equipment to enable calls was switched off.

"Hello."

Dee seemed alarmed as the voice boomed through the speaker. This was not how things went on her show, and she was pretty sure that it wasn't technically feasible either. She motioned the remaining studio techies to lower the volume as she continued the conversation:

> "Hello Sir, I'm not sure how you have managed to get through to us but we have finished this segment of the show. Try us again at the same time next week."

"Really? I believe I am the one who decides" said the voice with cold impassionate assurance.

"Now wait a minute! I'm the one …."

"No, my dear. You will take my call because I'm Klanmaster of 'USA Always and Forever (UAF)'and I would have words with you."

It was true and everyone in the studio knew it was an exposé too good to miss, no matter how late the hour, no matter how inexplicable the occurrence.

"Ok, I'll play. So how can we help you mister …."

"Its Klanmaster to you."

"Righhht …." Retorted Dee.

"I would have words with this fraud of a guest of yours, Lewis."

Lewis shifted uneasily. He, like Dee, sensed something was wrong. Back in the day he and his friends had joked that Black people in fact have something akin to a racial sixth sense, a product of racial survival. For example, when it looks like it's going to throw down, particularly in white majority settings, you can bet Black folks have already left. Think for a moment, when exactly did you last see a Black hostage reading a hostage letter? Added to this; to paraphrase Comedian Dave Chapelle, Black people make bad bargaining chips! Imagine five Black hostages are taken and terrorists call the White House, "Hello, we have 5 Black … hello?" (Chappelle & Bennan, 2004). Exactly. Black value is less. But back to the moment at hand.

Lewis's "Spidy sense" was tingling loudly. In fact, they were sitting by the exit just in case …. But he addressed this self-professed Klan Grandmaster with a defiant grin:

"O.K., I'm game. What do you want Klan Master Flash?"

"We will sue you. Then we will sue this sham of a radio station out of existence. You'll be back picking cotton with your dirty grubby hands in no time."

Unfazed by the racial dog whistle Lewis replies.

"For what reason?"

"Firstly, we of 'USA Always and Forever' are constitutional freedom fighters for the god given rights of US citizens. You sir are racist and so is this station and your hateful DEI pomposity harms the rights of disenfranchised innocent whites, Asians and Jewish

> professionals who simply want to be treated fairly. But luckily, we have Civil Rights legislation to defend them, they have the UAF to fight for them and they have the words of Martin Luther King, that it is the content of a person's character not the color of their skin that matters most, a lesson this English joker seems to have missed."

Bemused, Lewis had heard this line before. A different group America First Legal, had sent a cease and desist letter to PwC, one of the Big 4 global Accounting firms, charging it with Civil Rights violations relating to illegal PwC employment and contracting practices. The group alleged that whites and Asians were unfairly prevented from advantageous programs based on racial criteria. In this instance they seemed to have scared the Accounting firm into submission, as it did indeed open up its programs to whites and Asians (Foley, 2024; Legal, 2023). But he would not bend so easily, crouched over the microphone Lewis replied back.

> "Well, I have two answers for you right away. First, go back. And. Listen. To. What. I. Said earlier. I've seen this tactic before and explained it to the audience. You should try listening before speaking. Its helpful with a bunch of things like not looking stupid, on air."

Indeed, Lewis had pointed out to the audience that a DEI rollback was happening and such letters were often the first salvo, then followed by dogged legal challenges. The idea was to bully DEI into submission and unfortunately it was working. Yet, Lewis rebuked US business for backing down so easily to intimidation. Alternatively firms should ask the likes of *USA Always and Forever* and *America First Legal* what they would do better? If Civil Rights are so important to them then what is their solution for equity in the workplace? And if they come up with something how do we ensure their plan, based on the viewpoint of Equality of Opportunity actually works? Throw them this thorny ball and watch them fumble. They will.

Rain pelted hard against the window the minute the Klanmaster had taken to the air. Thunder rolled ominously, following the tempo of his argument, as if to double down on his points. So much so that the deafening thunderclap that followed WAS the Klanmaster's furious response to Lewis's jibe without him uttering a word. Static electricity filled the air. Dee received a shock from her coffee mug as she reached for it. The duel continued. Lewis held his own so far.

"Also, I hold to the idea of King and Tan's Moral Debt, originally culled from Gloria Ladson Billings, that people at the intersection of Dis/ability and race are owed a Moral Debt, due to years of racialized opportunity forfeiture, subjugation and forced sterilization, and incarceration in mental institutions for the 'feeble minded,' who were invariably Black (Thorius & Tan, 2016). I concede DEI is an imperfect tool but it is the best we have right now for paying back that debt and the associated interest of suffering which accompanied it. Yes, reparations would be a start but much damage has and is still being done along these lines. UAF has no solution to actioning this Moral Debt, in fact you deny its very history, while at the same time, in Florida you champion the removal of three hundred texts from schools which explain why this debt exists and why it must be paid. Instead, books like *Anti Racist baby* by Kendi, and Baldwin's *The Fire Next Time* are removed in an attempt to rewrite history to fit your own venal political ends" (Baptiste, 2024).

Another tremendous crack of lightning lights up the rain-drenched streets outside the Radio station, as the Klanmaster himself bellowes with indignant rage at the truth of Lewis's assertion. Then suddenly, it became lighter as his first response that was not a cataclysmic type weather event followed.

> "Ah Anton. You seem to have all the answers don't you. Well answer me this. Why should I or the audience out there or anybody believe a word you say when you are an outright liar of the highest order."

> "Liar? About what exactly."

Lewis was incredulous about the assertion and began to think of this Klan-fraud as a top rated imbecile.

> "Your brother Myron doesn't exist. He's a fiction of your imagination."

Lewis froze. Damnnn …. It's true! But how does he know and what will he say next? Terrified thoughts raced at a pace through his mind, trust and authenticity were his shield and weapon in this arena and the Klanmaster had torn them asunder.

> "The question is why? And I will tell you. It's because you are a coward Anton. The fiction of Myron is a proxy for you. His experiences are your experiences. You are ADHD inattentive and it was you who found out only a few years ago. But differently, you have Dyscalculia, not Dyslexia. You are the Accounting Professor who cannot count!" (Lewis, 2024b).

Being "outted" live on air! Lewis felt the ground swallow him up. It was all true. Destructive waves of guilt and shame washed over him, but the Klanmaster would not stop.

> "yes, you have lied to your family, to your University, to your students and a myriad of companies you worked for. And you wonder why you cannot hold a job!"

Silence filled the airways. Lewis shrank inside himself unable to respond. Dee stared at him somewhat aghast. It was true. It was he that stumbled in previous

Accounting roles, bungled basic bank reconciliations, and incorrectly posted journals regularly to the chagrin of previous line managers. But it did fuel his ingenuity as he ended up learning how to code to automate to avoid silly errors where he could. It was he who stumbled over basic arithmetic computations in Accounting review courses as he attempted and typically failed to gain formal Accounting qualifications caused by his dyscalculia. All the while, ever the imposter, ever the fake. The toll on his self-worth had been extraordinary. The pain was exquisite. But there is another side to this. What doesn't kill you makes you stronger right? What strength had Lewis gained from this? I proffer that an absurd level of fortitude was found to "carry on regardless" no matter what life throws at you. Understanding all need help, and that we all stumble and it is our responsibility to steady our brothers, sisters and ourselves when we do. They are not alone, we are not alone, none of us ever were, no matter what color, creed, sexuality or other marker of difference is presented. Pain can breed empathy at the deepest level. Shame and guilt reared a well of forgiveness within him. This was his strength. Fighting his neurological difficulties meant he worked hard to understand the needs of his students. He worked hard to ensure they never felt stupid or belittled in his classes because he understood this pain all too well. He encouraged students to be their best and show him their best. Helping them fight the fear of their own imposter phenomenon. It costs little and is worth so much. All this is done even as doubt, shame and fear accompay him as constant companions to this day. Perhaps this is all a tad dramatic, but at this moment, to him, he realized that all was not lost. Secrets and lies are just the worst! Truth wins in the end.

> "I'm sorry. It's all true. I've been wearing masks for the longest time. But before then I didn't even know. I just knew something wasn't right. To be fair I have always found damn inventive ways to solve my deficiencies but that didn't make them go away. I admit I was afraid. I am afraid."

But the Klanmaster had a response to drive the blade deeper.

> "I repeat you are a selfish lying coward and nobody should believe a word you say! Certainly not your audience who are still listening. I've made sure of that."

The howling wind was all that remained of the weather event outside. It knocked and clattered in victory at the behest of the Klanmaster. Mocking, victorious gusts blew. But Lewis, although physically and emotionally spent in this most arduous of evenings, had one more comment:

> "I am all these things Klanmaster, and worse. So much worse. But … I'm human. Was it not said that he who is without sin cast the first stone? It is my vulnerability, that is my humanity, its my guilt and my shame, my faults and inconsistencies that make me fight when I should give up. Make me fight for those who cannot

do so for themselves. THIS is why we must talk about race and racism in Accounting and its connection with and around neurodiversity for the raced professional. And why their voice must be heard. And what about you Klanmaster? How are you vulnerable? How are you relatable? Why should we believe you? Where is your humanity?"

"Yes! Speak Anton!"

Dee jumped up in triumph at his mini soliloquy. As dawn began to rise over the rain-soaked building containing the radio station. Dee took up the challenge.

"Well, Klanmaster, what do you have to say now?"

But her request was met with silence. The line was dead. In this joust, victory was theirs.

Dee signed off to the audience in a stunned muted fashion. It was early morning now. Looking at the disheveled man in front of her she felt his humanity. He had been in the most curious of contests and was fatigued to the point of near collapse. She offered him a beverage as a gesture of support.

"Do you want the last of the coffee Anton?"

"No thank you Dee, I only drink tea. It's an English thing …."

With that he made his goodbyes and walked into the early morning air, toward his car and away from this most dire and rewarding of radio shows.

References

AICPA. (2021). *2021 trends report*. https://www.aicpa.org/professional-insights/download/2021-trends-report

Alim, S., & Smitherman, G. (2012). *Articulate while Black. Barrack Obama, language, and race in the U.S.* Oxford University Press.

Baptiste, N. (2024). *In Florida, more than 300 books have been removed from school shelves.* https://www.huffpost.com/entry/florida-bans-300-books-schools_n_6508b7b6e4b0d98f39e7f759

Carbado, D., & Gulati, M. (2000). Working identity. *Cornell Law Review*, *85*, 1259–1308.

Chappelle, D., & Bennan, N. (2004). *Why terrorists won't take Black people as hostages* [Chappelle's Show]. https://youtu.be/_oNQxYIFDI4?si=fEdxXy03EshtiOSa

Connor, D., Ferri, B., & Annamma, S. (2016). *DisCrit. disability studies and critical race theory in education.* Teachers College Press.

Dudziak, M. L. (2009). Desegregation as a cold war imperative. In E. Taylor, D. Gillborn, & G. Ladson-Billings (Eds.), *Foundations of critical race theory in education* (pp. 85–95). Routledge.

Duff, A., & Ferguson, J. (2007). Disability and accounting firms: Evidence from the UK. *Critical Perspectives on Accounting*, *18*, 139–157.

Foley, S. (2024). *PwC drops some US diversity goals to meet changed legal landscape*. https://www.ft.com/content/20d1646d-2039-40de-abe1-f2270830b01f

Legal, A. F. (2023). *America first legal sends warning letter to big three accounting firm: Stop racial discrimination now*. https://aflegal.org/america-first-legal-sends-warning-letter-to-big-three-accounting-firm-stop-racial-discrimination-now/

Lewis, A. (2012). *A critical analysis of the Black accounting experience in the U.K. Tales of success and failure in the British professional workplace*. Lambert Academic Publishing.

Lewis, A. (2015). Counting Black and white beans. Why we need a critical race theory of accounting. *European Journal of Contemporary Economics and Management*, *2*(2), 1–13.

Lewis, A. (Producer). (2021, September 24). *Counting Black and White Beans. Episode 1 - Race Talk as Threat*. https://open.spotify.com/episode/3VKMHhHRcD8QwYO5QK0oHv

Lewis, A. (2022). Smoke and mirrors. Race and the Black CPA. *The CPA Journal*. https://www.cpajournal.com/2022/01/21/smoke-and-mirrors/

Lewis, A. (2024a). Black women in accounting and the backlash to DEI. *The CPA Journal*, *XCIV*(3/4), 1–80.

Lewis, A. (2024b). The divergent accountant. *The CPA Journal*, *January / February*, 72–75. https://www.cpajournal.com/2024/04/22/the-divergent-accountant/

Minute, A. (2020). *Kevin Cokley, University of Texas at Austin – Impostor syndrome*. https://academicminute.org/2020/01/kevin-cokley-university-of-texas-at-austin-imposter-syndrome/

Moorcraft, P. (2014). *It just doesn't add up. explaining dyscalculia and overcoming number problems for children and adults*. Tarquin.

Ovaska-Few, S. (2018). Promoting neurodiversity. *Journal of Accountancy*. https://www.journalofaccountancy.com/issues/2018/jan/ey-pilot-program-workers-with-autism.html

Saline, S. (2023). *How to control your anger when ADHD emotional reactivity kicks in*. https://www.additudemag.com/how-to-control-anger-emotional-reactivity-adhd/

Saltz, G. (2017). *The power of different. The link between disorder and genius*. Flatiron Books.

Smith, P. (2020). *BAME 2020: One in 250 partners is black at top eight accountancy firms*. https://www.accountancydaily.co/bame-2020-one-250-partners-black-top-eight-accountancy-firms

Thorius, K., & Tan, P. (2016). Expanding analysis of educational debt. Considering intersections of race and ability. In A. Artiles & E. Kozleski (Eds.), *DisCrit. disability studies and critical race theory in education* (pp. 46–71). Teachers College.

Wilmore, L. (2009). *I'd rather we got casinos*. Hyperion.

Chapter 8

8th Fable: Jinn and Tonic

> Tonic – *a medicinal substance taken to give a feeling of vigor or well-being.*
>
> Jinn – *spirit often capable of assuming human or animal form and exercising supernatural influence over people.*

The Black woman CPA was tired. It was all too much. The world was closing in and she couldn't see a way out. It was a long way down as she beheld her murky fate. Rippling waves colliding against the base of the Brooklyn bridge greeted her gaze, as she stood transfixed, high above, teetering on the edge. She knew it was all so cliché. She knew her long-standing chronic depression was to blame. She knew it had no doubt got the better of her good reason and yet she did not care. Still, the six or seven strong gin and tonics, downed in one, for Dutch courage at Satan's Whiskers Bar and Grill only an hour earlier, helped matters. She was drunk alright and didn't care a jot. On this bridge she would finally commit the suicide she had contemplated for so long, something only she knew. To everyone else she was the epitome of the successful, attractive strong Black woman. But inside, she wobbled over the edge in every conceivable way leaving her exhausted. Nonetheless, internally distressed or not she retained her poise, and was "dressed to the nines," in her Anne Taylor two-piece suit to meet her maker. Her deportment at this moment was due to her role as lead auditor at the AWF office in lower east Manhattan, where she had left a client meeting a number of hours earlier. Impulsively, on the drive home, she detoured into the Whiskers bar downtown to drown herself in quality gin, before actually drowning herself in the East River. Now her watch read three in the morning, cold gusts of wind howled past her head, mocking her to take the final plunge. So, not one to disappoint she did. No ceremony. No drama. Just death and gin-soaked freedom.

Hold and Swallow ...

They say as you approach your doom that time slows down and your life flashes before your eyes. Not for her though, in its place was what brought this all to pass, vivid images flashed across her retina.

Accounting Fables: Tales of Race and Racism in the Borderlands of Business, 133–150

Published under exclusive licence by Emerald Publishing Limited
doi:10.1108/978-1-80117-069-720251023

Her life, love, and professional dreams. Her fall, both figurative and literal is symptomatic of being Black, successful, and a woman in the US today. She is emblematic of Black women's experience in Accounting, or any area of commerce for that matter. At this moment in time, at work, she is of course a role model, not too threatening, regularly monitoring herself to avoid making white colleagues feel uncomfortable, something she excelled at. And wow did she work hard, only to receive half the plaudits, a curse experienced by Black professionals in the workplace ad infinitum (Colson et al., 2024). Typically, as with other Black women of a certain level, she found herself tasked with the hidden labor that is mentorship of Black women at All World Financial. Frustratingly, it did not count toward career assessment, but how could she refuse ambitious African Americans? Those looking to emulate her, believing the fabrication that their daily toil will cease once they reach her level and beyond. A myth of course, so easily peddled, so effortlessly believed, something she worked hard to rid them of. Yet, a sticky question remains, why do this when all that matters is ability in the profession? Authorized as copious amounts of elbow grease, grit and reward, the best way to progress. Because she had learned the hard way, knowing it to be a dangerous fallacy, one which accountants of color all too readily believe, one which conceals the existence of an innately raced and gendered "shadow structure" within Accounting's dispassionate hallowed halls (Lewis, 2012).

Career stagnation is the price paid for not knowing how to play the game of Accounting. A tournament of professionalism which sees some occupational activities as prized, and others not. On the surface, they may seem splendid, but are in fact valueless, time-sapping pursuits, worse than useless at impacting a career. Exemplar being the bringing together of employee resource groups, or formation of DEI initiatives. Worthy in the sense of giving back to the professional community of color in AWF, but of little significance where it counts. Why? Because to succeed, participants in the game (all employees bar none) must adhere to the values of pale males running the profession. Valuing socially responsible work is not what they truly care about even if pragmatic DEI pronouncements are uttered from their lying lips. What they value the Other must also if they are to survive let alone prosper.

However, to force the point and do devalued DEI is to quickly comprehend unpaid, unappreciated activities, typically undertaken by Black women (and sometimes Black men), embody an "opportunity career cost" (OCC), where doing what is right, in reality, is to harm your own job prospects (Harley, 2008; Lewis, 2020). Also, let us not forget that agency is a mirage of the game. For our Black woman protagonist, this lack of choice, cost her dearly in the end. Pressured by white seniors to take on ever greater Black mentorship because somebody has to do the DEI work, they anointed her, causing ever more OCC pain, the function of which was inevitable career stagnation. This no-win situation ailed her over time, coaxing into existence, chronic stress, irritable bowel syndrome, visual disturbance migraines with a side order of crippling depression. It was enough to make someone consider jumping off a bridge ....

It is against this brutal backdrop, Black women are fated to be superwomen, cape and all. A no-win situation sees them subtly appointed as the "DEI girl," expected to volunteer for all things related to diversity. Pressured institutionally, to be the unabashed advocate for Black problems, involuntary advisor on issues of race and racism, cultural interpreter, fixer in chief within the firm's DEI landscape, and extraneous to it. All the while being monitored by the institution for any perceived deviation from this set state of affairs (Harley, 2008). A Herculean task at best if not downright impossible which causes "Battle Fatigue," destructive daily racial/gendered workplace stress over time plaguing Black professionalism to this day (Acuff, 2018).

Advising mentees now, the Black woman CPA admonishes herself for lack of knowledge of the game when she first started. It's a Catch-22 for the Black employee who fights the system and tries to raise Black colleagues with them. It can't be done, making the task nothing but a fool's errand. To attempt to do so is to be cast as "Black Wonder Woman," a thankless role personifying sacrifice to community and profession, becoming overworked and underpaid in the process. Yet, the only viable path to attain any measure of professional authenticity as a Black woman knowledge worker in the Accounting landscape is to do it all. Without complaint. It's a trap. So, she cautions mentees about the dangers of idealism and to avoid her mistakes. Back then, fueled by a passion for social justice, she devoured literature critiquing the intersectional nature of racism and sexism experienced in the office setting, citing Critical Race Feminists like Adrienne Wing (2003) where possible, battling against a poisonous professional existence. Vocal in meetings, fighting for good projects for herself, standing her ground. She was a veritable Angela Davies of Accounting. But speaking truth to power is folly, for which she was awarded the moniker, "Mad, Black, Bad, Bitch." The quintessential Sapphire.[1] Accusations spread as white colleagues hissed untruths around the water cooler, utterings denoting her "difficult" and amateurish. Rumors grew rife finding their way into annual evaluations, hexing her burgeoning career (Upton & Arrington, 2012). This is how dirty work came her way and never left. Work that gave no glory. Although the bread and butter of all large multinational financial services firms, it's not the work that makes you a star, nor propels you toward partnership. She was boxed in.

The dilemma prompted her to recall a paper that laid the situation plainly. At its heart is the interplay of networked powerful white men. Arbiters choosing anointed ones, whose "right fit," is in part based on work quality, but far more importantly on nebulous, opaque traits. Characteristics like "ease" of being around, affability or "clubablity," i.e. who gets to play golf with the partners on Sundays. This is what counts as true merit in Accounting, naturally baked into the white male professional. To compete the stigmatized must find a way to "uncook themselves," be remolded again to fit white male standards. Meaning they can never truly be the real thing, only an imitation. She was disfavored in every sense of the word for her inability to do so, stalling her career. Regardless of meeting

[1]Sapphire is a demeaning trope perpetuated in early 20th-century racist media portrayals depicting Black women as noisy, mad and controlling (Austin, 2003; Doharty & Esoe, 2023).

benchmarks for promotion, her applications always lacked something that was never fully articulated. The subtext of feedback suggested that she simply lacked an unidentified X factor, and therefore was not partnership material (Anderson-Gough et al., 2024).

So, what happened next, you ask? Over time she believed she had rewritten the narrative around her sapphire trope, enough to put her back on track. But Accounting was not done with her yet. Instead, a new tale was weaved, moving her from hardened Black Wonder Woman to something else entirely. By default, years of working her identity out of one stereotype simply pushed her into another, that of "Mammy." The Black woman CPA was now too old to be an innovative young go getting achiever. Career stagnation ossified her in the eyes of the institution. Currently seen as "the fixer," an Accounting MacGyver of sorts, assigned to bad jobs, and hapless assignments to get the job done in time and on budget.[2] A helper of others to be fast tracked to greatness. Placed squarely within the mammy trope. Perceived as selfishly loyal, hardworking to a fault, but still not leadership material in any way.

Ominously, she was following a familiarly distressing path outlined by critical Accounting academics from the University of Memphis, for Black, Indigenous, or People of Color (BIPOC) professionals. Their research suggests BIPOC auditors expect racism to come their way, ruminating on likely stressful outcomes ahead. This manifests as a loss of psychological safety at the office and on engagements, harming relationships with Audit team colleagues. A condition worsened by having to code switch, to raise their professional profile to mitigate the inevitable racism. Diminishing racial identity forces change within themselves, mandating the altering of appearance, language, and countenance, to fit in with white cultural norms dominant in Auditing. The scholars point out that it's a vital process in being schooled to the "rules of the Audit" game if success is to be achieved. But they also point out that working identity in such a fashion comes at a high psychological cost for BIPOC auditors, leading to time off work away from unsafe colleagues, causing a withdrawal from work and the environment. A costly practice to be sure, something the Black woman CPA knew all too well and wished others knew too (Raddatz et al., 2024).

Patience was all she heard over the years, said to mollify her (which it did), and that her time would come (it never did), all typical comments heard by Black women professionals from white male managers (but not always), who are in reality "Barrier Bosses." They represent a small but destructive middle tranche of management steadfastly opposed to gender equality (Gyimah et al., 2022). Their trick is to gain the trust of Black women professionals by helping at first, but then subtly sabotaging progress over time of their women acolytes, converting Black

[2]MacGyver was a US series which aired from 2016 to 2021. The show explored the exploits of the analytical problem-solver Angus "Mac" MacGyver, an agent of a covert government agency. His trademark ability was to use his extraordinary technical and scientific imagination to crack difficult challenges on missions utilizing everyday materials or anything to hand at that moment.

women from "Pet to threat" (Donahue et al., 2021). It is somewhat reminiscent of Racial Gaslighting[3] because if barrier bosses are challenged on their behavior, it is denied as absurd. Instead, it is Black women who are accused of being "too angry" (Kretsedemas, 2010), too eager to "bite the hand that feeds them," of being all too Saphire-like. Flipping the table, it is Black women who engage in unfair race baiting with little evidence against innocent colorblind white managers. This trap had ensnared our Black woman CPA time and again, compelling her to question the many choices she had made, forcing her to question if life was worth living, even as she hurtled to her end.

But yet what option was best available to her at that time as a junior colleague? Could she afford to refuse help and support from powerful white males who can make or break your career? I don't think so. But to do so is to play the racialized, sexist game that is the Accounting profession, and never truly win. For her it was Barrier Boss behavior that is a perpetual elusive attack/help that is hindrance/help, that is unbearable to Black women, a daily, never-ending microaggression. It proved too much. From white women trying to touch a Black women's hair (a bad idea unless you like losing a hand …) in the workplace, to mispronouncing one's name. All the while enduring inappropriate racist/sexist jokes spoken casually by whites as mere banter at the expense of men and women of color (Sue, 2010).

This cut into her psyche with the cumulative force of a thousand razor blades, one or two slashes every day, no one inflicting a mortal wound, but over time severely debilitating her, now forcing her to look down at icy murky waters as salvation. And it is not just the Accounting workplace. When leaders like Justine Till, the first appointed Black woman president of Yale University, can be mauled at senate hearings,[4] when Black woman DEI officers endure such racism and sexism that they take their own life,[5] is it any surprise she, a capable Black woman CPA was about to take hers? Conditioned so by racist hostility, and habituated to isolation in Predominantly White Institutions, whose cultural ignorance in and of itself equates to an Environmental Microaggression.[6] They have come for us all; this DEI Winter is not just coming, it is here freezing Black women's advancement in its tracks (Lewis, 2023)!

---

[3]Stories told which erase the reality of white supremacist power structures while normalizing whiteness as the status quo (Davis & Ernst, 2017).

[4]The character Justine Till is a fictional proxy for ex Harvard University President Claudine Gay (Bisset, 2024).

[5]The suicide of the Vice President of Student Affairs at Lincoln University of Missouri, Dr. Antoinette Candia-Bailey is exemplar of the extreme psychological toll placed upon Black women professionals, and their experience of workplace bullying, invisibility, and diminishment of self-worth (RIVERA, 2024).

[6]This involves often non-verbal, structurally indirect inequitable behaviors which exist within the wider context of a society or institution, negatively affecting People of Color as a result. Typically, Environmental Microaggression is seen when one is the only Black person in a predominantly white organization, subtly suggesting that Black people are not wanted in this environment without a word ever being said (Sue, 2010).

The Black woman CPA saw little else, thought of nothing else, as she plunged deep into the East River. Her life force ebbing as did the last of her breath as she sunk toward the riverbed.

Sloshed ...

Hither and thither the accountant swirled, round and around the freezing cold depths of the East River. The waterway washed away her pain, angst, and depression. One last gasp remained. But wait, what was it she spied just a way away? Intrigued, she swam towards a glowing object in the murk. Radiant hexagonal forms met her gaze, which comprised much of the surface of an ancient bottle like structure half embedded in the mud. These shapes moved, ever so often slipping from one space to another, over and under, on its unusually smooth surface. A touch of beauty to witness before the end? Pulling it firmly out of its muddy tomb, she saw now that it was really a most peculiar lamp, the most ornate she had ever seen. Immediately captivating her. And so, it all began, with an outstretched hand reaching for an impossible lamp lodged at the bottom of the East River.

Smokeless fire engulfed her as she clutched greedily to the elaborate old lamp, swirling around her, darting this way and that as if sentient, which you have to admit is a damn unusual thing to experience at the bottom of a riverbed. Eventually, creating a pulsing, fiery dome, emanating intense light and air, finally establishing itself as a large burning bubble. Within it the accountant heaved in a lung full of impossible air into her starved chest. Neither was she scorched by the fire burning intensely all around. She was dry, not wet, or hypothermic, standing upright with lamp in tow. A mighty presence, mythic, defiantly ancient, otherworldly even, saturated her being. Peering upward, it was then she noticed an immense towering figure staring back. Primeval in nature, Arabic in some fashion to her mind, with gold bangles as jewelry around its neck and wrists. Dark flowing jet black hair tied deftly in a tight ponytail, hiding elven ears within. Powerful muscles, held up its enormous frame, which itself tailed off into a smokey nothingness.

Although startled initially, the Black woman CPA soon regained composure, beckoning the creature to her, indicating as best as she could she meant no harm. It did so, and a wordless conversation began their meeting. Communication with complete comprehension was something new to the accountant she had never experienced before, telepathy fused with empathy. A deep feeling conveyed that wants were known, and needs would soon be fulfilled. Something the rest of humanity could only dream of with its pronounced inability to deeply connect irrespective of human difference, let alone smokey entities beneath the waves. This is how she knew it to be Jinn. Mythic creatures, with the power to grant wishes, which humans classed as Genies in centuries past. It now wordlessly conveyed its tale of woe. It was Eldritch Jinn, those of Flameless Smoke, who for eons existed before humanity. He (for it was a he), was "التائب" or the penitent one.

But a quick sidebar is required to explain more. They are in reality "doemans" or "minor domainisz," a lesser sub species of Daemon. Created as a prototype of mankind eons ago by Elder gods. Unfortunately, many races of Jinn were found to be disobedient and sometimes cruel (an irony to be sure where Daemons are concerned), others carnivorous and power hungry. So much so they may one day be a threat to their master's unchallenged power. Although chances of this happening were infinitesimal, a threat is still a threat, and the Elder Gods don't play well with others. It was judged that the Jinn were sin itself, the most sinister of which were expelled to the great "Empty of the Damned," a small foul pocket dimension of unspeakable horrors, cursed with eternal atonement for something that was never done. The rest were cast out from the Daemon pantheon down to the earthly realm. Doomed never to return to the Galactic Temple, which is in fact another and far nicer sub universe of 18 dimensions. All Daemons exist here in some way or form. Cursed were fallen Earthly Jinn to obey the bidding of mortals, and when no mortal can be found, instead be automatically trapped in an assortment of small uncomfortable vessels, until released by the next unsuspecting human. Eternal subjugation and slavery were their fate. Of course it had fallen to the Grandmaster to do the deed, and it was he who forced Jinn to suffer this ignominious fate, bound into bottles, mugs, ceramic plates and even rust clad kettles, obliged to do the bidding of any human who comes across them.

The Jinn communicated this in silence, to the Black woman accountant. Telling a tale of how he was also Marid Jinn (Giant Jinn), able to grant wishes but now limited to three, by design of the Grandmaster, unable to access his own powers to resist their Daemon subjugators for the betterment of his people. Worse to grant a wish is to use up his very life essence. On top of all this, due to the deliverer of lies, obtaining wishes also comes at a cost to humans too. Upon release Jinn are compelled to give wishes, usually not telling of the price to follow, usually racialized in nature as per the way of the Grandmaster. Which brings us back to the odd scene, deep below the East River, below the Brooklyn bridge on the bottom of the riverbed. Where a mortal and a Jinn were laughing ....

First Wish

The Black woman CPA began to laugh at the absurdity of her predicament only to find the Jinn accompanying her. After all, he had not laughed in nearly a thousand years and thought he had better take advantage of the opportunity before it left for another millennia. Through noiseless giggles the Jinn communicated telepathically that she had three wishes that he would make come true. Anything was possible. Bemused, she wondered what to do. Then like a Thunderbolt it hit her! In her mind she roared "let's bring about the end of racism for Black people in Accounting." She thought she had hit the proverbial nail on the head until he informed her that in this instance that wish had already been taken, and a caveat of wishing granting was that wishes were forbidden to be repeated. In fact, true to form, it was his master, Daemon Enki Abyd, a far more powerful being than he, who had eradicated Anti-Black racism in Accounting a few years hence, this time at the behest of a Black male accountant in similar dire straits as she. But alas, it failed, and racism simply reappeared in another shape. Greater originality in wishing making was called for, but what exactly?

Then she recalled what took her to Brooklyn Bridge in the first place. Suffering carried her all the way to that iron precipice, caused by being a Black woman in Accounting. She had simply just wanted to be, but the profession would not tolerate it. Now she knew what she must wish for. Never again will another Black woman experience professional dismissal or feel her loss of self-worth in the field of Accounting. The first wish asked of the Jinn was to stop racism against Black women. Instead, now to be viewed as exemplary professionals she knew them to be, not eternal pariahs within Accounting space.

Underneath the East River a smokeless fire violently swirled once more, violet, then red with sparks of booming mauve. Traveling, in all directions at once, and then nothing. It was done. Speechlessly, the Jinn beseeched her to come nearer to observe the future effects of her wish. Intrigued, she obeyed, watching how with a small stick, he drew a large circle in the sand bed. Then abruptly expanding to three times his magnitude and with a sizeable inhale he sucked in the remaining glowing, flashing fire which had been all about them a moment ago. Holding it in his chest for a second or two, his eye bulging with effort, he eventually exhaled a cool smoke ring of "future sight." Steadily it floated, settling gently onto the sandy oval. As it landed intense heat flared up from the sand burning it into the clearest glass, creating a "scree pool" where both perceived what the future was to be.

And what happened next? Racism, sexism and any other intersecting facet of difference used against those considered Black women accountants in the United States instantly faded. Overnight, somewhat ironically, Black femininity, replaced Asian women as the model minority of the profession.[7] Racial advantage, a "rAce trump card" if you will, temporarily loaned to Asian femininity from Whiteness, transferred to Black women (Elise, 2004; Lewis, 2020). It was then that the Jinn told the tale of how the Grandmaster centuries ago gave all whites a rAce trump card, giving advantage in the game of life. To possess this is to have an egregious head start in all things over groups of Color who do not have it. However occasionally, the card is partially loaned out to favored racialized groups high in the racial hierarchy for further white advantage. To favor one racial group over another is a tried and tested strategy to sow discord and disunity among People of Color making racial coalition all but impossible. It gives the model minority, temporary but valuable access to more of life's benefits, but not to the same extent as whites, and it can always be removed at any time. Additionally, also gaining what critical legal scholar Derrick Bell called the "5th rule of superstanding," where those who align with white viewpoints on racial issues are taken more seriously and are paid more attention to, thus increasing their status in the eyes of whites and themselves.[8] The Jinn gave this card to Black women accountants with interesting results.

[7]It is the myth that Asian Americans are homogenous in their ability to excel academically, They are rewarded are simply hard-working immigrants who are rewarded through hard work. But are not leadership material, nor can they excel at sports.
[8]Bell (1992) attributed the rules of superstanding firstly to Blacks.

The first hurdle to fall was that of racial "Mental Gymnastics," a feat all Black women professionals must perform in an attempt to be accepted as authentic in the workplace (Gyimah et al., 2022). Black women no longer needed to fear braided or dreadlocked hair looking unprofessional. Instead, it was seen as unremarkable. Afro hair now remained untouched by white hands, something unheard of for Black women in dominant majority white spaces. Next, the sentiment surrounding Black woman professionalism inverted. In this future they were on par with white middle-class men in Accounting, competing equally for quality work and partnership positions. Prized career enhancing work flowed to Black women who took full advantage of this boon. Such jobs were no longer just for white boys in the office, and Black women were no longer a "round peg in a square professional hole" (Lewis & Allen, 2016). The next image in the oval filled the heart of the Black woman accountant with joy. It was a future Washington Post article citing the astonishing diminishment of mental health ailments for Black women accountants. It had basically reduced to zero, while metrics of happiness and progression at work for Black women CPAs went through the roof. Battle fatigue and work-based stress so often indicative of the Black woman professional experience (Rollock, 2019) now seemed a thing of the past.

Interestingly, as Black women accountants acquired the mantle of model minority, they soon found themselves fetishized, unwantedly, as an "acceptable" form of Jezebel. Her insatiable desire for sex, in the white male imaginary drove white male professionals both inside and outside of the industry wild. Making Black women accountants a curious mix, dangerous, wild, brilliant, and efficacious, akin to a professional version of the "fighting fuck toy trope," Hollywood's oft beloved stereotypical depiction of on screen women heroines as hyper-able and hyper sexualized (Corso, 2022). Still a Sapphire in essence, but with her negative characteristics now seen as deeply sensual and alluring in the addled white male mind. Deemed extremely desirable, Black women accountants became hot marital material, with white men coveting Black feminine favor, with the ultimate goal being marriage or long-term relationships. Perhaps the only "fly in the ointment" is the model minority hangover of an adherence to the 5th rule of superstanding cited earlier. Black women in Accounting, oddly, now supported white constructions of racial reality. A troubling turnaround indeed. Doubling down on negative tropes of Black masculinity, and unsuitability in certain circumstances. This state of affairs caused schisms with the vast majority of Black women in every other profession who have supported Black men since time immemorial and continue to do so today. Black women CPAs were becoming a breed apart for good and ill.

Despite this our Black woman accountant wrung her hands with glee. Finally, a feat never seen before in this country, the full recognition and acceptance of the worth of Black femininity. But the Jinn beckons her to look deeper still as, typically, racial physics had yet to play its role. Here, race and space are connected, as Black women ascend the racial hierarchy another group must take their subordinated place. And it was the fate of Asian femininity to take that role. Additionally, Black femininity came into serious competition with white women, who saw a threat to their position. Both professionally, and personally. More and more white men were marrying their fantasy of the incredibly confident, powerful, deeply fetishized Black woman accountant. But the power these Black women now possessed meant they couldn't be challenged by white femininity directly. As an alternative, Black women in the profession were befriended by powerful white women cliques as sisters under the guise of fellow "equally" gender-oppressed kin until weakness could be found and exploited. And find them they did. Sadly, for Asian women as the new undesirables in racialized Accounting space, they felt the full blast of unveiled animosity that is white female power unchallenged. White femininity punched down. Quickly finding ways to demote, harass, mock and demean Asian women, making all but the hardiest wary of the profession.

However, as subjugation rose groups of brilliant, brave, and resilient Asian women accountants arose as well. The scree pool showed this too, fighting for their rights not to be exploited. Dealing with everyday microaggressions and gendered harm. Fighting against deeply entrenched historic tropes of being meek, therefore unbefitting of leadership roles. As usual though, as happened with our Black woman CPA, telling truth to power comes at a cost, earning Asian women accountants the caustic nickname of "Firebricks." Asian women who could withstand any racialized "heat" in the workplace, and remain intact, durable in a way that was painted inhuman and unfeeling. They were the ones who could not experience pain or pleasure as humanity understands it. Mere animals perhaps, that no longer feel suffering as rest of humanity or conversely human-looking automatons, cold and calculating. Either way this was how Asian femininity gained its own specialized Sapphire trope, just as damaging as the last attached to Black women, through no fault of their own. It was Stuart Hall's floating racial signifier that with a single wish attached itself as a raced and gendered parasite to the eternal harm of Asian women CPAs.

The Black woman accountant pulled back from the pool and understood. In this game of racialized corporate life, no woman of color could win without another suffering, breeding an animosity continually pitting POC sister against sister. The procedure of divide and conquer, well-practiced, sees that despite any rAce card, no woman of Color can truly ever win. This wish was a curse. The Jinn asked her should this wish be made permanent? She declined. She would not see this affliction passed to her Asian sisters or any other.

Second Wish

Assorted fish and seldom-seen riverbed dwellers respectively swam, crawled, and bumbled cautiously toward the giant glowing air pocket. As if inexplicably drawn to it. Truly, what did they think of such a sight? Deep down in the depths of the East River, an ancient spirit beckoned the mortal woman forward once more, for she was required to make the second of her three wishes. The CPA was a little more collected now, shrewd even given the circumstance. A switch of tactic was required instead, where she would don her professional Accounting armor, a façade showing indomitable steely professionalism, an identity worked by Black professional women to buttress against raced and gendered tropes of incompetence or "Sapphire," which may harm career advancement. In the same manner she had to fortify herself against outward displays of feelings where this wishing business was concerned, quashing any passion, sorrow, or feelings which the Jinn might detect souring her next wish. She must reinforce her mind against strong emotion, enabling her to envisage something better. This was her downfall last time and so dispassion would be her watchword for the next. After all, being logical, cool, and calculated is a core trait of her profession, one she must employ currently. The last attempt was far too specific, heated, and easily manipulated toward harmful ends. This time she would frame her wish tightly, positively, in a manner where negative manipulation would be obfuscated. She moved toward the Jinn, meeting him eye to eye for what seemed the longest time. He sensed a difference in her poise, astuteness, missing just moments ago appeared. The mystic entity nodded with acceptance. Once again, he increased to titanic proportions, smokeless fire swirled all around, engulfing the woman, but not burning her, flashes and crackles of static electricity zoomed forth. Raging, the fire switched hue, red, charred amber, then radiant vermillion, and finally, that regal ancient lost pigment Tyrian Purple, the like of which people had not seen for a thousand years. So, I hear you ask, what did she wish for this time?

As before, both the Jinn and the accountant approached the scree pool once again, that mortal portal in which present and future events caused by her wishes could be perceived. This second wish was a simple ask for a change. But one that caused true, radical, meaningful change for the better for all in Accounting to happen. The idea being of course that a rising tide raises all ships. Life chances for all increase where the dominant majority and the subjugated benefit in equal measure. Deflating back to a more realistic 7 feet tall, the Jinn whispered a mixture of Enochian[9] and Aramaic incantations under its breath. The invocation initiated the grand "I" of Accounting (IoA), tenets for a better profession for all to be made real. This ideological bedrock now existed as pragmatic guidelines which Accounting held as its underlying theme, to be used in all circumstances and activities where possible. The IoA is in a sense a new conceptual framework for Accounting, rather than Federal Accounting Standards Board (FASB) led or International Accounting Standards Board (IASB) pronounced rules. An inherent playbook for better times.

And better times were sorely needed. The Jinn in images and telepathy, narrated facts and figures to the Black woman accountant as they peered once again into the ocean of future possibilities that is a scree pool. What she observed did not surprise her in the least as one particular future news article caught her eye:

Most pressing is the global shortage of accountants, felt most acutely in the United States. The overall number of Accounting graduates decreased through the 2019–2020 academic year, with a fall of 2.8% for bachelor's and 8.4% for master's degrees. Disturbingly, these declines in enrollment connected to the steep declines in candidates taking the CPA exam, where numbers declined from 48,004 first-time candidates in 2016 to 32,188 in 2021, a precipitous drop of 33%. Additionally, 2022

[9]A language supposedly used to commune with Angles, recorded in the 16th-century journals of John Dee and Edward Kelley.

saw the lowest number of exam takers since 2006. Compounding the problem, in 2021 30% less candidates passed the final section of the CPA exam in relation to students at the same level in 2016. To conclude, 75% of AICPA members have currently reached retirement age. This all is the resultant tumultuous effect of a leaky Accounting pipeline, where demand is subdued at entry level, and at the other end a sieve like supply, as Senior accountants retire out (Burke & Polimeni, 2023).

The profession has effectually boxed itself in. On the one hand it shackled itself to a non-sensical 150-hour requirement that adds extra costly tuition, which turns off the average student and represents an almost insurmountable wall to already impoverished Black, Brown, and poor white students. This dwindles the pipeline further, sending the message to potential Accounting students of color that they are not needed nor welcome, even though the field claims the opposite (Sutherland et al., 2023). Worse, on the other hand, should such students find a way to battle through, and enter the profession, they are greeted with lesser pay than equivalent credentialed industries like Finance or the Technology sector. This profession is seen by the laity as plain, dull, and images still pervade of the bespeckled "Bean counter," boring and precise, devoid of flair and living a life without meaning. Lines of work and life fulfillment are not identified to these potential accountants, and so they (Generation Z) opt for another path, much to the cost of the Accounting field.

At this juncture the Jin intervened in proceedings directly stating without a word leaving his lips:

> Be aware of this remembrance. Accounting as a concept originally arose from the imagination of people, in tandem with that of Mathematics and other classics, constituent of what is considered Civilization. For in the 2nd millennium, in the fabled city of fair Babylon, I was tasked, as muse to tradesmen, to inspire superior record keeping in transactional dealings in goods and services. It was here that I sowed the kernel of an idea into the mind of a little known but fated academic, Ahmad Arif Saba. It was he who was the driving force behind those of that period who claim to have devised Double Entry Booking keeping. This being some three thousand seven hundred years before the supposed western originator Friar Luca Pacioli penned his own version of the ubiquitous debit and credit exercise. The creation of this key concept was a leap of faith away from what was, to dream of what could be. As you can see this is needed now. And your Yale Academic, Shyam Sunder calls this out!
>
> "For accounting to advance as a discipline … we must allow ourselves to imagine the future alternative worlds of accounting."[10]

[10]P11 (Sunder, 2011).

The scree pool moved time forward showing that at first the problems of the Accounting industry just mentioned, seemed to many insurmountable. But the Jinn's charm of the I of Accounting began to take hold as a roadmap to better times. Leaving the fuzzy question of exactly how it happened? The Jinn moved away from the pool as the Black woman CPA wordlessly blurted out "I've done it!" After which she muzzily accepted, she had no idea how. The Jinn met her gaze in a rigid fashion, his countenance conveying the message "I will show you." Unexpectedly, from his eye erupted a flame of mauve shooting above her head and then extinguishing just as quickly, leaving a halo of smoke behind. Rapidly the smoke formed into a definition of the I of the IoA that read:

> Imagination – the faculty or action of forming new ideas, or images or concepts of external objects, not present to the senses.

The CPA gawked at the fumes arranging themselves into letters and then words floating above her. Its smokey voice in her mind possessed a lilt like quality, lulling her into a mesmeric state of sorts, where her mind wondered, floated, and dreamed of what could be. This was in fact the enacting of the first of the "I's." She thought of the pressing shortage of accountants at this very moment in her world currently. Her thoughts drifted dreamily out, coaxing her to think of her nephew, Richard. Was he talented? Was he bright? Yes, on both counts. Was he academic? Not at all. He had struggled through his education every step of the way, a source of concern to his ambitious mother, Janice, a Black MD employed at Johns Hopkins Hospital. Being the medical expert she was it wasn't too long before he was diagnosed with Autism and Tourette's Syndrome, with a side order of depression accompanying it. No doubt fostered by years of academic struggle without help. Unfortunately, even with a mother who was a highly trained medical professional, his neurological disability went unobserved for the longest time. By adulthood, the damage had been done, his self-confidence lay in tatters. At this moment Richard worked as a barista at his local Starbucks. It was good for him in a way, as he excelled at dealing with multiple orders, going into a world of his own most times. Managing difficult patrons had been a struggle for him, often finding himself shutting down as irate customers' anger at incorrect orders grew. But the managers of Starbucks implemented a system of referral, where a neurotypical colleague could swap tricky situations or tasks with willing neurodiverse workers should neurodiverse colleagues feel overwhelmed. She mused it was a system that would do well in Accounting and she wondered which enterprising out of the box manager dreamed that solution up.

But it was not the future he, nor his mother, had envisioned. Her mind drifted still further, settling upon a Thanksgiving meal, some years back. It was over the kitchen table of her sister's house where Richard and she were in deep conversation about his potential and that his skills with the right institutional support could help him thrive in Accounting. He of course rejected the notion as ridiculous, asserting he of all people could never pass the CPA exam in a thousand years. On top of that it is as dull as it gets and poorly paid. Why should he, or anybody else go through that hell? But she saw his potential, finding herself citing a radio show from a while back to refute him. It featured an academic called Anton who preached for greater neurodiversity in Accounting (Lewis, 2024), making strong points for the need for young People of Color like Richard to join. Anton at one point severely chided the industry for not doing more, saying it was a failure of Accounting's imagination not to see this as a part solution to severe pipeline issues afflicting the profession. But it was to no avail as Richard dismissed it all outright.

She had argued with nearly everybody at the dinner table about it. She agreed with the professor that Accounting right now is incapable of dreaming of what can be, of new concepts and ideas to resolve its crisis of dwindling numbers and is suffering for it. Accounting can do more and is desperate for candidates to enter its halls, ones who not only think out of the box, but take it, set it alight, and throw it out of the window! The neurodiverse, particularly those who are BIPOC, have the ability to be an engine of unexpected new thinking, and new ways of being with which to disrupt the status quo. But of course, that was the issue. Do gatekeepers in Accounting really want to upset the applecart? Or is it better to surreptitiously leave the ableist/racist/gendered cart in place, one which keeps powerful whites in Accounting at the center of power? Will the white elite concede space at the top for the Other? Arc they capable?

But as her mind returned from its dream state back to the present, it was the Jinn who connected the dots. For it was he who simply, but powerfully stated that imagination leads to **Inspiration**, an essential way to foster mental stimulation, to create something new, something needed. Sadly, the Jinn communicated its current lack across the field as particularly troublesome where race and racism policy, and DEI as a whole is concerned. The Jinn next implied inspiration begats **Ingenuity**, that aspect of cleverness, fueling the spark of originality, and inventiveness. Giving one space and time to slay shibboleths of old ways of thinking and doing, which for far too long have frozen the accountant into the anachronistic visage of a dull, bespeckled, white, male bean counter. But difference must have its day stated the swirling smoke in her mind once again, leaving room for the newfangled, thought-provoking, a stranger Accounting, that is unalike that which has come before, possessing darker kinds of beans to count. Finally, the last word of **Inventiveness**, that quality of ingenuity and creativity came into being, forming a perfect smoldering word circle with the other words hanging in the air. Together they were the three I's of Accounting which the Jinn had enchanted the future with, tools the profession could use to foster the equity and fairness it states it so keenly seeks. Hovering in the air interlinked, the Black woman CPA saw one cannot exist without the other.

In his speechless voice the Jinn signaled that this was the great circle of Imagination for Accounting. It is where it begins to actually learn from its mistakes in the DEI realm noting the folly of non-performativity and color evasiveness. It is this leap of imagination that enables empathy, which leads to the connection sought by all. This connection to those deemed minority and those classed majority results in a true chance to change race and racism, at the intersection of other inequities for the better.

Final Wish

The Black woman beneath the East River saw all too well. And faced now with her last wish it all seemed so simple. As usual the most complicated things usually are. She saw it is really about hope. Already she had set her profession's path in the right direction, and it was on its way toward a better future. All she needed to do was do it again. The Jinn peered at her once more for the final time, gesturing her forward for a concluding wish. Meeting his gaze, she stated without a voice:

> I wish for hope to return to Accounting, so that we can begin again, to believe that racial subjugation can be tamed, an ill, which has bedeviled our profession since its inception for far too long.

The creature, deep in the bowels of the river grew enormous one last time, to a point which may pop the life-giving bubble itself. Would he burst allowing the river to gush forth and consume her? In this state no flame ushered forth, it was the Jinn itself, its skin which swooshed, mysterious colors seldom seen in this world or the next, his skin becoming fire swirling and consuming perhaps himself! Then it was done. Reducing to familiar form he looked exhausted. What was to come now the Black women accountant wondered? Had the world changed in fantastic ways like her previous wish? And curiously why did the Jinn not ask her over to the scree pool to see future events?

"I must make my leave of you my lady."

It was the first time in 5,000 years that he had spoken out loud. It felt damn good. For his mystic voice is captivating to mortals, all treacle and honeysuckle. No wonder the Elder Gods grew fearful of him and his kind. Jin could sway you into anything if you weren't careful. Danger lurked within their siren persuasion contained in their vocal cadence.

> "I am free and can speak. I am free and must leave."

Why, said the Black accountant? But curiously, no words came from her mouth. She wasn't using reciprocal telepathy now. She tried to rouse her vocal cords into use but to no avail. The Jinn transformed further, now distilled into the form of a muscular Black man, and the bubble was shrinking. And so was the Black woman accountant ... now the "New Jinn of the bottle." Her form grew smaller and shrank toward the swirling magnificent bluish, mauve, color-churning lamp. But what is this? Why is this? She cried with no words, screamed voicelessly. The once – was – Jinn knew, understandably appreciating her plight, but callously stating in a tone sweeter than sugarcane:

> This is the cost of your final wish that I warned you of. All wishes come at a price, but for good or ill humans never seem to understand this.

Her eyes pleaded, her mouth motioned in familiar ways, but silence was her only friend. The roles inverted and it was the once – was – Jinn who communicated in words what she could not, growing more pleased with every audible syllable uttered.

> You believe I have reneged on your final wish of hope but this is not so. Your destiny was always to replace me should you get to your final wish. As such is the Grandmasters design. But Hope now has returned to the world through your action, your wish was honored. Admittedly, she has been away awhile, abducted by the one who plans racial traps, but I was bade here, freeing her from her chains, hence once more she goes into the world at your request. She is a fragile thing that is most resilient in the best and worst ways. She is here now in the Accounting profession, stirring ferment, challenging things in the way your first wish attempted but was doomed to fail. She is however the true engine behind the second, currently fueling creativity and dreaming. She was trapped by the Grandmaster for eons, he who is foe to Jinn. But she is Hope and Hope never dies. With it she bade you here, one who was going to sacrifice her life to the River. Now you sacrifice your life to the lamp. You really shouldn't have too many complaints. Therefore, sacrifice is your genuine gift, and your way to me that allowed all of this to happen. It is her way of getting people to find one another that is her greatest power. The ability for those who are different to treat one another as equals. An eternal truth Old Nick, and his scion the Grandmaster has long sought to hide from humanity. You are siblings to one another, possessed of love, support, faith, and wonder for all. "You are we." This is what Hope is now doing, she is connecting, reaching, touching the mind and the souls of all. Soon empathy will be everywhere, and the real work of creating a true meritocracy in the profession will begin anew, with a chance of succeeding this time.

The new Jinn-of-the-bottle shrieked in terror, as finally her form was sucked into this most disconcerting ancient carafe. Sadly, it would be another ten thousand years before she saw the light of day again. Perhaps somewhat ironic for a Black woman Accounting professional who had sought to end her life because of the institutionally raced and gendered apathy of a profession. One she had single handedly put on a path to real diversity, equity, and inclusion. Making belonging a watchword to guide its rosy future. A profession soon to be guided by Hope herself who will employ peerless imagination that will alter Accounting in ways nobody thought possible, right here and now. Change is afoot in ways seldom dreamt of.

And what of the once – was – Jinn? He returned to report in detail the events of that night. The instant he disappeared back to the Elder realm the East River finally crashed into the pocket previously sustaining this curious duo, at the bottom of the riverbed. Nothing remained, no tale could be told of this night by any person on Earth. Familiar darkness once again covered the multicolored swirling lamp, hidden in the depths for what would seem like eternity for the person inside. In truth the task of the once – was – Jinn had been one of the hardest and most perilous, which the daemon Enki Abyd had commanded of his most trusted lieutenant. An eon in the making, daring in the extreme. This plan had to be breathtakingly simple to stand a chance. To get a human, to wish Hope into freedom (she being the Grandmasters only weakness) and away from his grasp. For it takes more than most have to outwit the Grandmaster and his father Beelzebub at their own game. It takes the guile and slyness of a Trickster God.

References

Acuff, J. (2018). Confronting racial battle fatigue and comforting my blackness as an educator. *Multicultural Perspectives*, *20*(3), 174–181.

Anderson-Gough, F., Edgley, C., Robson, K., & Sharma, N. (2024). Diversity and the evaluation of talent in the accounting profession: The enigma of merit. *Accounting Horizons*, *38*(1), 27–37.

Austin, R. (2003). Sapphire bound! In A. K. Wing (Ed.), *Critical race feminism* (2nd ed., pp. 301–308). New York University Press.

Bell, D. (1992). *Faces at the bottom of the well: The permanence of racism*. Basic Books.

Bisset, V. (2024). *Claudine Gay says critics attacked her in 'war' against trusted institutions*. https://www.washingtonpost.com/education/2024/01/04/claudine-gay-harvard-op-ed/

Burke, J. A., & Polimeni, R. S. (2023). The accounting profession is in crisis. *The CPA Journal*, *XCIII*(9/10), 6–8. https://www.cpajournal.com/2023/12/01/the-accounting-profession-is-in-crisis/

Colson, C., McWilliams, D., Oliver, D., Sharma, D., & Witherspoon, C. (2024). The ledger does not balance for all: Experiences of underrepresented individuals in accounting academia. *Issues in Accounting Education*, *39*(3), 7–30.

Corso, E. (2022). The strong female character and the fighting fuck toy: A comparative analysis of Katniss and Glimmer in The Hunger Games. *Binghamton University Undergraduate Journal*, *8*(1), 1–16.

Davis, A. M., & Ernst, R. (2017). Racial gaslighting. *Politics, Groups, and Identities*, *7*(1), 1–14.

Doharty, N., & Esoe, M. (2023). Demonstrable experience of being a Mammy or Crazy Black Bitch'(essential). A critical race feminist approach to understanding Black women headteachers' experiences in English schools. *Race Ethnicity and Education*, *26*(3), 318–334.

Donahue, K., Gilbert, T., Halpert, M., & Migas, P. (2021). *The infuriating journey from pet to threat: How bias undermines Black women at work*. https://www.forbes.com/sites/forbeseq/2021/06/29/the-infuriating-journey-from-pet-to-threat-how-bias-undermines-black-women-at-work/?sh=253e3b296490

Elise, S. (2004). How whites play their rAce card: DRYLONGSO stories reveal "The Game". *Sociological Perspectives*, *47*(4), 409–438.

Gyimah, M., Azad, Z., Begum, S., Kapoot, A., Ville, L., Henderson, A., & Dey, M. (2022). *Broken ladders: The myth of meritocracy for women of colour in the workplace*. Runnymede Trust, Fawcett Society.

Harley, D. A. (2008). Maids of academe: African American women faculty at predominately white institutions. *Journal of African American Studies*, *12*, 19–36.

Kretsedemas, P. (2010). "But She's Not Black!" Viewer interpretations of "Angry Black Women" on Prime Time TV. *Journal of African American Studies*, *14*, 149–170.

Lewis, A. (2012). *A critical analysis of the Black accounting experience in the U.K. Tales of success and failure in the British professional workplace*. Lambert Academic Publishing.

Lewis, A. (2020). *Counting Black and white beans. Critical race theory in accounting*. Emerald Publishing Limited.

Lewis, A. (2023). Keeping our promise. *The CPA Journal*, *November-December*, 1–80. https://www.cpajournal.com/2024/02/07/keeping-our-promise/

Lewis, A. (2024). The divergent accountant. *The CPA Journal*, *January-February*, 72–75. https://www.cpajournal.com/2024/04/22/the-divergent-accountant/

Lewis, A., & Allen, T. (2016). Looking through a glass darkly: Reflections on power, leadership and the Black female professional. *The Journal of Values Based Leadership*, *9*(2), 1–16.

Raddatz, N., Raddatz, P., Sorensen, K., & Ogunade, K. (2024). The adverse effects of the "Anticipation of Racial Discrimination" on auditors who are Black, Indigenous, or People of Color (BIPOC): An exploratory study with research propositions. *Accounting Horizons*, *38*(1), 139–147.

Rivera, G.-I. (2024). *Dr. Antoinette Candia-Bailey's tragic end reminds me how much empathetic leadership can literally be a matter of life or death for Black women*. https://www.essence.com/op-ed/opinion-dr-antoinette-candia-bailey-death-empathetic-leadership/

Rollock, N. (2019). *Staying power. The career experiences and strategies of UK Black female professors*. Project Report. University and College Union, London. https://www.ucu.org.uk/media/10075/Staying-Power/pdf/UCU_Rollock_February_2019.pdf

Sue, D. W. (2010). *Microaggressions in everyday life: Race, gender and sexual orientation*. John Wiley & Sons.

Sunder, S. (2011). Imagined worlds of accounting. *Accounting Economics and Law*, *1*(1), 1–12.

Sutherland, A., Uckert, M., & Vetter, F. (2023). Occupational licensing and minority participation in professional labor markets. *Journal of Accounting Research*, *62*(2), 453–503.

Upton, D. R., & Arrington, E. (2012). Implicit racial prejudice against African Americans in balanced scorecard performance evaluations. *Critical Perspectives on Accounting*, *23*, 281–297.

Wing, A. K. (2003). Introduction. In A. K. Wing (Ed.), *Critical race feminism. A reader* (2nd ed., pp. 1–19). New York University Press.

Conclusion

I am, therefore, I imagine.

The quotation above which closes this book is a riff on René Descartes' famous line, "I think therefore, I am," where through the act of thinking, a person realizes their own being. But where do they exist? What is the environment that they exist within? Without slipping down a philosophical hole, this book has sought to show that the practice of race and racism in professions such as Accounting and the wider business world is this place. Racism confounds and alters reality for People of Color, pressing the racialized to question what and how they think in the workplace, challenging their right to exist in that space. Reshaping Descartes' quote again, "I do not trust what I think, therefore I am not," a professional erasure if you like. Relentlessly challenging the authenticity and right to exist in places they work. So, what is to be done?

An acceptance of racial reality is the starting point but it is difficult for some. Our journey together through each fable was a call to reveal the extent of racial harm befalling Black professionals, and others of Color in a myriad of fantastical settings, depicting issues in a way to foster comprehension of their plight. Much scholarship, as stated at the beginning of this book, points toward a parlous state of affairs for the raced accountant especially if they are Black. It's a life saturated with mental health hazards, as explored in the 8th Fable "Jinn and Tonic," which opens with the attempted suicide of a Black woman accountant. Fanciful thinking? Perhaps, but as the tale illustrates, the presence of Black women in Accountancy has, for many, been one of implicit (and explicit) maltreatment in one way or another (Fearfull & Kamenou, 2006; Robinson-Backmon & Weisenfeld, 2002). Finding themselves caught in shifting cultural eddies to their detriment, women of color might very well find themselves pressured to extreme acts. The 6th Fable of "The Great White Hope" studies what might take place when the world is made aware of Black plight in a fashion I have just described. Will this momentous action begin to move the needle of raced suffering as powerful white men step up to help and change the situation? The narrative suggests not, looking at what it means when even they cannot shift racial sentiment so deeply entrenched in the Accounting profession and society as a whole. While some suggest this view to be too gloomy, Frank B Wilderson's formulation of "Afropessimism" charges that ever thus was this the case. That Blackness endures as an anathema to civilized society and cannot be tolerated as such (Wilderson, 2020), and to think

Accounting Fables: Tales of Race and Racism in the Borderlands of Business, 151–156

Published under exclusive licence by Emerald Publishing Limited
doi:10.1108/978-1-80117-069-720251026

elsewise is wishful thinking. A state of affairs I have alluded to as being severe in Accounting in previous work (Lewis, 2015).

Yet, let us not forget that the stories described in some instances show racial optimism. An observational dare to readers to join in the reimagining of Accounting and business locales as accepting and allied to the ways of being of the Other. To envisage a setting where institutional racism is absent. A world where professionals of color do not replay workday events in their mind, when at home, scanning for veiled racism. A place where mental resources are actually employed to unwind and relax from the day rather than catalog potential microaggressions. It is a call for a home in which Descartes promulgation rings true for the racially stigmatized and Others running the gamut of differing inequities too. Critical Race Theory counterstories presented in this book simply ask the racialized being that is the professional, what can be dreamed that is better? Because one way or another I worry the opposite is true, we have in fact run out of imagination to do this, and stamina to stay in the fight where racial fair play is concerned.

These imagined worlds ask us how we might do better in our own. For me it seems that we are doomed to live the faux Chinese curse *may you live in interesting times,* the origin of which is about as elusive as finding a meaningful solution to propagate Black progress. Making those of us committed to anti-racism and social justice in the Accounting profession and beyond wonder at this present moment what have we done to deserve such severe interest (Martin, 2024)! Interestingly, this phrase is of Western, not Chinese origin, and was amended from "interesting age" to "interesting times." The phase was made more famous through its utterance by Robert Kennedy in a speech in Cape Town in June 1966, adding that tumultuous times are also a period of opportunity for the inventive imagination of people to flourish to meet and beat such times. A call is made for the world to take notice, that it needs that quality of youth which is:

> [...] a state of mind, a temper of the will, that is a quality of imagination, a predominance of courage over timidity. (Kennedy, 1966)

It is a call that I echo for Accounting as a profession. For it to meet the challenge of race and racism with inspiration and bravery. For me, given the current supply side shortages of new accountants entering the field, and Generations Z's commitment to working in diverse accepting environments, President John F. Kennedy's words look prophetic as ever. And perhaps in this lies a solution. The ability to get young accountants who can envision a unique way forward, demanding change which ignites the spark of inspiration required. Can we dream of something more than counting beans? However, to do so requires a change in outlook right now, a change in pedagogy right now and shaking of the status quo right now, if we are to enable real transformation as I and others have argued elsewhere (Alston et al., 2023). It is a recurrent theme one way or another I have broached throughout this text.

Accounting for Upheaval. The Shadow/Vorlon War … Build or Destroy?

Now, wait a minute, a change of tact is needed. Never mind my prattling, what do bright young things making their way at the start of their careers in Accounting academe and industry think about all this? They are the future after all. To be sure, what I say next is anecdotal, but still fascinating. Time and again, the phrase "it needs blowing up" occurs in my conversations with young scholars. They seem tired and frustrated with inaction, and I wonder if this is the eye of the oncoming storm. The last vestiges of millennials and surging numbers of Generation Z entering the workplace have no time for apathy, they wryly critique the status quo as not fit for purpose and certainly ill-suited to their needs. Blowing it all up from their perspective is the only imaginative and perhaps sensible option left.

Yet, for all my fire and brimstone when it comes to counseling the careers of young scholars, I have counseled silence. And yes, I have made hypocrisy a close confidant on this one! But here's the thing, I want them to stay quiet for now, waiting until the time is right to light the fuse … frankly I agree with them. For too long I have muted my own voice, in favor of majoritarian narratives suggesting Accounting does not do radical. Ever. I'm tired of waiting too. Aren't you? It's risky though, because inciting such a thing is to be doomed as an outcast and be laughed out of the academy or possibly industry with one's career in tatters. Try getting published in a top-rated journal with a title of blowing things up! Yet, this is the change that is necessary. One that is real. It is without irony, that I invoke Economist Joseph Schumpeter's classical idea of "Creative Destruction" as a euphemism for "Blowing it all up." His was the notion that new innovations replace older ones.

Typically I see the matter through a science fiction lens, and in doing so my mind turns to the classic 1990s US space opera, Babylon 5, set in the mid-23rd century. The series followed the fate of Babylon 5, a lone space station at the far reaches of space, humanity's last best chance for peace in a fractious, warring galaxy. Onboard alien races of all types engaged in diplomatic negotiations, seeking to avoid war and promote trade. As the story progressed, two powerful factions become apparent. The Shadows, one of the oldest, and most advanced races emerge as the champions of disorder and devastation. They believe chaos through destruction is the only true path to innovation and progress (shout to Schumpeter here), that the younger races must follow them or be annihilated. In opposition the Vorlons, another of the first races rise up to challenge them. Conversely, it is their conviction that order, compliance, and adherence to the established way of things, best promotes steady growth in opposition to the disordered growth of Chaos. For them it is the only genuine path to invention and evolution for the younger races that they must follow. Both have been at war for eons.

Boom Time!

For me, Babylon 9 is analogous to the conundrum we currently face in the profession when it comes to the question of race and Accounting, especially where Black accountancy is concerned. The frustration of youthful scholars and accountants dedicated to battling racism is my own as just mentioned. Simply because the old ways don't work. Numbers of Black and Brown colleagues haven't improved, and this is why creative destruction looks so attractive. The Shadows have a point! Let's sweep away the pieces of the chess board and start again. It might have merit as an idea but what does the "creative destruction" of Accounting look like? No surprise here, I propose that the first order of business is the removal of underlying stock stories of Accounting as a white male profession. Although tacitly denied by the industry, a quick peek at the majority of pale male Accounting partners who the make up the boardrooms in large firms says all that needs to be said. They would have to make way, irrespective of their power, because it's damn difficult to make people alter their behavior. And if this doesn't happen, I believe disruption will be stifled, extinguishing the creative destruction called for.

Alarming as it all sounds it is not. Disruption defines everyday life as seen with the car company Tessla. Some years ago, it entered the global car market as a disruptor, thinking about and doing things in a completely new way, and is now the vanguard of many electric vehicles omnipresent on our roads today. Innovative ideas of production, of the relationship of car to driver, rocked the automotive industry. Today most large car manufacturers possess a line of electric cars, forced to do so, where just a few years ago it was not the case, arguably benefiting the environment in the process.

In the context of US Accounting, an equivalent pedagogical disruption would be the dismissal of the 150 hour requirement for CPA licensure. It is a well-documented costly layer of the Accounting professionalization process, whose removal many call for, including myself. At best it is an anachronistic weed out mechanism in the guise of quality protection. At worse it is a barrier keeping Black and Brown students, poor whites and other POC from entering Accounting in substantial numbers.

Humor me for a moment. Imagine that it is those with top educational capital who have the best chance of winning at the game of Accounting. Think here for a minute, who exactly is best suited to succeed in the present system? It is white, upper middle class males, preferably those who have attended one of the Big Accounting schools. At these predominantly white institutions (PWIs), it is not unusual for them to be grandfathered into master's level Accounting courses once undergraduate study is completed. Traditionally during term time, on campus recruiters, seek to interview this pool of quality students for employment in the best firms. Completion of master's level study triggers a summer invitation to on campus fast track courses with CPA Exam pass rates nearing 95%. The upshot? Those who succeed in this process are admitted into coveted multinational Accounting firms, leapfrogging ahead of those not able to afforded similar opportunities. Possessing a prestigious undergraduate degree, master's qualification and CPA license, it is they who customarily make up the "chosen," who succeed in large Accounting organizations. As you might have guessed the numbers of Black and Brown students enjoying this ride is minimal. And therein lies the problem. It is an inherently unfair process. So "blowing it all up" sounds that much more attractive now, doesn't it? Disrupt educational exclusivity, allowing inclusivity to determine true talent, allowing a Blacker, Browner and poorer white candidates to compete in a fairer space. This is not fiction but the state of play as explained to me a few years ago by an Accounting professor at a PWI Big 10 Accounting program. This should concern us all.

Brick by Brick We Make It

But perhaps the Vorlon way is better. As an alternative, the Accounting powers that be could choose to build upon change. Seeking steady DEI improvement over time. What would this mean? As far back as 2004 celebrated scholar Theresa Hammond cited benchmarking progress in the Financial Services arena as key to developing greater Black representation over time to a Congressional hearing on the subject (Hammond, 2004). Establishing assessable criteria holds DEI policy to account, assisting progress. However true to form, in years subsequent to Congressional inquiry, little systematic benchmarking of racial metrics has taken place. Neither National Association of States Boards of Accountancy (NASBA) nor the American Institute of Certified Public Accountants (AICPA), as Accounting's regulatory bodies have taken issue with the lack of basic racialized numbers from multinational firms or mid-sized ones. Nor are they keen to release their own data on the matter either. It's like they are not really trying .... To me it's curious, because as I see it, annual mandating of systemic racial metrics as national policy, and then publicly reporting said data, makes all Accounting actors answerable for failures in policy. Growth is represented by firm policies that work, showing positive improvement in the number of Black and Brown accountants. It is to have open and frank discussions about the institutionally racist and gendered environment of both Accounting industry and academe and resist any and all calls to mute DEI for expedient political or business needs. It is to recognize that if the Vorlon concept is to be taken on then no quick fixes exist, data will be awful for a number of years, and yet remain bound to the task at hand irrespective of any set back. Nevertheless, that level of commitment takes money and effort with little immediate return, because change in this fashion is slow yet solid when it does finally arrive.

Both Worlds

As we conclude what it means to tell tales of Accounting, we cannot escape the inevitable inference that change in Accounting is crucial. Perhaps, the Shadows and Vorlons of Accounting can work together, blowing some things up that don't work and replacing them with nimble alternatives that do. Where possible, building firm policies which demonstrably increase representation, producing a better environment for the raced Other, and all who are stigmatized for a variety of reasons.

Lastly, Accounting Fables as I present them are intended to provoke discovery of "Worldscapes" of racial possibility of what can be, while illuminating what can't. They exist to "menace" what is considered irrefutable, unchangeable, and sacred in Accounting space. Tales to problematize the Accounting establishment, questioning its VERY existence. Is it fit for purpose? Can inaction, and adherence to "the way things are," save the DEI day? Has it ever? In my judgment the status quo means forever trying to get to Accounting's Shangri-La,[1] but always failing, never to arrive. Nonetheless, agitation remains the work of Critical Accounting scholars and industry activists who see the "Upside down of Accounting," as it is today, but wish to see it the right way up tomorrow. It's an invitation to make agitation everyday labor. As youth ever declares, bringing forth rebellion of thought, deed, and action is the only way. Certainly, important to a profession which, in my opinion, has no idea what this is. It continues to be an institutionally racist profession that cannot alter without fundamental action. This must be admitted to. Accounting leaders know racial Shangri-La is a myth, but a useful one though to pacify change, freezing the racialized traditional "way of things" in place. Simply put the profession MUST risk more if it wants more. These are the stakes at play if it wants to greet the bright inclusive future it claims. I implore it to do so because it risks much if it does not.

References

Alston, C., Rukasuwan, L., & Lewis, A. (2023). What can the profession do? Looking closely at each piece of the puzzle. *The CPA Journal* (September/October), 36. https://www.cpajournal.com/2023/12/04/what-can-the-profession-do/

Fearfull, A., & Kamenou, N. (2006). How do you account for it? A critical exploration of career opportunities for and experiences of ethinic minority women. *Critical Perspectives on Accounting*, *17*, 883–901.

Hammond, T. (2004). Testimony of Theresa A. Hammond. *Hearing on diversity in the financial services industry and access to capital for minority-owned businesses: Challenges and opportunities*. United States House of Representatives. https://archives-financialservices.house.gov/media/pdf/071504th.pdf

Kennedy, J. (1966). *'Freedom & democracy' University of Cape Town, Cape Town, South Africa*. Retrieved March 6, 2024, from https://www.jfklibrary.org/learn/about-jfk/the-kennedy-family/robert-f-kennedy/robert-f-kennedy-speeches/day-of-affirmation-address-university-of-capetown-capetown-south-africa-june-6-1966

Lewis, A. (2015). Frankenstein is Black. A tale of Black accountancy. International Journal of Linguistics, *Literature and Culture*, *2*(1), 1–21.

Martin, G. (2024, June 3). *What's the meaning of the phrase 'May you live in interesting times'?* https://www.phrases.org.uk/meanings/may-you-live-in-interesting-times.html

Robinson-Backmon, I. B., & Weisenfeld, L. W. (2002). An historical overview and comparison of women and African-Americans in the accounting profession: 1960s–1990s. *Accounting and the Public Interest*, *2*, 41–67.

Wilderson, F. (2020). *Afropessimism*. Liveright Publishing Corporation.

---

[1] I conceive Accounting Shangri-La as a harmonious racial Utopia for the profession, a final destination of true equity, implicitly implied by DEI policies doomed to fail.

Epilogue

I have something to say! It's better to burn out than to fade away!"[1]
The Kurgan

And now we return to the moment amid moments, that is the endless empty between one reality and another, home to Daemon kind. Once more, we find our central character Enki Abyd, sitting on the Rock of Pondering, next to the foggy sulfur Lake of Shame and Desolation, still pondering. Next to him lies the unwieldy "Fable Stone," the magical object that made so much of his victory possible. Tapping into its power allowed him to peer into new futures yet to be created by the vagaries of mortal decisions and imaginings. Exploiting its tremendous energy to move through time and space at will, setting a Jinn trap for an unhappy accountant, pushing unsuspecting academics to appear on peculiar radio shows, among a myriad of other machinations, all to keep The Grandmaster preoccupied, unaware of his true design. Disbelief was a feeling no Elder God ever admitted to, for it contravened the fact that they are the very essence of disbelief itself. At least from the mortal perspective anyway. Still, it was a bit embarrassing for Enki to admit to himself that on some level he disbelieved his own victory. Coming to terms with the fact he had finally beaten the Grandmaster at his own game would take time. Enki peered down at his palm, looking with pride at the newly emancipated Daemon Hope. She was tiny, fragile, beautiful, and most importantly free, her liberty obtained by the one holding her as she slept. He sighed; this is what victory feels like.

"Victory?"

A familiar bubble burp popped into existence from the surface of the now choppy sulfuric acid lake. A belch of indignation if you can imagine a lake to do such a thing (and you probably shouldn't).

"And why shouldn't I celebrate?" retorted Enki.

The lake now boiled quizzically, stinky vapors escaping at will.

"I alone have engineered the freeing of the one being the Grandmaster truly fears that Old Nick himself has tried to vanquish in unseen and unadmitted ways for eons. She alone can bring humanity together, embracing harmony with all things. She has done it before with other beings, such as the Dwarf Star Alliance, who at her behest created the 'Nova Galactic Trade Confederation' of a thousand worlds. A league dedicated to the propagation of peace, harmony and plenty

[1]This is a line from the arch villain of the movie *Highlander*, uttered by the immortal Kurgan in a church (Mulcahy, 1986).

throughout countless galaxies. Earth is but one world and its time has finally come. Soon racial suffering and harm will cease faster than many will believe."

With a near ear-splitting pop the lake produced the most prestigious gaseous gurgle, hissing noxiously.

"Him."

Understanding this, Enki turned slowly to his left and gazed upward. Leaning over him was a bemused Grandmaster, his frame wide, his hair like his wizened skin, alabaster white.

"Hmm … she is smaller and frailer than I remember, this delicate, little Hope you pin your dreams upon Abyd."

He said so in a sneering manner, but beneath was genuine concern and Enki knew it. The Lord of racial lies and falsehood looked altered somehow. Still white, still powerful, still older-looking but not quite as all-mighty. Hesitation lurked within. And he looked … tired. Something Enki thought impossible. An ageless one, a demon of never ending dimension and incomprehension does not concern themselves with exhaustion. It's so unbecoming. Enki judged it as a front and told him so.

"Whatever your pretense of tiredness, to unbalance me you must admit defeat. I have bested you and you know it. Hope will grow as you grow weak. Every connection she incites nurtures greater humanity and empathy for the Other. Diminishing your power, day by day, year by year as the former God of Race and Racism. And you've never seen your father Old Nick displeased, have you? That strange feeling within in you is called fear, something you have delt out so much of as the prince of racial misrule. Now you are the one on the verge of losing the one ill he, Beelzebub has taken so much pride in for so long. I can't wait to see his faces! You've basically gotten me out of a longstanding bind caused by a bet turned sour a millennia ago that kicked this whole thing with race and racism off in the first place."[2]

Enki's taunt evoked a wince that painfully made its way across the Grandmaster's face. Lingering there for far too long. After all what could he actually do to him? No daemon can ever harm another. But that wince soon changed to a crafty half smile.

"Ah … Abyd. You overstate matters. As usual you overplay your hand. This is not victory but stalemate."

"How so?" a bemused Enki replied.

"For so long you have assumed that underneath it all I have sole control over people's willingness to embrace race and racism. I do not possess this ability. Agency has always existed in humanity to turn away from my seductive path. Hope may exist, she may dent my work, but in the end, mine is the temptation of pleasure and righteousness (it just feels so good to blame the Other), coupled with

---

[2]It was a bet between Enki Abyd and the Devil himself, "Old Nick," that Enki lost after suggesting that he was unable to create new all-encompassing harm in the world. It was a jibe gone wrong which created the woe of race and racism in the first place, that Enki felt responsible to defeat.

home grown fear (it's the only true narcotic in town) and loathing (the product of shame and guilt over past and present racial practice) that it is ordained that race and racism will return. When they do it will be in a newer more powerful form, impervious to the positivity of Hope and her ways. I have been told that a mortal once bid you remove race and racism from Accounting and you attempted to do so. You failed, because race and racism, (the heart of me and my reason for being) is central to dominant majority white society that much of white humanity exists within. And they have the power and with it they do my bidding and follow my way, for I am the permeance of race and racism itself, and I am going nowhere. You the Trickster god should dare to bet on that."

And the Grandmaster did indeed have an excellent point. For it was Critical Race Theorists who latched onto the idea of the everlasting nature of race and racism in society, a notion first advocated by the peerless Derick Bell (1992). Many ridiculed the concept at the time, suggesting its nihilism was unwarranted. Yet, decades later race and racism are still as intractable as ever without a solution in sight. It was at this juncture that diminutive Hope awoke, blinking from her sleep, staring at the two gods arguing their case. Fluttering lightly, delicate, gossamer wings she flew to the faces of the two Daemons and addressed them thus in the sweetest of voices.

"You are both right. Grandmaster, it is most likely that race and racism will never be defeated in the manner so many mortals have hoped for. It is obdurate in nature given the way mortals live their lives and treat one another. However many in their field of sociology have identified it as a social construction, something made up by humans, that can be unmade. This is true. But given the fact that you exist Grandmaster and have the strength that you have this unlikely to happen either."

"And me?" uttered Enki, a little dumb founded.

"And you Enki Abyd. Thank you. For you show all the way. It has been said that it's not the destination but the journey which matter most. The journey that is the defeat of race and racism may never end, but the fact we walk it, together, as racial allies and ambassadors of difference is all important. If humans do not try, they will never understand the nonsensicality of believing in what does not exist. They will never truly understand that race is a fiction that objectively does not exist unless people make it so. They will not gain the empathy needed to minimize race and racism or possess sympathy at the intersection of race and other inequalities for those who are stigmatized as different also. Those without power, who live in reduced life circumstances. Our journey must be one which makes anti racism akin to breathing for people. Even though they know they will take a final breath one day, they fight with the core of their being for their breath today and every other day they can. My role is to inspire new ways to help them on their voyage, to help them help themselves and one another to be better. I rouse them to get up when they fall, be humble and try again. To engage with difference that they might not understand but respect, nonetheless. This is how the existence of race and racism can be minimized. And perhaps one day in the far, far future humanity will recognize race as the figment of their imagination it always was. Then you Grandmaster, for all your power will cease to exist, and humanity will then take their place finally, in the 'Nova Galactic Trade Confederation', rightfully taking their place among those who fight for social justice for all beings everywhere. *All it takes is a little hope.*"

With a grudging nod the Grandmaster commends Enki on a game well played so far. Then he vanishes because he has work to do in the mortal realm. For his part, Enki understands that he jumped the gun believing race and racism to be vanquished so easily. Annoyed in particular that he had been contradicted by a Lake of all things and it was right! But he let Hope know that he is not yet done. The eternal battle continues. With that he popped out of sight, slipping left behind an electron, and followed the Grandmaster down to earth to do his bit once more. In a similar fashion Hope for her part, made her way to Earth, to begin the instigation of inspiration, education and empathy. Of course, where she could, she pointed those who wished to stand and fight against racial tyranny to the Daemon God Enki Abyd. He always had an idea or two about what to do next ….

The End.

References

Bell, D. (1992). *Faces at the bottom of the well: The permanence of racism*. Basic Books.

Mulcahy, R. (Writer). (1986). *Highlander* [Movie]. In P. S. Davis (Producer). Thorn EMI.

Index

Printed and bound by CPI Group (UK) Ltd, Croydon, CR0 4YY

19/05/2025

14672888-0001